Memoirs of the
Duc de Saint-Simon

Memoirs of the
Duc de Saint-Simon

Edited by

W. H. LEWIS

The Macmillan Company

NEW YORK

Translated by Bayle St. John

LIBRARY OF CONGRESS CATALOG CARD NUMBER: 64-13352
FIRST PUBLISHED 1829–1830
REVISED EDITION © W. H. LEWIS 1964

First published in the United States of America
by the Macmillan Company, 1964
Made and printed in Great Britain
by William Clowes and Sons, Limited
London and Beccles

Contents

The Illustrations

Acknowledgment

The Publishers wish to thank the following for permission to reproduce the illustrations included in this book:

The Trustees of the British Museum for the illustrations facing pages 67 (bottom right), 131 (bottom) and 146 (bottom); the Mansell Collection for pages 66 (top), 130, 131 (top) and 146 (top); Giraudon, Paris, for pages 51 and 67 (top); the *Radio Times* Hulton Picture Library for page 66 (bottom); the Réunion des Musées Nationaux for pages 50 and 147; the Trustees of the Wallace Collection for 67 (bottom left).

The jacket is reproduced, by courtesy of the Réunion des Musées Nationaux, from the first page of the Memoirs of the Duc de Saint-Simon.

Introduction

It is commonly assumed that Saint-Simon is the outstanding example of a type, the French Peer of the seventeenth century, but in fact he was an anachronism. Seeing him always foremost in asserting the privileges of his order we tend to regard him as the leader of a rout of little-minded nobles, whereas his leadership of the Peers in so many precedence claims is a coincidence arising out of his own peculiar political theories. His fellows, almost without exception, had no ambitions beyond the aggrandizement of their Houses, but Saint-Simon longed for the return to an old France which probably never existed outside his own imagination. He was in fact Trollope's Miss Thorne of Ullathorne; who, I may say, for the benefit of non-Trollopians, in the England of the 1850's sighed for the good old days of the Saxon Kings. So did Saint-Simon dream of a reversion to the times when the Peers were the *Parlement*, an hereditary oligarchy controlling a *roi fainéant*, with the hated "men of the gown", the present-day bureaucrats, in their proper places as recorders of the Peers' decisions. In his reading he was as divorced from his century as in his political theories; he devoured old memoirs, genealogies, and the like, and from them he acquired a style which derives nothing from the great writers of his own day. And apparently in his favourite books he found nothing to disturb his belief that rule by the Peers was the ideal government for France. He surely must have heard of the Fronde, the civil war of 1649–54 from old men who had fought in it and who could tell him of the most recent experiment in rule by the Peers; but if he did, their information apparently made no impression upon him.

Such being his views it is easy to understand his hatred of Louis XIV whose theory of government was the very antithesis of that of Saint-Simon. Louis XIV had his faults, but at least he had grasped the vital necessity of reducing his nobility to Court ornaments whilst entrusting executive power exclusively to his new bourgeois civil service. And whatever Saint-Simon may say to the contrary, Louis was not a fool; he understood Saint-Simon a great deal better than Saint-Simon understood him, which did nothing to reconcile the Duke to the King.

In writing on Saint-Simon it is usual to call attention to his intense absorption with trifles and label it childish. But it is anything but childish, granted Saint-Simon's premises. The King was always on the alert to reduce his subjects to one dead level in the interests of despotic power, and Saint-Simon felt, quite rightly, that in such a dispute as the *affaire du bonnet* for instance, he was doing something, however small, to prevent that dead level from being attained. He was in fact in every precedence quarrel fighting a rearguard action for the old order.

Saint-Simon's life is a tragedy, or if you like, a tragi-comedy. He thought that in the Duke of Burgundy he had found the king of his dreams; but Burgundy died suddenly in 1712. Then in 1715 his oldest friend the Duke of Orléans became Regent and once more Saint-Simon's hopes rose high. One brief triumph over the hated *Parlement* he achieved, then he exasperated Orléans into snubbing him into self-banishment. In 1723 he disappeared from Court. He lived on until 1755, outliving both his sons, and died the last of his House, the last Duc de Saint-Simon.

Readers unfamiliar with the period may be confused by *Court* as opposed to legal titles, so I give a list of these *Court* titles and their holders.

Monseigneur: Louis de France, the Dauphin, Louis XIV's only legitimate son. *Monseigneur* had three sons, the Dukes of Burgundy, Anjou and Berri. When *Monseigneur* died in 1711, the Duke of Burgundy let it be known that he wished to be styled not *Monseigneur* but simply *M. le Dauphin*. In 1700 the Duke of Anjou became King Philip V of Spain. Berri died without issue in 1714.

Monsieur: The Court title of the second son of a king of France. During the period with which we are concerned this was Philippe de France, Duke of Orléans, the only brother of Louis XIV. His wife was *Madame*. Their only son, Philippe, Duke of Chartres, succeeded his father as Duke of Orléans in 1701, but was of course ineligible to become *Monsieur*.

M. le Prince: The Prince de Condé, head of a collateral branch of the House of Bourbon. In this case the fifth prince, who died in 1709, whereupon Louis XIV decreed that this Court title should fall into abeyance. His wife was *Madame la Princesse*.

M. le Duc: Eldest son of *M. le Prince*, officially the Duc de Bourbon. His wife was *Mme. la Duchesse*. There were two holders of the title during this period, Louis III (1668–1710) and his son Louis Henri (1692–1740).

M. le Grand: The Grand Equerry of France, Louis de Lorraine, Comte d'Armagnac.

M. le Premier: The First Equerry of France, the Marquis de Beringhen.

Finally it should be noted that Bishops were nearly always referred to by the names of their Sees. The two with whom we shall be most concerned are M. de Meaux (Bossuet) and M. de Cambrai (Fénelon).

I should perhaps add a word on the difficult subject of money. It is not really possible to give any adequate comparison between the cost of living in England today and in seventeenth-century France, but the following table is at least a rough guide.

1 livre, silver	= 1 franc, seventeenth century	= 1 franc 1914 = 10*d*.
6 livres, silver	= 1 crown, seventeenth century	= 6 francs 1914 = 5*s*.
4 crowns, silver	= 1 gold louis, seventeenth century	= 24 francs 1914 = 20*s*.

1675

I was born on the night of the 15th of January, 1675, of Claude, Duc de Saint-Simon, Peer of France; and of his second wife Charlotte de l'Aubépine. I was the only child of that marriage.

I bore the name of the Vidame de Chartres; and was educated with great care and attention. My mother, who was remarkable for virtue, perseverence, and sense, busied herself continually in forming my mind and body. She feared for me the usual fate of young men, who believe their fortunes made, and who find themselves their own masters early in life. It was not likely that my father, born in 1606, would live long enough to protect me from this danger; and my mother repeatedly impressed on me how necessary it was for a young man, the son of the favourite of a King long dead,—with no new friends at Court,—to acquire some personal value of his own. She succeeded in stimulating my courage; and in exciting in me the desire to make the acquisitions she laid stress on; but my aptitude for study and the sciences did not come up to my desire to succeed in them. However, I had an innate inclination for reading, especially works of history; and thus was inspired with ambition to emulate the examples presented to my imagination,—to do something and become somebody, which partly made amends for my distaste for letters.

What I read of my own accord, of history, and, above all, of the personal memoirs of the times since Francis I, bred in me the desire to write down what I might myself see. The hope of advancement, and of becoming familiar with the affairs of my time, stirred me. The annoyances I might thus bring upon myself did not fail to present themselves to my mind; but the firm resolution I made to keep my writings secret from everybody, appeared to me to remedy all evils. I commenced my memoirs then in July, 1694, being at that time colonel of a cavalry regiment.

1691

In 1691 I was studying my philosophy and beginning to learn to ride at an academy at Rochefort,—getting mightily tired of masters and books, and anxious to join the army. The siege of Mons, formed by the King in person, at the commencement of the spring, had drawn away all the young men of my age to commence their first campaign; and, what piqued me most, the Duc de Chartres was there too. I had been, as it were, educated with him. I was younger than he by eight months; and if the expression be allowed in speaking of young people, so unequal in position, friendship had united us. I made up my mind, therefore, to escape from my leading-strings; but pass lightly over the artifices I used in order to attain success. I addressed myself to my mother. I soon saw that she trifled with me. I had recourse to my father, whom I made believe that the King, having led a great siege this year, would rest the next.

My father took me, therefore, to Versailles, where he had not been for many years, and begged of the King admission for me into the Musketeers. It was on the day of St. Simon and St. Jude, at half-past twelve, and just as his Majesty came out of the council.

The King did my father the honour of embracing him three times, and then turned towards me. Finding that I was little and of delicate appearance, he said I was still very young; to which my father replied, that I should be able in consequence to serve longer. Thereupon the King demanded in which of the two companies he wished to put me; and my father named that commanded by Maupertuis, who was one of his friends. My mother, after a little vexation and pouting at finding me enrolled by my father against her will, did not fail to bring him to reason, and to make him provide me with an equipment of thirty-five horses or mules, and means to live honourably.

1692

The King set out on the 10th of May, 1692, with the ladies; and I performed the journey on horseback with the soldiers and all the attendants, like the other Musketeers, and continued to do so through the whole campaign.

This was the fifth campaign of the War of the League of Augsburg, 1688–1697. It was an offensive-defensive war launched by Louis XIV to forestall action by the hostile forces encircling him, and, from the French point of view, had been rendered necessary by the downfall of James II in 1688; an event which had transformed England from a French dependency into the most dangerous enemy. The French king's capture of Namur was the highlight of the 1692 campaign.

The King was very anxious to establish his illegitimate children, whom he advanced day by day; and had married two of them, daughters, to Princes of the blood. For some time past Madame de Maintenon, even more than the King, had thought of nothing else than how to raise the remaining illegitimate children, and wished to marry Mademoiselle de Blois (second daughter of the King and of Madame de Montespan) to Monsieur the Duc de Chartres. The Duc de Chartres was the sole nephew of the King, and was much above the Princes of the blood by his rank of *Grandson of France*, and by the Court that *Monsieur* his father kept up.

The marriages of the two Princes of the blood, of which I have just spoken, had scandalised all the world. The King was not ignorant of this; and he could thus judge of the effect of a marriage even more startling; such as was this proposed one. But for four years he had turned it over in his mind and had even taken the first steps to bring it about. It was the more difficult because the father of the Duc de Chartres was infinitely proud of his rank, and the mother belonged to a nation which abhorred illegitimacy and misalliances, and was indeed of a character to forbid all hope of her ever relishing this marriage.

In order to vanquish all these obstacles, the King applied to *M. le Grand*. This person was brother of the Chevalier de Lorraine, the favourite, by

3

disgraceful means, of *Monsieur*, father of the Duc de Chartres. The two brothers, unscrupulous and corrupt, entered willingly into the scheme, but demanded as a reward, paid in advance, to be made Chevaliers of the Order.

The young Duc de Chartres had at that time for teacher Dubois (after-wards the famous Cardinal Dubois,) whose history was singular. He had formerly been a valet; but displaying unusual aptitude for learning, had been instructed by his master in literature and history, and in due time passed into the service of Saint Laurent, who was the Duc de Chartres' first instructor. He became so useful and showed so much skill, that Saint Laurent made him become an abbé. Thus raised in position, he passed much time with the Duc de Chartres, assisting him to prepare his lessons, to write his exercises, and to look out words in the dictionary. I have seen him thus engaged over and over again, when I used to go and play with the Duc de Chartres. When St. Laurent died Dubois aspired to succeed to him. He had paid his court to the Chevalier de Lorraine, by whose influence he was much aided in obtaining his wish.

It was, then, Dubois that the Chevalier de Lorraine made use of to gain the consent of the young Duc de Chartres to the marriage proposed by the King.

The affair ended as might have been anticipated, and Chartres was wheedled into believing or pretending to believe that Mlle de Blois was the lady of his choice. Madame, *though furious, could do nothing, and a few days later the wedding took place.*

The King spoke very obligingly to the Duc de Chartres, said that he wished to see him married; that he offered him his daughter, but that he did not intend to constrain him in the matter, but left him quite at liberty. This discourse, however, pronounced with that terrifying majesty so natural to the King, and addressed to a timid young prince, took away his voice, and quite unnerved him. He thought to escape from his slippery position by throwing himself upon *Monsieur* and *Madame*, and stammeringly replied that the King was master, but that a son's will depended upon that of his parents. 'What you say is very proper,' replied the King; 'but as soon as you consent to my proposition your father and mother will not oppose it.' And then turning to *Monsieur* he said, 'Is this not true, my brother?' *Monsieur* consented, as he had already done, and the only person remaining to consult was *Madame*, who was immediately sent for.

That evening an 'Apartment' was held at the palace, as was customary three times a week during the winter; the other three evenings being set

4

apart for comedy, and the Sunday being free. An Apartment, as it was called, was an assemblage of all the Court in the grand saloon, from seven o'clock in the evening until ten, when the King sat down to table; and, after ten, in one of the saloons at the end of the grand gallery towards the tribune of the chapel. In the first place there was some music: then tables were placed all about for all kinds of gambling; there was a *lansquenet*, at which *Monsieur* and *Monseigneur* always played; also a billiard-table; in a word, every one was free to play with every one, and allowed to ask for fresh tables if all the others were occupied. Beyond the billiards was a refreshment-room. All was perfectly lighted. At the outset, the King went to the 'apartments' very often and played, but lately he had ceased to do so. He spent the evening with Madame de Maintenon, working with different ministers one after the other. But still he wished his courtiers to attend assiduously.

This evening, directly after the music had finished, the King sent for *Monseigneur* and *Monsieur*, who were already playing at *lansquenet*; *Madame*, who scarcely looked at a party of *ombre* at which she had seated herself; the Duc de Chartres, who, with a rueful visage, was playing at chess; and Mademoiselle de Blois, who had scarcely begun to appear in society, but who this evening was extraordinarily decked out, and who, as yet, knew nothing and suspected nothing; and therefore, being naturally very timid, and horribly afraid of the King, believed herself sent for in order to be reprimanded, and trembled so that Madame de Maintenon took her upon her knees, where she held her, but was scarcely able to reassure her. The fact of these royal persons being sent for by the King at once made people think that a marriage was in contemplation. In a few minutes they returned, and then the announcement was made public. I arrived at that moment. *Madame* was walking in the gallery with Châteauthiers—her favourite, and worthy of being so. She took long strides, her handkerchief in her hand, weeping without constraint, speaking pretty loudly, gesticulating, and looking like Ceres after the rape of her daughter Proserpine, seeking her in fury, and demanding her back from Jupiter. Every one respectfully made way to let her pass.

The Apartment, which, however heavy in appearance, was full of interest to me, seemed quite short. It finished by the supper of the King. His Majesty appeared quite at ease. *Madame's* eyes were full of tears, which fell from time to time as she looked into every face around, as if in search of all our thoughts. Her son, whose eyes too were red, she would not give a glance to; nor to *Monsieur*: all three ate scarcely anything. I remarked that the King offered *Madame* nearly all the dishes that were before him, and that she refused with an air of rudeness which did not, however, check his politeness. It was furthermore noticeable that, after leaving the table, he made to *Madame* a very marked and very low reverence, during which she performed so complete a pirouette, that the King on raising his head found nothing but her back before him, removed about a step further towards the door.

M. du Maine wished to marry. The King tried to turn him from it, and said frankly to him, that it was not for such as he to make a lineage. But pressed by Madame de Maintenon, who had educated M. du Maine, and who felt for him as a nurse, the King resolved to marry him to a daughter of the Prince de Condé. The marriage once arranged, was celebrated on the 19th of March, much in the same manner as had been that of the Duc de Chartres.

1693

My year of service in the Musketeers being over, the King, after a time, gave me, without purchase, a company of cavalry in the Royal Roussillon, in garrison at Mons, and just then very incomplete. I thanked the King, who replied to me very obligingly. The company was entirely made up in a fortnight. This was towards the middle of April.

On May 3rd, 1693, at ten o'clock in the morning, I had the misfortune to lose my father. He was eighty-seven years of age, and had been in bad health for some time, with a touch of gout during the last three weeks. After having paid the last duties to my father I betook myself to Mons to join the Royal Roussillon cavalry regiment, in which I was captain.

We gained some successes this year. Maréchal de Villeroy took Huy in three days, losing only a sub-engineer and some soldiers. On the 29th of July we attacked the Prince of Orange at Neerwinden, and after twelve hours of hard fighting, under a blazing sun, entirely routed him. I was of the third squadron of the Royal Roussillon, and made five charges. One of the gold ornaments of my coat was torn away, but I received no wound. During the battle our brigadier, Quoadt, was killed before my eyes. The Duc de Feuillade became thus commander of the brigade. We missed him immediately, and for more than half an hour saw nothing of him; he had gone to make his toilette. When he returned he was powdered and decked out in a fine red surtout, embroidered with silver, and all his trappings and those of his horse were magnificent; he acquitted himself with distinction.

6

Our cavalry stood so well against the fire from the enemy's guns, that the Prince of Orange lost all patience, and turning away, exclaimed—'Oh, the insolent nation!' He fought until the last, and retired with the Elector of Hanover only when he saw there was no longer any hope. After the battle my people brought us a leg of mutton and a bottle of wine, which they had wisely saved from the previous evening, and we attacked them in good earnest, as may be believed. The enemy lost about twenty thousand men, including a large number of officers; our loss was not more than half that number.

The season finished with the taking of Charleroy. Charleroy taken, our troops went into winter-quarters, and I returned to Court, like the rest. The roads and the posting service were in great disorder. At Pont Saint-Maxence all the horses were retained by M. de Luxembourg. Fearing I might be left behind, I told the postmaster that I was a governor (which was true), and that I would put him in jail if he did not give me horses. I should have been sadly puzzled how to do it; but he was simple enough to believe me, and gave the horses.

My mother, who had been much disquieted for me during the campaign, desired strongly that I should not make another without being married. Although very young, I had no repugnance to marry, but wished to do so according to my own inclinations. With a large establishment I felt very lonely in a country where credit and consideration do more than all the rest. Without uncle, aunt, cousins-german, or near relatives, I found myself, I say, extremely solitary.

Among my best friends, as he had been the friend of my father, was the Duc de Beauvilliers. He had always shown me much affection, and I felt a great desire to unite myself to his family. My mother approved of my inclination, and gave me an exact account of my estates and possessions. I carried it to Versailles, and sought a private interview with M. de Beauvilliers. At eight o'clock the same evening he received me alone in the cabinet of Madame de Beauvilliers. After making my compliments to him, I told him my wish, showed him the state of my affairs, and said that all I demanded of him was one of his daughters in marriage, and that whatever contract he thought fit to draw up would be signed by my mother and myself without examination.

The Duc, who had fixed his eyes upon me all this time, replied like a man penetrated with gratitude by the offer I had made. He said, that of his eight daughters the eldest was between fourteen and fifteen years old; the second much deformed, and in no way marriageable; the third between twelve and thirteen years of age, and the rest were children: the eldest

7

wished to enter a convent, and had shown herself firm upon that point. He seemed inclined to make a difficulty of his want of fortune; but, reminding him of the proposition I had made, I said that it was not for fortune I had come to him, not even for his daughter, whom I had never seen; that it was he and Madame de Beauvilliers who had charmed me, and whom I wished to marry!

'But,' said he, 'if my eldest daughter wishes absolutely to enter a convent?'

'Then,' replied I, 'I ask the third of you.' To this he objected, on the ground that if he gave the dowry of the first to the third daughter, and the first afterwards changed her mind and wished to marry, he should be thrown into an embarrassment. I replied that I would take the third as though the first were to be married, and that if she were not, the difference between what he destined for her and what he destined for the third, should be given to me. The Duc, raising his eyes to heaven, protested that he had never been combated in this manner, and that he was obliged to gather up all his forces in order to prevent himself yielding to me that very instant.

On the next day, at half-past three, I had another interview with M. de Beauvilliers. With much tenderness he declined my proposal, resting his refusal upon the inclination his daughter had displayed for the convent,—upon his little wealth, if, the marriage of the third being made, she should change her mind—and upon other reasons. He spoke to me with much regret and friendship, and I to him in the same manner; and we separated, unable any longer to speak to each other. Two days after, however, I had another interview with him by his appointment. I endeavoured to overcome the objections that he made, but all in vain. He could not give me his third daughter with the first unmarried, and he would not force her he said, to change her wish of retiring from the world. His words, pious and elevated, augmented my respect for him, and my desire for the marriage. In the evening, at the breaking up of the appointment, I could not prevent myself whispering in his ear that I should never live happy with anybody but his daughter, and without waiting for a reply hastened away. I had the next evening, at eight o'clock, an interview with Madame de Beauvilliers. I argued with her with such prodigious ardour that she was surprised, and, although she did not give way, she said she should be inconsolable for the loss of me, repeating the same tender and flattering things her husband had said before, and with the same effusion of feeling.

There was nothing left for me but to look out for another marriage. One soon presented itself, but as soon fell to the ground; and I went to La Trappe to console myself for the impossibility of making an alliance with the Duc de Beauvilliers.

Although I was very young then, M. de la Trappe charmed me, and the sanctity of the place enchanted me. Every year I stayed some days there, sometimes a week at a time, and was never tired of admiring this great and distinguished man. He loved me as a son, and I respected him as though he were my father. This intimacy, singular at my age, I kept secret from everybody, and only went to the convent clandestinely.

It was while our proceedings[1] were making some little stir that fresh favours were heaped upon the King's illegitimate sons, at the instance of the King himself, and with the connivance of Harlay, who, for the part he took in the affair, was promised the chancellorship when it should become vacant. The rank of these illegitimate sons was placed just below that of the princes of the blood, and just above that of the peers even of the oldest creation. This gave us all exceeding annoyance: it was the greatest injury the peerage could have received, and became its leprosy and sore. All the peers who could, kept themselves aloof from the parliament, when M. du Maine, M. de Vendôme, and the Comte de Toulouse, for whom this arrangement was specially made, were received there.

By the spring, preparations were ready for fresh campaigns. I went first to Soissons to see my regiment. I stopped six days at Strasbourg and then went by the Rhine to Philipsburg. On the next day after arriving there, I joined the cavalry, which was encamped at Obersheim.

We encamped for forty days at Gaw-Boecklheim, and it was in the leisure of that long camp that I commenced these memoirs, incited by the pleasure I took in reading those of Marshal Bassompierre, which invited me thus to write what I should see in my own time.

1694

On the 16th of October I received permission to return to Paris. Upon my arrival there I learnt that many things had occurred since I left. During that time some adventures had happened to the Princesses, as the three illegitimate daughters of the King were called for distinction sake. *Monsieur* wished that the Duchesse de Chartres should always call the others 'sister,' but that the others should never address her except as 'Madame.' The Princesse de Conti submitted to this; but the other (*Madame la Duchesse*, being

---

[1] A dull and complicated lawsuit which I have omitted.

the produce of the same love) set herself to call the Duchesse de Chartres 'mignonne.' But nothing was less *mignonne* than her face and her figure; and *Monsieur*, feeling the ridicule, complained to the King. The King prohibited this familiarity very severely.

While at Trianon these Princesses took it into their heads to walk out at night and divert themselves with crackers. Either from malice or imprudence they let off some one night under the windows of *Monsieur*, rousing him thereby out of his sleep. He was so displeased, that he complained to the King, who made him many excuses (scolding the Princesses), but had great trouble to appease him. His anger lasted a long time, and the Duchesse de Chartres felt it. I do not know if the other two were very sorry. *Madame la Duchesse* was accused of writing some songs upon the Duchesse de Chartres.

M. de Luxembourg very strangely married his daughter at this time to the Chevalier de Soissons (an illegitimate son of the Count de Soissons), brought out from the greatest obscurity by the Comtesse de Nemours, and adopted by her to spite her family. M. de Luxembourg did not long survive this fine marriage. At sixty-seven years of age he believed himself twenty-five, and lived accordingly. Nothing could be more exact than the *coup d'œil* of M. de Luxembourg—nobody could be more brilliant, more sagacious, more penetrating than he before the enemy or in battle, and this, too, with an audacity, an ease, and at the same time a coolness, which allowed him to see all and foresee all under the hottest fire, and in the most imminent danger. It was at such times that he was great. For the rest he was idleness itself. He rarely walked unless absolutely obliged,—spent his time in gaming, or in conversation with his familiars; and had every evening a supper with a chosen few (nearly always the same); and if near a town, the sex were always agreeably mingled with them. At last, age, temperament, and constitution betrayed him. He fell ill at Versailles. Given over by Fagon, the King's physician, Coretti, an Italian, who had secrets of his own, undertook his cure, and relieved him, but only for a short time. His door during this illness was besieged by all the Court. The King sent to inquire after him, but it was more for appearance sake than from sympathy, for I have already remarked that the King did not like him. The brilliancy of his campaigns, and the difficulty of replacing him, caused all the disquietude. Becoming worse, M. de Luxembourg received the sacraments, showed some religion and firmness, and died on the morning of the 4th of January, 1695, the fifth day of his illness, much regretted by many people, but personally esteemed by none, and loved by very few.

1695

Towards the end of the summer and the commencement of the winter of 1695, negotiations for peace were set on foot by the King. Harlay was sent to Maestricht to sound the Dutch. But in proportion as they saw peace desired they were less inclined to listen to terms. Harlay was rather roughly dismissed, and hastened to regain our frontier.

Two events followed each other very closely this winter. The first was the death of the Princess of Orange in London, at the end of January. The King of England[1] prayed our King to allow the Court to wear no mourning, and it was even prohibited to M. de Bouillon and M. de Duras, who were both related to the Prince of Orange. The order was obeyed, and no word was said; but this sort of vengeance was thought petty. Hopes were held out of a change in England, but they vanished immediately, and the Prince of Orange appeared more accredited there and stronger than ever. The Princess was much regretted, and the Prince of Orange, who loved her and gave her his entire confidence, and even most marked respect, was for some days ill with grief.

The King, entirely occupied with the aggrandisement of his natural children, had heaped upon the Comte de Toulouse every possible favour. He now (in order to evade a promise he had made to his brother, that the first vacant government should be given to the Duc de Chartres) forced M. de Chaulnes to give up the government of Brittany, which he had long held, and conferred it upon the Comte de Toulouse, giving to the friend and heir of the former the successorship to the government of Guyenne, by way of recompense.

M. de Chaulnes was old and fat, but much loved by the people of Brittany. He was overwhelmed by this determination of the King, and his wife, who had long been accustomed to play the little Queen, still more so; yet there was nothing for them but to obey. They did obey, but it was with a sorrow and chagrin they could not hide.

The appointment was announced one morning at the rising of the King. *Monsieur*, who awoke later, heard of it at the drawing of his curtains, and

[1] James II, in exile.

was extremely piqued. The Comte de Toulouse came shortly afterwards, and announced it himself. *Monsieur* interrupted him, and before everybody assembled there said, 'The King has given us a good present; but I know not if what he has done is good policy.' *Monsieur* went shortly afterwards to the King, and reproached him for giving, under cover of a trick, the government of Brittany to the Comte de Toulouse, having promised it to the Duc de Chartres. The King heard him in silence: he knew well how to appease him. Some money for play and to embellish Saint-Cloud, soon effaced *Monsieur's* chagrin.

All this winter my mother was solely occupied in finding a good match for me. Some attempt was made to marry me to Mademoiselle de Royan. It would have been a noble and rich marriage; but I was alone, Mademoiselle de Royan was an orphan, and I wished a father-in-law and a family upon whom I could lean. During the preceding year there had been some talk of the eldest daughter of Maréchal de Lorges for me. The affair had fallen through, almost as soon as suggested, and now, on both sides, there was a desire to recommence negotiations. The probity, integrity, the freedom of Maréchal de Lorges pleased me infinitely, and everything tended to give me an extreme desire for this marriage. Madame de Lorges by her virtue and good sense was all I could wish for as the mother of my future wife. Mademoiselle de Lorges was a blonde, with complexion and figure perfect, a very amiable face, an extremely noble and modest deportment, and with I know not what of majesty derived from her air of virtue, and of natural gentleness. The Maréchal had five other daughters, but I liked this one best without comparison, and hoped to find with her that happiness which she since has given me. As she has become my wife, I will abstain here from saying more about her, unless it be that she has exceeded all that was promised of her, and all that I myself had hoped.

My marriage being agreed upon and arranged, the Maréchal de Lorges spoke of it to the King, who had the goodness to reply to him that he could not do better, and to speak of me very obligingly. The marriage accordingly took place at the Hôtel de Lorges, on the 8th of April, 1695, which I have always regarded, and with good reason, as the happiest day of my life. My mother treated me like the best mother in the world. On the Thursday before Quasimodo the contract was signed; a grand repast followed; at midnight the curé of Saint Roch said mass, and married us in the chapel of the house. On the eve, my mother had sent forty thousand livres' worth of precious stones to Mademoiselle de Lorges, and I six hundred louis in a corbeille filled with all the knick-knacks that are given on these occasions. We slept in the grand apartment of the Hôtel de Lorges. On the morrow, after dinner, my wife went to bed, and received a crowd of visitors, who came to pay their respects and to gratify their curiosity. The next evening we went to Versailles, and were received by Madame de Maintenon and the King. On arriving at the supper-table, the King said to the new Duchesse:— 'Madame, will you be pleased to seat yourself?'

His napkin being unfolded, he saw all the duchesses and princesses still standing; and rising in his chair, he said to Madame de Saint-Simon— 'Madame, I have already begged you to be seated'; and all immediately seated themselves. On the morrow, Madame de Saint-Simon received all the Court in her bed—in the apartment of the Duchesse d'Arpajon, as being more handy, being on the ground floor. Our festivities finished by a supper that I gave to the former friends of my father, whose acquaintance I had always cultivated with great care.

Almost immediately after my marriage the second daughter of the Maréchal de Lorges followed in the footsteps of her sister. She was fifteen years of age, and at the reception of Madame de Saint-Simon had attracted the admiration of M. de Lauzun, who was then sixty-three. Since his return to the Court he had been reinstated in the dignity he had previously held. He flattered himself that by marrying the daughter of a General he should re-open a path to himself for command in the army. Full of this idea he spoke to M. de Lorges, who was by no means inclined towards the marriage. M. de Lauzun offered, however, to marry without dowry; and M. de Lorges, moved by this consideration, assented to his wish. The affair concluded, M. de Lorges spoke of it to the King. 'You are bold,' said his Majesty, to 'take Lauzun into your family. I hope you may not repent of it.'

Nobody was able to understand this marriage; and all foresaw that a rupture would speedily be brought about by the well-known temper of M. de Lauzun. In effect, this is what soon happened. The Maréchal de Lorges, remaining still in weak health, was deemed by the King unable to take the field again, and his army was given over to the command of another General. M. de Lauzun thus saw all his hopes of advancement at an end, and, discontented that the Maréchal had done nothing for him, broke off all connection with the family, took away Madame de Lauzun from her mother (to the great grief of the latter, who doted upon this daughter), and established her in a house of his own adjoining the Assumption, in the Faubourg St. Honoré. There she had to endure her husband's continual caprices, but little removed in their manifestation from madness. Everybody cast blame upon him, and strongly pitied her and her father and mother; but nobody was surprised.

13

A few days after the marriage of M. de Lauzun, as the King was being wheeled in his easy chair in the gardens at Versailles, he asked me for many minute particulars concerning the family of the Maréchal de Lorges. He then set himself to joke with me upon the marriage of M. de Lauzun—and upon mine. He said to me, in spite of that gravity which never quitted him, that he had learnt from the Maréchal I had well acquitted myself, but that he believed the Maréchale had still better news.

The loss of two illustrious men about this time, made more noise than that of two of our grand ladies. The first of these men was La Fontaine, so well known by his 'Fables' and stories, and who, nevertheless, was so heavy in conversation. The other was Mignard—so illustrious by his pencil: he had an only daughter—perfectly beautiful: she is repeated in several of those magnificent historical pictures which adorn the grand gallery of Versailles and its two salons, and which have had no slight share in irritating all Europe against the King, and in leaguing it still more against his person than his realm.

At the usual time the armies were got ready for active service, and everybody set out to join them. That of the Rhine, in which I was, was commanded by the Maréchal de Lorges.

The campaign of 1695 was uneventful and Saint-Simon's account of it consists mainly of a violent attack on the Duc du Maine for his cowardice in Flanders. I omit the passage because Maine is vindicated by eyewitness evidence.

M. de Brias, archbishop of Cambrai, had died, and the King had given that valuable preferment to the Abbé de Fénelon, preceptor of the children of France, Fénelon was a man of quality, without fortune,—whom the consciousness of wit—of the insinuating and captivating kind—united with much ability, gracefulness of intellect, and learning, inspired with ambition. He had been long going about from door to door, knocking for admission, but without success. Piqued against the Jesuits, to whom he had addressed himself at first, as holding all favours in their hands, and discouraged because unable to succeed in that quarter, he turned next to the Jansenists, and succeeded at last in being of the private parties that some of the important Jansenists then held once or twice a week at the house of the Duchesse de Brancas. But little by little his intimacy with them cooled; and by dint of turning around Saint-Sulpice, he succeeded in forming another connection there, upon which he built greater expectations. The Sulpicians appeared a middle party, very useful to the prelates; who equally feared the Court, on account of suspicions of doctrine, and the Jesuits: for as soon as the latter had insinuated themselves into the good graces of the prelates, they imposed their yoke upon them, or ruined them hopelessly; thus the Sulpicians grew apace. None amongst them could compare in any way with the Abbé de Fénelon; so that he was able easily to play first fiddle, and to make himself protectors who were interested in advancing him, in order that they might be protected in turn. His piety, which was all things to all men, and his doctrine that he formed upon theirs (abjuring, as it were, in whispers, the impurities he might have contracted amongst those he had abandoned)—the charms, the graces, the sweetness, the insinuation of his mind, rendered him a dear friend to this new congregation, and procured for him what he had long sought,—people upon whom he could lean, and who could and would serve him. Whilst waiting opportunities, he carefully courted these people, without thinking, however, of positively joining them, his views being more ambitious; so that he ever sought to make new acquaintances and friends. He was as anxious to captivate a lackey as a lord; and his talents for this work perfectly seconded his desires.

At this time, and while still obscure, he heard speak of Madame Guyon. He saw her. There was an interchange of pleasure between their minds. Their *sublimes* amalgamated. I know not if they understood each other very clearly in that system, and that new tongue which they hatched subsequently, but they persuaded themselves they did, and friendship grew up between them. Although more known than he, Madame Guyon was nevertheless not much known, and their intimacy was not perceived, because nobody thought of them; Saint-Sulpice even was ignorant of what was going on.

The Duc de Beauvilliers, Governor of the Children of France, had to choose a preceptor for Monseigneur le Duc de Bourgogne. He addressed himself to Saint-Sulpice, for he liked and protected it. He had heard Fénelon well spoken of: the Sulpicians vaunted his piety, his intelligence, his knowledge, his talents; at last they proposed him for preceptor. The Duc de Beauvilliers saw him, was charmed with him, and appointed him to the office.

As soon as installed, Fénelon saw of what importance it would be to gain the entire favour of the Duc de Beauvilliers, and of his brother-in-law the Duc de Chevreuse, both very intimate friends, and both in the highest confidence of the King and Madame de Maintenon. This was his first care, and he succeeded beyond his hopes, becoming the master of their hearts and minds, and the director of their consciences. He was almost as successful with Madame de Maintenon as he had been with the two Dukes. His spirituality enchanted her: the Court soon perceived the giant strides of the fortunate Abbé, and eagerly courted him. But, desiring to be free and entirely devoted to his great object, he kept himself aloof from their flatteries—made for himself a shield with his modesty and his duties of preceptor—and thus rendered himself still more dear to the persons he had captivated, and that he had so much interest in retaining in that attachment.

Among these cares he forgot not his dear Madame Guyon; he had already praised her to the two Ducs and to Madame de Maintenon. He had even introduced her to them, but as though with difficulty and for a few moments, as a woman all in God, whose humility and whose love of contemplation and solitude kept her within the strictest limits, and whose fear above all, was that she should become known. The tone of her mind pleased Madame de Maintenon extremely; her reserve, mixed with delicate flatteries, won upon her. Madame de Maintenon wished to hear her talk upon matters of piety; with difficulty she consented to speak. She seemed to surrender herself to the charms and to the virtue of Madame de Maintenon, and Madame de Maintenon fell into the nets so skilfully prepared for her.

Such was the situation of Fénelon when he became Archbishop of Cambrai; increasing the admiration in which he was held by taking no step to gain that great benefice.

Cambrai was a thunderbolt for this little flock. It was the archbishopric of Paris they wished. Cambrai they looked upon with disdain as a country diocese, the residence in which (impossible to avoid from time to time) would deprive them of their pastor. Their grief was then profound at what the rest of the world took for a piece of amazing luck, and the Countess of Guiche was so affected as to be unable to hide her tears. The new prelate had not neglected such of his brethren as made the most figure: they, in turn, considered it a distinction to command his regard. Saint-Cyr, that spot so valuable and so inaccessible, was the place chosen for his consecration; and M. de Meaux (Bossuet), dictator then of the episcopacy and of doctrine, consecrated him. The Children of France were among the spectators, and Madame de Maintenon was present with her little court of familiars. No others were invited; the doors were closed to those who sought to pay their court.

The new archbishop of Cambrai, gratified with his influence over Madame de Maintenon and with advantages it had brought him, felt that unless he became completely master of her, the hopes he still entertained could not be satisfied. But there was a rival in his way—Godet, Bishop of Chartres, who was much in the confidence of Madame de Maintenon, and had long discourses with her at Saint-Cyr. M. de Cambrai believed he could easily overthrow him. To do this, he determined to make use of Madame Guyon, whose new spirituality had already been so highly relished by Madame de Maintenon. He persuaded this latter to allow Madame Guyon to enter Saint-Cyr, where they could discourse together much more at their ease than at the Hôtel de Chevreuse or Beauvilliers. Madame Guyon went accordingly to Saint-Cyr two or three times. Soon after, Madame de Maintenon, who relished her more and more, made her sleep there, and their meetings grew longer. Madame Guyon admitted that she sought persons proper to become her disciples, and in a short time she formed a little flock, whose maxims and language appeared very strange to all the rest of the house, and, above all, to M. de Chartres. That prelate was not so simple as M. de Cambrai imagined. As soon as he got wind of this strange doctrine, he caused two ladies, upon whom he could count, to be admitted to Saint-Cyr, as if to become disciples of Madame Guyon. He gave them full instructions, and they played their parts to perfection. They communicated everything to M. de Chartres, who quietly looked on, allowed things to take their course, and, when he believed the right moment had arrived, disclosed all he had learnt to Madame de Maintenon. She was strangely surprised when she saw the extraordinary drift of the new doctrine. Troubled and uncertain, she consulted with M. de Cambrai, who, not suspecting she had been so well instructed, became, when he discovered it, embarrassed, and thus augmented her suspicions.

Suddenly Madame Guyon was driven away from Saint-Cyr, and prohibited from spreading her doctrine elsewhere. But the admiring disciples she had made still gathered round her in secret, and this becoming known, she was ordered to leave Paris. She feigned obedience, but in effect went no further than the Faubourg St. Antoine, where, with great secrecy, she continued to receive her flock.

1696

Monsieur de Cambrai, stunned but not overpowered by the reverse he had sustained, and by his loss of favour with Madame de Maintenon, stood firm in his stirrups. After Madame Guyon's abuse of her liberty, and the conferences of Issy, he bethought himself of confessing to M. de Meaux, by which celebrated trick he hoped to close that prelate's mouth. These circumstances induced M. de Meaux to take pen in hand, in order to expose to the public the full account of this affair, and of Madame Guyon's doctrine; and he did so in a work under the title of *Instruction sur les États d'Oraison.*

Before M. de Meaux's book was ready, M. de Cambrai's, entitled *Maximes des Saints*, was published and distributed.

This book, written in the strangest manner, did M. de Cambrai little service. Nobody, except the theologians, understood it, and even they not without reading it three or four times. Not a word was heard in praise of the book; everybody was opposed to it, and it was the means of making Madame de Maintenon more unfavourable to M. de Cambrai than ever. He sent the King a copy, without informing her. This completed her annoyance against him. In the mean time, M. de Meaux's book appeared in two volumes octavo, well written, clear, modest, and supported upon the authority of the Scriptures. It was received with avidity, and absolutely devoured. M. de Cambrai asked permission to go to Rome to defend his cause in person, but this the King refused. He sent his book, therefore, to the Pope, and had the annoyance to receive a dry, cold reply, and to see M. de Meaux's book triumph. His good fortune was in effect at an end. He remained at Court some little time, but the King was soon irritated against him, sent him off post-haste to Paris, and from there to his diocese, whence he has never returned.

The end of the year was stormy at Marly. One evening, after the King had gone to bed, and while Monseigneur was playing in the saloon, the Duchesse de Chartres and *Madame la Duchesse* (who were bound together by their mutual aversion to the Princesse de Conti) sat down to a supper in the chamber of the first-named. Monseigneur, upon retiring late to his own room, found them smoking with pipes, which they had sent for from the Swiss Guards. Knowing what would happen if the smell were discovered, he made them leave off, but the smoke had betrayed them. The King next day severely scolded them, at which the Princesse de Conti triumphed. Nevertheless, these broils multiplied, and the King at last grew so weary of them that one evening he called the Princesses before him, and threatened that if they did not improve he would banish them all from the Court. The measure had its effect; calm and decorum returned, and supplied the place of friendship.

Madame de Sévigné, so amiable and such excellent company, died some time after at Grignan, at the house of her daughter, her idol, but who little deserved to be so. I was very intimate with the young Marquis de Grignan, her grandson. This woman, by her natural graces, the sweetness of her wit communicated these qualities to those who had them not; she was besides extremely good, and knew thoroughly many things without ever wishing to appear as though she knew anything.

The public lost soon after a man illustrious by his genius, by his style, and by his knowledge of men,—I mean La Bruyère, who died of apoplexy at Versailles, after having surpassed Theophrastus in his own manner, and after painting, in the new Characters, the men of our days in an inimitable manner. He was besides a very honest man, of excellent breeding, simple, very disinterested, and without anything of the pedant. I had sufficiently known him to regret his death, and the works that might have been hoped from him.

Our campaign was undistinguished by any striking event. From June to September we did little but subsist and observe, after which we recrossed the Rhine at Philipsburg, where our rear guard was slightly inconvenienced by the enemy. In Italy there was more movement. The King sought to bring about peace by dividing the forces of his enemies, and secretly entered into a treaty with Savoy. The conditions were, that every place belonging to Savoy which had been taken by our troops should be restored, and that a marriage should take place between Monseigneur the Duc de Bourgogne and the daughter of the Duke of Savoy, when she became twelve years of age. In the mean time she was to be sent to the Court of France, and preparations were at once made there to provide her with a suitable establishment.

The household of the Princess of Savoy being completed, the members of it were sent to the Pont Beauvosin to meet their young mistress. She arrived early on the 16th of October, slept at the Pont Beauvosin that night, and on the morrow parted with her Italian attendants without shedding a single tear. On the 4th of November she arrived at Montargis, and was received by the King, *Monseigneur*, and *Monsieur*. The King handed her down from her coach, and conducted her to the apartment he had prepared for her. Her respectful and flattering manners pleased him highly. Her cajoleries, too, soon bewitched Madame de Maintenon, whom she never addressed except as 'Aunt'; whom she treated with a respect, and yet with a freedom, that ravished everybody. She became the doll of Madame de Maintenon and the King, pleased them infinitely by her insinuating spirit, and took greater liberties with them than the children of the King had ever dared to attempt.

As the Duchesse de Bourgogne makes a great figure in these Memoirs, it will be well to give a description of her personal appearance from the pen of Louis XIV himself. Writing to Madame de Maintenon, he says, 'She is most graceful and has the handsomest figure I have ever seen; dressed to be the model of a painter, with lively and beautiful eyes, eyelashes black and admirable, a clear complexion, white and red; the most beautiful flaxen hair that can be seen, and very plentiful. She is thin, as is proper at her age; with a vermilion mouth; full lips; white teeth long and ill-arranged; hands well made, but of the colour of her age.'

1697

Our campaign was brought to an end by the peace of Ryswick. The first news of that event arrived at Fontainebleau on the 22nd of September.

There was, however, another claimant to the throne of Poland; I mean the Elector of Saxony, who had also been elected, and who had many partisans; so many, indeed, that when the Prince de Conti arrived at Dantzig, he found himself almost entirely unsupported. The people even refused provision to his frigates. However, the Prince's partisans at length arrived to salute him.

By the above-mentioned peace of Ryswick, the King acknowledged the Prince of Orange as King of England. It was, however, a bitter draught for him to swallow, and for these reasons. Some years before, the King had offered his illegitimate daughter, the Princesse de Conti, in marriage to the Prince of Orange, believing he did that Prince great honour by the proposal. The Prince did not think in the same manner, and flatly refused; saying that the House of Orange was accustomed to marry to legitimate daughters of great kings and not their bastards. These words sank so deeply into the heart of the King, that he never forgot them; and often, against even his most palpable interest, showed how firmly the indignation he felt at them had taken possession of his mind. Since then, the Prince of Orange had done all in his power to efface the effect his words had made, but every attempt was rejected with disdain. The King's ministers in Holland had orders to do all they could to thwart the projects of the Prince of Orange, to excite people against him, to protect openly those opposed to him, and to be in no way sparing of money in order to secure the election of magistrates unfavourable to him. The Prince never ceased, until the breaking-out of this war, to use every effort to appease the anger of the King. At last, growing tired, and hoping soon to make his invasion of England, he said publicly, that he had uselessly laboured all his life to gain the favours of the King, but that he hoped to be more fortunate in meriting his esteem. It may be imagined, therefore, what a triumph it was for him when he forced the King to recognise him as monarch of England, and what that recognition cost the King.

Towards the end of the year, and not long after my return from the army, the King fixed the day for the marriage of the Duc de Bourgogne to the young Princess of Savoy. He announced that on that occasion he should be glad to see a magnificent Court; and he himself, who for a long time had worn only the most simple habits, ordered the most superb. This was enough; no one thought of consulting his purse on his state: everyone tried to surpass his neighbour in richness and invention. Gold and silver scarcely sufficed: the shops of the dealers were emptied in a few days; in a word the most unbridled luxury reigned over Court and city, for the fête had a huge crowd of spectators. Things went to such a point, that the King almost repented of what he had said, and remarked, that he could not understand how husbands could be such fools as to ruin themselves by dresses for their wives; he might have added, by dresses for themselves. But the impulse had been given; there was now no time to remedy it, and I believe the King at heart was glad; for it pleased him during the fêtes to look at all the dresses. He loved passionately all kinds of sumptuosity at his Court, and he who should have held only to what had been said, as to the folly of expense, would have grown little in favour. There was no means, therefore, of being wise among so many fools. Several dresses were necessary. Those for Madame Saint-Simon and myself cost us twenty thousand francs. Workmen were wanting to make up so many rich habits. Madame la Duchesse actually sent her people to take some by force who were working at the Duc de Rohan's. The King heard of it, did not like it, and had the workmen sent back immediately to the Hôtel de Rohan, although the Duc de Rohan was one of the men he liked least in all France. The King did another thing, which showed that he desired everybody to be magnificent: he himself chose the design for the embroidery of of the Princess. The embroiderer said he would leave all his other designs for that. The King would not permit this, but caused him to finish the work he had in hand, and to set himself afterwards to the other; adding, that if it was not ready in time, the Princess could do without it.

The marriage was fixed for Saturday, the 7th of December; and, to avoid disputes and difficulties, the King suppressed all ceremonies. The day arrived. At an early hour all the Court went to Monseigneur the Duc de

Bourgogne, who went afterwards to the Princess. A little before mid-day the procession started from the *salon*, and proceeded to the chapel. Cardinal de Coislin performed the marriage service. As soon as the ceremony was finished, a courier, ready at the door of the chapel, started for Turin. The day passed wearily. The King and Queen of England came about seven o'clock in the evening, and some time afterwards supper was served. Upon rising from the tables, the Princess was shown to her bed, none but ladies being allowed to remain in the chamber. Her chemise was given her by the Queen of England through the Duchesse de Lude. The Duc de Bourgogne undressed in another room, in the midst of all the Court, and seated upon a folding-chair. The King of England gave him his shirt, which was presented by the Duc de Beauvilliers. As soon as the Duchesse de Bourgogne was in bed, the Duc de Bourgogne entered, and placed himself at her side, in the presence of all the Court. Immediately afterwards everybody went away from the nuptial chamber, except *Monseigneur*, the ladies of the Princess, and the Duc de Beauvilliers, who remained at the pillow by the side of his pupil, with the Duchesse de Lude on the other side. *Monseigneur* stopped a quarter of an hour talking with the newly-married couple, then he made his son get up, after having told him to kiss the Princess, in spite of the opposition of the Duchesse de Lude. As it proved, too, her opposition was not wrong. The King said he did not wish that his grandson should kiss the end of the Princess's finger until they were completely on the footing of man and wife. Monsieur le Duc de Bourgogne after this redressed himself in the ante-chamber, and went to his own bed as usual. The little Duc de Berry, spirited and resolute, did not approve of the docility of his brother, and declared that he would have remained in bed. The young couple were not, indeed, allowed to live together as man and wife until nearly two years afterwards. The Princess continued to live just as before, and the ladies had strict orders never to leave her alone with her husband.

1698

The King of England was, as I have before said, at the height of satisfaction at having been recognised by the King (Louis XIV), and at finding himself secure upon the throne. But a usurper is never tranquil and content. William was annoyed by the residence of the legitimate King and his family at Saint Germains. It was too close to the King (of France), and too near England to leave him without disquietude. He had tried hard at Ryswick to obtain the dismissal of James II from the realm, or at least from the Court of France, but without effect. Afterwards he sent the Duke of St. Albans to our King openly, in order to compliment him upon the marriage of the Duc de Bourgogne, but in reality to obtain the dismissal.

The Duke of St. Albans meeting with no success, the Duke of Portland was sent to succeed him. The Duke of Portland came over with a numerous and superb suite; he kept a magnificent table, and had horses, liveries, furniture, and dresses of the most tasteful and costly kind. He was on his way when a fire destroyed Whitehall, the largest and ugliest palace in Europe, and which has not since been rebuilt; so that the kings are lodged, and very badly, at St. James's Palace.

Portland had his first audience of the King on the 4th of February, and remained four months in France. His politeness, his courtly and gallant manners, and the good cheer he gave charmed everybody, and made him universally popular. It became the fashion to give fêtes in his honour; and the astonishing fact is, that the King, who at heart was more offended than ever with William of Orange, treated this ambassador with the most marked distinction. One evening he even gave Portland his bedroom candlestick, a favour only accorded to the most considerable persons, and always regarded as a special mark of the King's bounty.

Notwithstanding all these attentions, Portland was as unsuccessful as his predecessor. The King had firmly resolved to continue his protection to James II, and nothing could shake this determination. Portland was warned from the first, that if he attempted to speak to the King upon the point, his labour would be thrown away: he wisely therefore kept silence, and went home again without in any way having fulfilled the mission upon which he had been sent.

M. de Cambrai's affair still continued to make a great stir among the prelates and at the Court. Madame Guyon was transferred from the Vincennes to the Bastille, and it was believed she would remain there all her life. The Ducs de Chevreuse and Beauvilliers lost all favour with M. de Maintenon, and narrowly escaped losing the favour of the King. An attempt was in fact made, which Madame de Maintenon strongly supported, to get them disgraced; and, but for the Archbishop of Paris, this would have taken place. But this prelate, thoroughly upright and conscientious, counselled the King against such a step, to the great vexation of his relations, who were the chief plotters in the conspiracy to overthrow the two Ducs. As for M. de Cambrai's book, 'Les Maximes des Saints,' it was as little liked as ever, and underwent rather a strong criticism at this time from M. de La Trappe, which did not do much to improve its reputation. At the commencement of the dispute M. de Meaux had sent a copy of 'Les Maximes des Saints' to M. de La Trappe, asking as a friend for his opinion of the work. M. de La Trappe read it, and was much scandalized. The more he studied it, the more shocked he became. At last, after having well examined the book, he sent his opinion to M. de Meaux, believing it would be considered as private, and not be shown to anybody. He did not measure his words, therefore, but wrote openly, that if M. de Cambrai was right he might burn the Evangelists, and complain of Jesus Christ, who could have come into the world only to deceive us. The frightful force of this phrase was so terrifying, that M. de Meaux thought it worthy of being shown to Madame de Maintenon; and she, seeking only to crush M. de Cambrai with all the authorities possible, would insist upon this opinion of M. de La Trappe being printed.

It might be imagined what triumphing there was on the one side, and what piercing cries on the other. The friends of M. de Cambrai complained most bitterly that M. de La Trappe had mixed himself up in the matter, and had passed such a violent and cruel sentence upon a book then under the consideration of the Pope. M. de La Trappe on his side was much afflicted that his letter had been published. He wrote to M. de Meaux protesting against this breach of confidence; and said that, although he had only expressed what he really thought, he should have been careful to use more measured language, had he supposed his letter would have seen the light. He said all he could to heal the wounds his words had caused, but M. de Cambrai and his friends never forgave him for having written them.

The affair of M. de Cambrai was not finally settled until the commencement of the following year, 1699, but went on making more noise day by day. At the date I have named the verdict from Rome arrived. Twenty-three propositions of the 'Maximes des Saints' were declared rash, dangerous, erroneous—*in globo*—and the Pope excommunicated those who read the book or kept it in their houses. The King was much pleased with this condemnation, and openly expressed his satisfaction. Madame de Maintenon appeared at the summit of joy. As for M. de Cambrai, he learnt his fate in a moment which would have overwhelmed a man with less resources in himself. He was on the point of mounting into the pulpit: he was by no means troubled; put aside the sermon he had prepared, and, without delaying a moment, took for subject the submission due to the Church; he treated this theme in a powerful and touching manner; announced the condemnation of his book; retracted the opinions he had professed; and concluded his sermon by a prefect acquiescence and submission to the judgment the Pope had just pronounced. Two days afterwards he published his retraction, condemned his book, prohibited the reading of it, acquiesced and submitted himself anew to his condemnation, and in the clearest terms took away from himself all means of returning to his opinions. A submission so prompt, so clear, so perfect was generally admired, although there were not wanting censors who wished he had shown less readiness in giving way. His friends believed the submission would be so flattering to the Pope, that M. de Cambrai might rely upon advancement to a cardinalship, and steps were taken, but without any good result, to bring about that event.

On the 29th of May, in the morning Madame de Saint-Simon was happily delivered of a child. God did us the grace to give us a son. He bore, as I had the name of Vidame of Chartres. I do not know why people have the fancy for these odd names, but they seduce in all nations, and they who feel the triviality of them, imitate them. It is true that the titles of Count and Marquis have fallen into the dust because of the quantity of people without wealth, and even without land, who usurp them; and that they have become so worthless, that people of quality who are Marquises or Counts are silly enough to be annoyed if those titles are given to them in conversation. It is certain, however, that these titles emanated from landed creations, and that in their origin they had functions attached to them, which they have since outlived. The *vidames*, on the contrary, were only principal officers of certain bishops, with authority to lead all the rest of their seigneur's vassals to the field, either to fight against other lords, or in the armies that our kings used to assemble to combat their enemies before the creation of a standing army put an end to the employment of vassals, and to all the power and authority of the seigneurs. There is thus no comparison between the title of *Vidame*, which only marks a vassal, and the titles which by fief emanate from the King. Yet because the few Vidames who have been known were illustrious, the name has appeared grand, and for this reason was given to me, and afterwards by me to my son.

Some little time before this, the King resolved to show all Europe, which believed his resources exhausted by a long war, that in the midst of profound peace, he was as fully prepared as ever for arms. He gave all the necessary orders, therefore, for forming a camp at Compiègne, to be commanded by the Maréchal de Boufflers. On Thursday, the 28th of August, all the Court set out for the camp. Sixty thousand men were assembled there.

Colonels, and even simple captains, kept open table; but the Maréchal de Boufflers outstripped everybody by his expenditure, by his magnificence, and his good taste. There was everything which can be the most widely, and the most splendidly comprehended under the term refreshment: French and foreign wines, and the rarest liqueurs in the utmost abundance. Measures were so well taken that quantities of game and venison arrived from all sides; and the seas of Normandy, of Holland, of England, of Brittany, even the Mediterranean, furnished all they contained—the most unheard-of, extraordinary, and most exquisite—at a given day and hour with inimitable order, and by a prodigious number of horsemen and little express carriages. Even the water was fetched from Sainte-Reine, from the Seine, and from the most esteemed sources; and it is impossible to imagine anything of any kind which was not at once ready for the obscurest as for the most distinguished visitor, the guest most expected, and the guest not expected at all. Wooden houses and magnificent tents stretched all around, in number sufficient to form a camp of themselves, and were furnished in the most superb manner, like the houses in Paris. Kitchens and rooms for every purpose were there, and the whole was marked by an order and cleanliness that excited surprise and admiration.

The King arrived at the camp on Saturday, the 30th of August, and went with the Duc and Duchesse de Bourgogne and others to the quarters of Maréchal de Boufflers, where a magnificent collation was served up to them—so magnificent that when the King returned, he said it would be useless for the Duc de Bourgogne to attempt anything so splendid; and that whenever he went to the camp he ought to dine with Maréchal de Boufflers. In effect, the King himself soon after dined there, and led to the Maréchal's table the King of England, who was passing three or four days in the camp. On these occasions the King pressed Maréchal de Boufflers to be seated. He would never comply, but waited upon the King while the Duc de Grammont, his brother-in-law, waited upon *Monseigneur*.

The King left the camp on Monday the 22nd of September, much pleased with the troops. He gave, in parting, six hundred francs to each cavalry captain, and three hundred francs to each captain of infantry. He gave as much to the majors of all the regiments, and distributed some favours to his household. To Maréchal de Boufflers he presented one hundred thousand francs. All these gifts together amounted to something: but separately were as mere drops of water. There was not a single regiment that was not ruined, officers and men, for several years. As for Maréchal de Boufflers, I leave it to be imagined what a hundred thousand francs were to him whose magnificence astounded all Europe, described as it was by foreigners who were witnesses of it, and who day after day could scarcely believe their own eyes.

1699

Here we have a typical example of those precedence squabbles which bedevilled the Court of Louis XIV, and in which victory was to Saint-Simon the breath of life.

On the 6th of January, upon the reception of the ambassadors at the house of the Duchesse de Bourgogne, an adventure happened which I will here relate. M. de Lorraine belonged to a family which had been noted for its pretensions, and for the disputes of precedency in which it engaged. He was as prone to this absurdity as the rest, and on this occasion incited the Princesse d'Harcourt, one of his relations, to act in a manner that scandalised all the Court. Entering the room in which the ambassadors were to be received and where a large number of ladies were already collected, she glided behind the Duchesse de Rohan, and told her to pass to the left. The Duchesse de Rohan, much surprised, replied, that she was very well placed already. Whereupon, the Princesse d'Harcourt, who was tall and strong, made no further ado, but with her two arms seized the Duchesse de Rohan, turned her round, and sat down in her place. All the ladies were strangely scandalised at this, but none dared say a word, not even Madame de Lude, lady in waiting on the Duchesse de Bourgogne, who, for her part also, felt the insolence of the act, but dared not speak, being so young. As for the Duchesse de Rohan, feeling that opposition must lead to fisticuffs, she curtseyed to the Duchesse, and quietly retired to another place. A few minutes after this, Madame de Saint-Simon, who was then with child, feeling herself unwell, and tired of standing, seated herself upon the first cushion she could find. It so happened, that in the position she thus occupied, she had taken precedence of Madame d'Armagnac by two degrees. Madame d'Armagnac, perceiving it, spoke to her upon the subject. Madame de Saint-Simon who had only placed herself there for a moment, did not reply, but went elsewhere.

As soon as I learnt of the first adventure, I thought it important that such an insult should not be borne, and I went and conferred with M. de la Rochefoucauld upon the subject, at the same time that Maréchal de Boufflers spoke of it to M. de Noailles. I called upon other of my friends, and the opinion was that the Duc de Rohan should complain to the King on the morrow of the treatment his wife had received.

In the evening while I was at the King's supper, I was sent for by Madame de Saint-Simon, who informed me that the Lorraines, afraid of the complaints that would probably be addressed to the King upon what had taken place between the Princesse d'Harcourt and the Duchesse de Rohan, had availed themselves of what happened between Madame de Saint-Simon and Madame d'Armagnac, in order to be the first to complain, so that one might balance the other. Here was a specimen of the artifice of these gentlemen, which much enraged me. On the instant I determined to lose no time in speaking to the King; and that evening I related what had occurred, in so far as Madame de Saint-Simon was concerned, but made no allusion to M. de Rohan's affair, thinking it best to leave that to be settled by itself on the morrow. The King replied to me very graciously, and I retired, after assuring him that all I had said was true from beginning to end.

The next day the Duc de Rohan made his complaint. The King who had already been fully informed of the matter, received him well, praised the respect and moderation of Madame de Rohan, declared Madame d'Harcourt to have been very impertinent, and said very hard words upon the Lorraines.

I found afterwards, that Madame de Maintenon, who much favoured Madame d'Harcourt, had all the trouble in the world to persuade the King not to exclude her from the next journey to Marly. She received a severe reprimand from the King, a good scolding from Madame de Maintenon, and was compelled publicly to ask pardon of the Duchesse de Rohan. This she did; but with a crawling baseness equal to her previous audacity. Such was the end of this strange history.

Nearly at the same time we lost the celebrated Racine, so known by his beautiful plays. No one possessed a greater talent or a more agreeable mien. There was nothing of the poet in his manners: he had the air of a well-bred and modest man, and at last that of a good man. He had friends, the most illustrious, at the Court as well as among men of letters. I leave it to the latter to speak of him in a better way than I can. He wrote, for the amusement of the King and Madame de Maintenon, and to exercise the young ladies of Saint-Cyr, two dramatic masterpieces, *Esther* and *Athalie*. They were very difficult to write, because there could be no love in them, and because they are sacred tragedies, in which, from respect to the Holy Scriptures, it was necessary rigidly to keep to the historical truth. They were several times played at Saint-Cyr before a select Court. Racine was charged with the history of the King, conjointly with Despreaux, his friend. This employment, the pieces I have just spoken of, and his friends, gained for Racine some special favours. It sometimes happened that the King had no ministers with him, as on Fridays, and, above all, when the bad weather of winter rendered the sittings very long; then he would send for Racine to amuse him and Madame de Maintenon.

M. de Vendôme began at last to think about his health, which his debauches had thrown into a very bad state. He took public leave of the King and of all the Court before going away, to put himself in the hands of the doctors. It was the first and only example of such impudence. From this time he lost ground. The King said, at parting, that he hoped he would come back in such a state that people might kiss him without danger. His going in triumph, where another would have gone in shame and secrecy, was startling and disgusting. He was nearly three months under the most skilful treatment—and returned to the Court with half his nose, his teeth out, and a physiognomy entirely changed, almost idiotic. The King was so much struck by this change, that he recommended the courtiers not to appear to notice it, for fear of afflicting M. de Vendôme. That was taking much interest in him assuredly. As, moreover, he had departed in triumph upon his medical expedition, so he returned triumphant by the reception of the King, which was imitated by all the Court. He remained only a few days, and then, his mirror telling sad tales, went away to Anet, to see if nose and teeth would come back to him with his hair.

On the night between the 3rd and 4th of June, a daring robbery was effected at the grand stables of Versailles. All the horse-cloths and trappings, worth at least fifty thousand crowns, were carried off, and so cleverly and with such speed, although the night was short, that no traces of them could ever afterwards be found. This theft reminds me of another which took place a little before the commencement of these memoirs. The grand apartment at Versailles, that is to say, from the gallery to the tribune, was hung with crimson velvet, trimmed and fringed with gold. One fine morning the fringe and trimmings were all found to have been cut away. This appeared extraordinary in a place so frequented all day, so well closed at night, and so well guarded at all times. Bontems, the King's valet was in despair, and did his utmost to discover the thieves, but without success.

Five or six days afterwards, I was at the King's supper, with nobody but Daquin, chief physician, between the King and *me*, and nobody at all between *me* and the table. Suddenly I perceived a large black form in the air, but before I could tell what it was, it fell upon the end of the King's table just before the cover which had been laid for *Monseigneur* and

Madame. By the noise it made in falling, and the weight of the thing itself, it seemed as though the table must be broken. The plates jumped up, but none were upset, and the thing, as luck would have it, did not fall upon any of them, but simply upon the cloth. The King moved his head half round, and without being moved in any way said, 'I think that is my fringe!'

It was indeed a bundle, larger than a flat-brimmed priest's hat, about two feet in height, and shaped like a pyramid. It had come from behind me, from towards the middle door of the two ante-chambers, and a piece of fringe getting loose in the air, had fallen upon the King's wig, from which it was removed by Livry, a gentleman-in-waiting. Livry also opened the bundle, and saw that it did indeed contain the fringes all twisted up, and everybody saw likewise. A murmur was heard. Livry wishing to take away the bundle found a paper attached to it. He took the paper and left the bundle. The King stretched out his hand and said, 'Let us see.' Livry, and with reason, would not give up the paper, but stepped back, read it, and then passed it to Daquin, in whose hands I read it. The writing counterfeited and long like that of a woman, was in these words:—'Take back your fringes, Bontems; they are not worth the trouble of keeping—my compliments to the King.'

Nothing has since been discovered respecting this theft or its bold restitution.

On the 12th August, Madame de Saint-Simon was happily delivered of a second son, who bore the name of Marquis de Ruffec. A singular event which happened soon after, made all the world marvel.

There arrived at Versailles a farrier, from the little town of Salon, in Provence, who asked to see the King in private. In spite of the rebuffs he met with, he persisted in his request, so that at last it got to the ears of the King. The King sent word that he was not accustomed to grant such audiences to whoever liked to ask for them. Thereupon the farrier declared that if he was allowed to see the King he would tell him things so secret and so unknown to everybody else that he would be persuaded of their importance, demanding, if the King would not see him, to be sent to a minister of state. Upon this the King allowed him to have an interview with one of his secretaries, Barbezieux. But Barbezieux was not a minister of state, and to the great surprise of everybody, the farrier, who had only just arrived from the country, and who had never before left it or his trade, replied, that not being a minister of state he would not speak with him. Upon this he was allowed to see Pomponne, and converse with him; and this is the story he told.

He said, that returning home late one evening he found himself surrounded by a great light, close against a tree and near Salon. A woman clad in white—but altogether in a royal manner, and beautiful, fair, and very dazzling—called him by his name, commanded him to listen to her, and spake to him more than half an hour. She told him she was the Queen, who had been the wife of the King; to whom she ordered him to go and say what she had communicated; assuring him that God would assist him through all the journey, and that upon a secret thing he should say, the King, who alone knew that secret, would recognize the truth of all he uttered. She said that in case he could not see the King he was to speak with a minister of state, telling him certain things, but reserving certain others for the King alone. She told him, moreover, to set out at once, assuring him he would be punished with death if he neglected to acquit himself of his commission. The farrier promised to obey her in everything, and the Queen then disappeared. He found himself in darkness near the tree. He laid down and passed the night there, scarcely knowing whether he was awake or asleep. In the morning he went home, persuaded that what he had seen was a mere delusion and folly and said nothing about it to a living soul.

Two days afterwards he was passing by the same place when the same vision appeared to him, and he was addressed in the same terms. Fresh threats of punishment were uttered if he did not comply, and he was ordered to go at once to the Intendant of the province, who would assuredly furnish him with money, after saying what he had seen. This time the farrier was convinced there was no delusion in the matter; but, halting between his fears and doubts, knew not what to do, told no one what had passed, and was in great perplexity. He remained thus eight days, and at last had resolved not to make the journey; when, passing by the same spot, he saw and heard the same vision, which bestowed upon him so many dreadful menaces that he no longer thought of anything but setting out immediately. In two days from that time he presented himself, at Aix, to the Intendant of the province, who, without a moment's hesitation, urged him to pursue his journey, and gave him sufficient money to travel by a public conveyance. Nothing more of the story was ever known.

The farrier had three interviews with M. de Pomponne, each of two hours' length. M. de Pomponne rendered, in private, an account of these to the King, who desired him to speak more fully upon the point in a council composed of the Ducs de Beauvilliers, Pontchartrain, Torcy, and Pomponne himself; *Monseigneur* to be excluded. This council sat very long, perhaps because other things were spoken of. Be that as it may, the King after this wished to converse with the farrier, and did so in his cabinet. Two days afterwards he saw the man again, at each time was nearly an hour with him, and was careful that no one was within hearing.

The day after the first interview, as the King was descending the staircase, to go a-hunting, M. de Duras, who was in waiting, and who was upon such a footing that he said almost what he liked, began to speak of this farrier with contempt, and, quoting the bad proverb, said, 'The man was mad, or the King was not noble.' At this the King stopped, and, turning round, a thing he scarcely ever did in walking, replied, 'If that be so, I am not noble, for I have discoursed with him long, he has spoken to me with much good sense, and I assure you he is far from being mad.'

These last words were pronounced with a sustained gravity which greatly surprised those near, and which in the midst of deep silence opened all eyes and ears. After the second interview the King felt persuaded that one circumstance had been related to him by the farrier, which he alone knew, and which had happened more than twenty years before. It was that he had seen a phantom in the forest of Saint-Germains. Of this phantom he had never breathed a syllable to anybody.

The King on several other occasions spoke favourably of the farrier; moreover, he paid all the expenses the man had been put to, gave him a gratuity, sent him back free, and wrote to the Intendant of the province to take particular care of him, and never to let him want for anything all his life.

The most surprising thing of all this is, that none of the ministers could be induced to speak a word upon the occurrence. Their most intimate friends continually questioned them, but without being able to draw forth a syllable. The ministers either affected to laugh at the matter or answered evasively. This was the case whenever I questioned M. de Beauvilliers or M. de Pontchartrain, and I knew from their most intimate friends that nothing more could ever be obtained from M. de Pomponne or M. de Torcy. As for the farrier himself, he was equally reserved. He was a simple honest, and modest man, about fifty years of age. Whenever addressed upon this subject, he cut short all discourse by saying, 'I am not allowed to speak,' and nothing more could be extracted from him. When he returned to his home he conducted himself just as before, gave himself no airs, and never boasted of the interview he had had with the King and his ministers. He went back to his trade, and worked at it as usual.

The King bestowed at this time some more distinctions on his illegitimate children. M. du Maine, as grand-master of the artillery, had to be received at the Chambre des Comptes; and his place ought to have been, according to custom, immediately above that of the senior member. But the King wished him to be put between the first and second president; and this was done. The King accorded also to the Princesse de Conti that her two ladies of honour should be allowed to sit at the Duchesse de Bourgogne's table. It was a privilege that no lady of honour to a Princess of the blood had ever been allowed. But the King gave these distinctions to the ladies of his illegitimate children, and refused it to those of the Princesses of the blood.

Boucherat, chancellor and keeper of the seals, died on the 2nd of September. Harlay, as I have previously said, had been promised this appointment when it became vacant. But the chancellorship was given to Pontchartrain, and the office of comptroller-general, which became vacant at the same time, was given to Chamillart, a very honest man, who owed his first advancement to his skill at billiards, of which game the King was formerly very fond.

The Comtesse de Fiesque died very aged, while the Court was at Fontainebleau this year. She had passed her life with the most frivolous of the great world. She was very straitened in means, because she had frittered away all her substance, or allowed herself to be pillaged by her business people. When those beautiful mirrors were first introduced she obtained one, although they were then very dear and very rare. 'Ah, Countess!' said her friends, 'where did you find that?'

'Oh!' replied she, 'I had a miserable piece of land,' which only yielded me corn; I have sold it, and I have this mirror instead. Is not this excellent? Who would hesitate between corn and this beautiful mirror?'

The Duc de Gesvres, a malicious old man, a cruel husband and unnatural father, sadly annoyed Maréchal de Villeroy towards the end of this year. M. de Gesvres and M. de Villeroy had both had fathers who made large fortunes and who became secretaries of state. One morning M. de Gesvres was waiting for the King, with a number of other courtiers, when M. de Villeroy arrived, with all that noise and those airs he had long assumed, and which his favour and his appointments rendered more superb. I know not whether this annoyed de Gesvres, more than usual, but as soon as the other had placed himself, he said, 'Monsieur le Maréchal, it must be admitted that you and I are very lucky.' The Maréchal, surprised at a remark which seemed to be suggested by nothing, assented with a modest air, and, shaking his head and his wig, began to talk to some one else. But M. de Gesvres had not commenced without a purpose. He went on, addressed M. de Villeroy point-blank, admiring their mutual good fortune, but when he came to speak of the father of each, 'Let us go no further,' said he, 'for what did our fathers spring from? From tradesmen; even tradesmen they were themselves. Yours was the son of a dealer in fresh fish at the markets, and mine of a pedlar, or, perhaps, worse. Gentlemen,' said he, addressing the company, 'have we not reason to think our fortune prodigious—the Maréchal and I?' The Maréchal would have liked to strangle M. de Gesvres, or to see him dead—but what can be done with a man who, in order to say something cutting to you, says it to himself first?

1700

The year 1700 commenced by a reform. The King declared that he would no longer bear the expense of the changes that the courtiers introduced into their apartments. It had cost him more than sixty thousand francs since the Court left Fontainebleau. It is believed that Madame de Mailly was the cause of this determination of the King; for during the last two or three years she had made changes in her apartments every year.

From just before Candlemas-day to Easter of this year, nothing was heard of but balls and pleasures of the Court. The King gave at Versailles and at Marly several masquerades, by which he was much amused, under pretext of amusing the Duchesse de Bourgogne. No evening passed on which there was not a ball. Madame de Saint-Simon and I passed the last three weeks of this time without ever seeing the day. I was delighted when Ash Wednesday arrived; and I remained a day or two dead beat, and Madame de Saint-Simon could not get over Shrove Tuesday.

Madame la Duchesse, whose heavy tradesmen's debts the King had paid not long since had not dared to speak of her gambling debts, also very heavy. They increased, and, entirely unable to pay them, she found herself in the greatest embarrassment. She feared, above all things, lest *M. le Prince* or *M. le Duc* should hear of this. In this extremity she addressed herself to Madame de Maintenon, laying bare the state of her finances, without the slightest disguise. Madame de Maintenon had pity on her situation, and arranged that the King should pay her debts, abstain from scolding her, and keep her secret. Thus, in a few weeks, *Madame la Duchesse* found herself free of debts, without anybody whom she feared having known even of their existence.

Langlée was entrusted with the payment and arrangement of these debts. He was a singular kind of man at the Court, and deserves a word. Born of obscure parents, who had enriched themselves, he had early been introduced into the great world, and had devoted himself to play, gaining an immense fortune; but without being accused of the least unfairness. With but little or no wit, but much knowledge of the world, he had succeded in securing many friends, and in making his way at the Court. He joined in all the King's parties, at the time of his mistresses. Similarity of tastes attached Langlée to *Monsieur*, but he never lost sight of the King. At all the fêtes Langlée was present, he took part in the journeys, he was invited to Marly, was intimate with all the King's mistresses; then with all the daughters of the King, with whom indeed he was so familiar that he often spoke of them with the utmost freedom. He had become such a master of fashions and of fêtes that none of the latter were given, even by Princes of the blood, except under his directions; and no houses were bought, built, furnished, or ornamented, without his taste being consulted. There were no marriages of which the dresses and the presents were not chosen, or at least approved, by him. He was on intimate terms with the most distinguished people of the Court; and often took improper advantage of his position. To the daughters of the King and to a number of female friends he said horribly filthy things, and that too in their own houses, at St. Cloud or at Marly. He was often made a confidant in matters of gallantry, and continued to be made so all his life. For he was a sure man, had nothing disagreeable about him, was obliging, always ready to serve others with his purse or his influence, and was on bad terms with no one.

At the marriage of Monseigneur the Duc de Bourgogne, the King had offered to augment considerably his monthly income. The young Prince, who found it sufficient, replied with thanks, and said that if money failed him at any time he would take the liberty of asking the King for more. Finding himself short just now, he was as good as his word. The King praised him highly, and told him to ask whenever he wanted money, not through a third person, but direct, as he had done in this instance. The King, moreover, told the Duc de Bourgogne to play without fear, for it was of no consequence how much such persons as he might lose. The King was pleased with confidence, but all the same liked to see himself feared; and when timid people who spoke to him, grew embarrassed in their discourse, nothing better made their court, or advanced their interests.

Le Nôtre died about this time, after having been eighty-eight years in perfect health, and with all his faculties and good taste to the very last. He was illustrious, as having been the first designer of those beautiful gardens which adorn France, and which, indeed, have so much surpassed the gardens of Italy, that the most famous masters of that country come here to admire and learn. Le Nôtre had a probity, an exactitude, and an uprightness which made him esteemed and loved by everybody. He never forgot his position, and was always perfectly disinterested. He worked for private people as for the King, and with the same application—seeking only to aid nature, and to attain the beautiful by the shortest road. He was of a charming simplicity and truthfulness. The Pope, upon one occasion, begged the King to lend him Le Nôtre for some months. On entering the Pope's chamber, instead of going down upon his knees, Le Nôtre ran to the Holy Father, clasped him round the neck, kissed him on the two cheeks, and said—'Good morning, Reverend Father; how well you look, and how glad I am to see you in such good health.'

The Pope, who was Clement X, Altieri, burst out laughing with all his might. He was delighted with this odd salutation, and showed his friendship towards the gardener in a thousand ways.

A month before Le Nôtre's death, the King who liked to see him and to make him talk, led him into the gardens, and on account of his great age, placed him in a wheeled chair, by the side of his own. Upon this Le Nôtre said, 'Ah, my poor father, if you were living, and could see a simple gardener like me, your son, wheeled along in a chair by the side of the greatest King in the world, nothing would be wanting to my joy!'

For the last two or three years the King of Spain had been in very weak health, and in danger of his life several times. He had no children, and no hope of having any. The question, therefore, of the succession to his vast empire began now to agitate every European Court. The King of England undertook to arrange this question in a manner that should prevent war when the King of Spain died. His plan was to give Spain, the Indies, the Low Countries, and the title of King of Spain to the Archduke, second son of the Emperor; Guipuscoa, Naples, Sicily, and Lorraine to France; and the Milanese to M. de Lorraine, as compensation for taking away from him his territory.

The King of England made this proposition first of all to our King; who, tired of war, and anxious for repose, as was natural at his age, made few difficulties, and soon accepted. M. de Lorraine was not in a position to refuse his consent to a change recommended by England, France, and Holland. This much being settled, the Emperor was next applied to. But he wished to inherit the entire succession, and would not tolerate the idea of seeing the House of Austria driven from Italy, as it would have been if the King of England's proposal had been carried out. He therefore declared that he would hear nothing upon the subject until after the death of the King of Spain. The resistance he made caused the whole scheme to come to the ears of the King of Spain, instead of remaining a secret, as was intended.

The King of Spain made a great stir in consequence of what had taken place, as though the project had been formed to strip him, during his lifetime, of his realm. The Emperor next endeavoured to strengthen his party in Spain. But just at this time, a small party arose in Spain, equally opposed to the Emperor, and to the propositions of the King of England. This party consisted at first of only five persons: namely, Villafranca, Medina-Sidonia, Villagarcias, Villena, and San Estevan, all of them nobles, and well instructed in the affairs of government. Their wish was to prevent the dismemberment of the Spanish kingdom by conferring the whole succession upon the son of the only son of the Queen of France, Maria Theresa, sister of the King of Spain.

One of the first resolutions of this little party was to bind each other to secrecy. Their next was to admit into their confidence Cardinal Portocarrero, a determined enemy to the Queen. Then they commenced an attack upon the Queen in the council; and being supported by the popular voice, succeeded in driving out of the country Madame Berlips, a German favourite of hers, who was much hated on account of the undue influence she exerted, and the rapacity she displayed. The next measure was of equal importance. Madrid and its environs groaned under the weight of a regiment of Germans commanded by the Prince of Darmstadt. The council decreed that this regiment should be disbanded, and the Prince thanked for his assistance. These two blows following upon each other so closely, frightened the Queen, isolated her, and put it out of her power to act during the rest of the life of the King.

There was yet one of the preliminary steps to take, without which it was thought that success would not be certain. This was to dismiss the King's Confessor, who had been given to him by the Queen, and who was a zealous Austrian.

Cardinal Portocarrero was charged with this duty. The Confessor was dismissed, and another was put in his place, who could be relied upon to do and say exactly as he was requested. Thus, the King of Spain was influenced in his conscience, which had over him so much the more power, because he was beginning to look upon the things of this world by the glare of that terrible torch that is lighted for the dying. The Confessor and the Cardinal, after a short time, began unceasingly to attack the King upon the subject of the succession. The King, enfeebled by illness, and by a lifetime of weak health, had little power of resistance. Pressed by the many temporal, and afrighted by the many spiritual reasons which were brought forward by the two ecclesiastics, with no friend near whose opinion he could consult, no Austrian at hand to confer with, and no Spaniard who was not opposed to Austria;—the King fell into a profound perplexity, and in this strait, proposed to consult the Pope, as an authority whose decision would be infallible. The Cardinal, who felt persuaded that the Pope would declare in favour of France, assented to this step; and the King of Spain accordingly wrote a long letter to Rome, feeling much relieved by the course he had adopted.

The Pope replied at once and in the most decided manner. He said he saw clearly that the children of the Dauphin were the next heirs to the Spanish throne, and that the House of Austria had not the smallest right to it. He recommended therefore the King of Spain to render justice to whom justice was due, and to assign the succession of his monarchy to a son of France. This reply, and the letter which had given rise to it, were kept so profoundly secret that they were not known in Spain until after the King's death.

The King, meantime, was drawing near to his end. A few days after he had signed the new will he was at the last extremity, and in a few days more he died. In his last moments the Queen had been kept from him as much as possible, and was unable in any way to interfere with the plans that had been so deeply laid. As soon as the King was dead the first thing to be done was to open his will. The council of state assembled for that purpose, and all the grandees of Spain who were in the capital took part in it. All the foreign ministers besieged the door. Every one sought to be the first to know the choice of the King who had just died, in order to be the first to inform his court. Blécourt, our ambassador, was there, without knowing more than they; and Count d'Harrach, ambassador from the Emperor, who counted upon the will in favour of the Archduke, was there also, with a triumphant look, just opposite the door, and close by it.

At last the door opened, and immediately closed again. The Duc d'Abrantes, a man of much wit and humour, but not to be trifled with, came out. He wished to have the pleasure of announcing upon whom the successorship had fallen, and was surrounded as soon as he appeared. Keeping silence, and turning his eyes on all sides, he fixed them for a moment on Blécourt, then looked in another direction, as if seeking some one else. Blécourt interpreted this action as a bad omen. The Duc d'Abrantes feigning at last to discover the Count d'Harrach, assumed a gratified look, flew to him, embraced him, and said aloud in Spanish, 'Sir, it is with much pleasure;' then pausing, as though to embrace him better, he added: 'Yes, sir, it is with an extreme joy that for all my life,'—here the embraces were redoubled as an excuse for a second pause, after which he went on— 'and with the greatest contentment that I part from you, and take leave of the very august House of Austria for ever.' So saying he clove the crowd, and every one ran after him to know the name of the real heir.

The astonishment and indignation of Count d'Harrach disabled him from speaking, but showed themselves upon his face in all their extent. He remained motionless some moments, and then went away in the greatest confusion at the manner in which he had been duped.

Blécourt, on the other hand, ran home without asking other information, and at once despatched to the King a courier. The news arrived at Court in the month of November. The King was going out shooting but, upon learning what had taken place, at once countermanded the sport, announced the death of the King of Spain, and at three o'clock held a council of the ministers in the apartments of Madame de Maintenon. This council lasted until past seven o'clock in the evening. *Monseigneur*, who had been out wolf-hunting, returned in time to attend it. On the next morning, Wednesday, another council was held, and in the evening a third, in the apartments of Madame de Maintenon.

The King, *Monseigneur*, the Chancellor, the Duc de Beauvilliers, Torcy, and Madame de Maintenon, were the only persons who deliberated upon this affair. Madame de Maintenon preserved at first a modest silence; but the King forced her to give her opinion after everybody had spoken except herself. The council was divided. Two were for keeping to the treaty that had been signed with King William, two for accepting the will.

Monseigneur, drowned as he was in fat and sloth, appeared in quite another character from his usual one, at these councils. To the great surprise of the King and his assistants, when it was his turn to speak he expressed himself with force in favour of accepting the testament. Then, turning towards the King in a respectful but firm manner, he said that he took the liberty of asking for his inheritance, that the monarchy of Spain belonged to the queen his mother, and consequently to him; that he surrendered it willingly to his second son for the tranquillity of Europe; but that to none other would he yield an inch of ground. These words, spoken with an inflamed countenance, caused excessive surprise. The King listened very attentively, and then said to Madame de Maintenon, 'And you, Madame, what do you think about all this?' She began by affecting modesty; but pressed, and even commanded to speak, she expressed herself with becoming confusion; briefly sang the praises of *Monseigneur,* whom she feared and liked but little—sentiments perfectly reciprocated—and at last was for accepting the will.

The King did not yet declare himself. He said that the affair might well be allowed to sleep for four-and-twenty hours, in order that they might ascertain if the Spaniards approved the choice of their King. He dismissed the council, but ordered it to meet again the next evening at the same hour and place. Next day, several couriers arrived from Spain, and the news they brought left no doubt in the King's mind as to the wishes of the Spanish nobles and people upon the subject of the will. When therefore the council reassembled, the King, after fully discussing the matter, resolved to accept the will.

At the first receipt of the news the King and his ministers had been overwhelmed with a surprise that they could not recover from for several days. When the news was spread abroad, the Court was equally surprised. Nothing else was spoken of but this matter. The King one evening, to divert himself, asked the princesses their opinion. They replied that he should send M. le Duc d'Anjou (the second son of *Monseigneur*) into Spain, and that this was the general sentiment. 'I am sure,' replied the King, 'that whatever course I adopt many people will condemn me.'

At last, on Tuesday, the sixteenth of November, the King publicly declared himself. The Spanish ambassador had received intelligence which proved the eagerness of Spain to welcome the Duc d'Anjou as its King. There seemed to be no doubt of the matter. The King, immediately after getting up, called the ambassador into his cabinet, where M. le Duc d'Anjou had already arrived. Then, pointing to the Duc, he told the ambassador he might salute him as King of Spain. The ambassador threw himself upon his knees after the fashion of his country, and addressed to the Duc a tolerably long compliment in the Spanish language. Immediately afterwards, the King, contrary to all custom, opened the two folding doors of his cabinet, and commanded everybody to enter. It was a very full Court that day. The King, majestically turning his eyes towards the numerous company, and showing them M. le Duc d'Anjou said—'Gentlemen, behold the King of Spain. His birth called him to that crown: the late King also has called him to it by his will; the whole nation wished for him, and has asked me for him eagerly; it is the will of heaven: I have obeyed it with pleasure.' And then, turning towards his grandson, he said, 'Be a good Spaniard, that is your first duty; but remember that you are a Frenchman born, in order that the union between the two nations may be preserved; it will be the means of rendering both happy, and of preserving the peace of Europe.'

When the hubbub of the courtiers had subsided, the two other sons of France, brothers of M. d'Anjou, arrived, and all three embraced each other tenderly several times, with tears in their eyes. The ambassador of the Emperor immediately entered, little suspecting what had taken place, and was confounded when he learned the news. The new King of Spain, during the rest of his stay in France, was publicly treated in every respect as a sovereign, by the King and all the Court.

The joy of *Monseigneur* at all this was very great. The King himself was so overcome, that at supper he turned to the Spanish ambassador and said that the whole affair seemed to him like a dream. In public, as I have observed, the new King of Spain was treated in every respect as a sovereign, but in private he was still the Duc d'Anjou. He passed his evenings in the apartments of Madame de Maintenon, where he played at all sorts of children's games, scampering to and fro with his brothers, with Madame la Duchesse de Bourgogne, and with the few ladies to whom access was permitted.

On Saturday, the 4th of December, the King of Spain set out for his dominions. The King rode with him in his coach as far as Sceaux, surrounded in pomp by many more guards than usual, gendarmes and light horse, all the road covered with coaches and people; and Sceaux, where they arrived a little after midday, full of ladies and courtiers, guarded by two companies of Musketeers. There was a good deal of leave-taking and all the family was collected alone in the last room of the apartment; but as the doors were left open, the tears they shed so bitterly could be seen. In presenting the King of Spain to the Princes of the blood, the King said—'Behold the Princes of my blood and of yours; the two nations from this time ought to regard themselves as one nation; they ought to have the same interests; therefore I wish these Princes to be attached to you as to me; you cannot have friends more faithful or more certain.' All this lasted a good hour and a half. But the time of separation at last came. The King conducted the King of Spain to the end of the apartment, and embraced him several times, holding him a long while in his arms. *Monseigneur* did the same. The spectacle was extremely touching.

The King returned into the palace for some time, in order to recover himself and the King of Spain, with his brother, M. de Noailles, and a large number of courtiers, set out on his journey. The King gave to his grandson twenty-one purses of a thousand louis each, for pocket-money, and much money besides for presents.

The King of Spain arrived in Madrid on the 19th February. From his first entrance into the country he had everywhere been most warmly welcomed. Acclamations were uttered when he appeared; *fêtes* and bull-fights were given in his honour; the nobles and ladies pressed around him. He had been proclaimed in Madrid some time before, in the midst of demonstrations of joy. Now that he had arrived among his subjects there, that joy burst out anew. The King was just then in the flower of his first youth —fair like the late King Charles, and the Queen his grandmother; grave, silent, measured, self-contained, formed exactly to live among Spaniards. With all this, very attentive in his demeanour, and paying everybody the attention due to him, having taken lessons from d'Harcourt on the way. Indeed he took off his hat or raised it to nearly everybody, so that the Spaniards spoke on the subject to the Duc d'Harcourt, who replied to them that the King in all essential things would conform himself to usage, but that in others he must be allowed to act according to French politeness.

Shortly after his arrival in Madrid, the new King of Spain began to look about him for a wife, and his marriage with the second daughter of M. de Savoie (younger sister of Madame de Bourgogne) was decided upon. An extraordinary ambassador was sent to Turin to sign the contract of marriage, and bring back the new Queen into Spain, and the Princesse des Ursins was selected as her *Camarera Mayor*, a very important office. The Princesse des Ursins seemed just adapted for it. A Spanish lady could not have been relied upon: a lady of our court would not have been fit for the post. The Princesse des Ursins was, as it were, both French and Spanish—French by birth, Spanish by marriage. She had passed the greater part of her life in Rome and Italy, and was a widow without children.

The royal marriage was celebrated at Turin, on the 11th of September, with but little display, the King being represented by procuration, and the bride set out on the 13th for Nice, where she was to embark on board the Spanish galleys for Barcelona. The King of Spain left Madrid on the 5th of September, to journey through Aragon and Catalonia to Barcelona to meet his wife. He was much welcomed on his route, above all by Saragossa, which received him magnificently.

The new Queen of Spain, brought by the French galleys to Nice, was so fatigued with the sea when she arrived there, that she determined to finish the rest of the journey by land, through Provence and Languedoc. Her graces, her presence of mind, the aptness and the politeness of her short replies, and her judicious curiosity, remarkable at her age, surprised everybody, and gave great hopes to the Princesse des Ursins.

When within two days' journey of Barcelona, the Queen was met by a messenger, bearing presents and compliments from the King. All her household joined her at the same time, being sent on in advance for that purpose, and her Piedmontese attendants were dismissed. Upon arriving at Figueras, the King, impatient to see her, went on before on horseback. In this first embarrassment Madame des Ursins, although completely unknown to the King, and but little known to the Queen, was of great service to both.

Upon arriving at Figueras, the bishop diocesan married them anew, with little ceremony, and soon after they sat down to supper, waited upon by the Princesse des Ursins and the ladies of the palace, half the dishes being French, half Spanish. This mixture displeased the ladies of the palace and several of the Spanish grandees, who plotted with the ladies openly to mark their displeasure; and they did so in a scandalous manner. Under one pretext or another—such as the weight or heat of the dishes—not one of the French dishes arrived upon the table; all were upset; while the Spanish dishes, on the contrary, were served without any accident. The affectation and the air of chagrin, to say the least of it, of the ladies of the palace, were too visible not to be perceived. But the King and Queen were wise enough to appear not to notice this; and Madame des Ursins, much astonished, said not a word.

After a long and disagreeable supper, the King and Queen withdrew. Then feelings which had been kept in during supper overflowed. The Queen wept for her Piedmontese women. Like a child, as she was, she thought herself lost in the hands of ladies so insolent; and when it was time to go to bed, she said flatly that she would not go, and that she wished to return home. Everything was done to console her; but the astonishment and embarrassment were great indeed when it was found that all was of no avail. The King had undressed, and was awaiting her. Madame des Ursins was at length obliged to go and tell him the resolution the Queen had taken. He was piqued and annoyed. He had until that time lived with the completest regularity; which had contributed to make him find the Princesse more to his taste than he might otherwise have done. He was therefore affected by her *fantaisie*, and by the same reason easily persuaded that she would not keep to it beyond the first night.

Madame des Ursins consulted with two of the courtiers, as to the best measures to be adopted with a child who showed so much force and resolution. The night was passed in exhortations and in promises upon what had occurred at the supper; and the Queen consented at last to remain Queen. The Duke of Medina-Sidonia and Count San Estevan were consulted on the morrow. They were of opinion that in his turn the King should not visit the Queen on the following night. This opinion was acted upon. The

King and Queen did not see each other in private that day. In the evening the Queen was very sorry. Her pride and her little vanity were wounded; perhaps also she had found the King to her taste.

The ladies and the grand seigneurs who had attended at the supper were lectured for what had occurred there. Excuses, promises, demands for pardon, followed; all was put right; the third day was tranquil, and the third night more agreeable to the young people. On the fourth day they went to Barcelona where only fêtes and pleasures awaited them. Soon after they set out for Madrid.

From the moment that Philip V ascended the Spanish throne it was seen that a war was certain. Italy, it was evident at once, would be the spot on which hostilities would commence, and our King lost no time in taking measures to be ready for events. By land and by sea every preparation was made for the struggle about to take place.

Here follows a long account of the Italian campaign of 1701 which I omit. It is of itself neither very important nor interesting, and Saint-Simon's account of it is difficult to follow.

1701

But it is time now for me to go back to other matters, and to start again from the commencement of 1701, from which I have been led by reciting in a continuous story, the particulars of our first campaign in Italy.

Barbezieux[1] had viewed with discontent the elevation of Chamillart. His pride and presumption rose in arms against it; but as there was no remedy he gave himself up to debauch, to dissipate his annoyance, and committing excesses above his strength, was seized with a fever, and died in a few days, looking death steadily in the face.

He was thirty-three years of age, with a striking and expressive countenance, and much wit and aptitude for labour. He was remarkable for grace, fine manners, and winning ways; but his pride and ambition were excessive, and when his fits of ill-temper came, nothing could repress them. Resistance always excited and irritated him. He had accustomed the King—whenever he had drunk too much, or when a party of pleasure was

[1] Secretary for War.

44

toward—to put off work to another time. It was a great question, whether the State gained or lost most by his death.

Chamillart was appointed in the place of Barbezieux, as Secretary of State; and wanted to give up the Finances, but the King, remembering the disputes of Louvois and Colbert, insisted on his occupying both posts. Chamillart was a very worthy man, with clean hands and the best intentions, polite, patient, obliging, a good friend, and a moderate enemy, loving his country, but his King better; and on very good terms with him and Madame de Maintenon. His mind was limited, and like all persons of little wit and knowledge, he was obstinate and pig-headed—smiling affectedly with a gentle compassion on whoever opposed reasons to his, but utterly incapable of understanding them. The most remarkable thing is that the chief origin of the King's tender regard for him was his incapacity. He used to confess it to the King at every opportunity; and the King took pleasure in directing and instructing him, so that he was interested in his successes as if they had been his own, and always excused him. The world and the Court excused him also, charmed by the facility with which he received people, the pleasure he felt in granting requests and rendering services, the gentleness and regretfulness of his refusals, and his indefatigable patience as a listener. His memory was so great that he remembered all matters submitted to him, which gave pleasure to people who were afraid of being forgotten. He wrote excellently; and his clear, flowing, and precise style was extremely pleasing to the King and Madame de Maintenon, who were never weary of praising him, encouraging him, and congratulating themselves for having placed upon such weak shoulders two burdens, each of which was sufficient to overwhelm the most sturdy.

Rose, secretary in the King's cabinet, died, aged about eighty-six, at the commencement of the year. For nearly fifty years he had held the office of the 'pen,' as it is called. To have the 'pen,' is to be a public forger, and to do what would cost anybody else his life. This office consists in imitating so exactly the handwriting of the King, that the real cannot be distinguished from the counterfeit. In this manner are written all the letters that the King ought or wishes to write with his own hand, but which, nevertheless, he will not take the trouble to write. It is not possible to make a great King speak with more dignity than did Rose; nor with more fitness to each person, and upon every subject. The King signed all the letters Rose wrote, and the characters were so alike it was imposible to find the smallest difference. Many important things had passed through the hands of Rose. He was extremely faithful and secret, and the King put entire trust in him.

For some time past *Monsieur* had been sorely grieved that his son, M. le

Duc de Chartres, had not been appointed to the command of an army. When M. de Chartres married, the King, who had converted his nephew by force into a son-in-law, promised him all kinds of favours; but except those which were written down in black and white had not given him any. M. de Chartres, annoyed at this, and at the manner in which the illegitimate children were promoted over his head, had given himself up to all kinds of youthful follies and excesses. The King was surprised to find *Monsieur* agree with his son's ambition; but gave a flat refusal when overtures were made to him on the subject. All hope of rising to a high command was thus forbidden to the Duc de Chartres; so that *Madame* had a fine excuse for sneering at the weakness which had been shown by *Monsieur*, who, on his part, had long before repented of it. He winked, therefore, at all the escapades performed or threatened by his son, and said nothing, not being sorry that the King should become uneasy, which was soon the case.

The King at last spoke to *Monsieur*; and being coldly received, reproached him for not knowing how to exercise authority over his son. Upon this *Monsieur* fired up; and asked the King what was to be done with a son at such an age: who was sick of treading the galleries of Versailles and the pavement of the Court; of being married as he was, and of remaining, as it were, naked, whilst his brothers-in-law were clothed in dignities, governments, establishments, and offices,—against all policy and all example. His son, he said, was worse off than any one in the King's service, for all others could earn distinction; added, that idleness was the mother of all vice, and that it gave him much pain to see his only son abandon himself to debauchery and bad company; but that it would be cruel to blame a young man, forced as it were into these follies, and to say nothing against him by whom he was thus forced.

Who was astonished to hear this straightforward language? Why, the King. *Monsieur* had never let out to within a thousand leagues of this tone, which was only the more annoying because supported by unanswerable reasons. However, the King answered as a brother rather than as a sovereign; endeavouring, by gentle words, to calm the excitement of *Monsieur*. But *Monsieur* was stung to the quick by the King's neglect of M. de Chartres, and would not be pacified. The conversation lasted very long, and was pushed very far; *Monsieur* throughout taking the high tone, the King very gentle. They separated in this manner,—*Monsieur* frowning, but not daring to burst out; the King annoyed, but not wishing to estrange his brother, much less to let their squabble be known.

As *Monsieur* passed most of his summers at St. Cloud, the separation which this occasioned put them at their ease whilst waiting for a reconciliation; and *Monsieur* came less often than before, but when he did filled all their private interviews with bitter talk.

Ordinarily, whenever *Monsieur* or *Madame* were unwell, even if their little finger ached, the King visited them at once; and continued his visits if the sickness lasted. But now, *Madame* had been laid up for six weeks with a tertian fever. The King had not been to see her, although *Monsieur* had urged him to do so. This was taken by *Monsieur*, who was ignorant of the private cause of indignation alluded to, for a public mark of extreme disrespect; and being proud and sensitive, he was piqued thereby to the last degree.

He had other mental troubles to torment him. For some time past he had had a Confessor, who although a Jesuit, kept as tight a hand over him as he could. He was a gentleman of good birth, and of Brittany, by name le Père du Trévoux. As a penance for his past life he forbade *Monsieur*, not only certain strange pleasures, but many which he thought he could innocently indulge in. He often told him that he had no mind to be damned on his account; and that if he was thought too harsh let another Confessor be appointed. He also told him to take great care of himself, as he was old, worn out with debauchery, fat, short-necked, and, according to all appearance, likely to die soon of apoplexy. These were terrible words to a prince, the most voluptuous and the most attached to life that had been seen for a long time; who had always passed his days in the most luxurious idleness, and who was the most incapable by nature of all serious application, of all serious reading, and of all self-examination. He was afraid of the devil; and he remembered that his former Confessor had resigned for similar reasons as this new one was actuated by. He was forced now, therefore, to look a little into himself, and to live in a manner, that for him, might be considered rigid. From time to time he said many prayers; he obeyed his Confessor, and rendered an account to him of the conduct he had prescribed in respect to play and many other things, and patiently suffered his Confessor's long discourses. He became sad, dejected, and spoke less than usual—that is to say, only about as much as three or four women— so that everybody soon saw this great change. It would have been strange if all these troubles together had not made a great revolution in a man like *Monsieur*, full-blooded, and a great eater, not only at meals, but all the day.

On Thursday, the 8th of June, he went from St. Cloud to dine with the King at Marly; and, as was his custom, entered the Cabinet, as soon as the

Council of State went out. He found the King angry with M. de Chartres for neglecting his wife, and allowing her to seek consolation for this neglect in the society of others. M. de Chartres was at that time enamoured of Mademoiselle de Sery, maid of honour to *Madame*, and carried on his suit in the most open and flagrant manner. The King took this for his theme, and very stiffly reproached *Monsieur* for the conduct of his son. *Monsieur*, who needed little to exasperate him, tartly replied, that fathers who had led certain lives had little authority over their children, and little right to blame them. The King, who felt the point of the answer, fell back on the patience of his daughter, and said that at least she ought not to be allowed to see the truth so clearly. But *Monsieur* was resolved to have his fling, and recalled, in the most aggravating manner, the conduct the King had adopted towards his queen, with respect to his mistresses, even allowing the latter to accompany him in his journeys—the queen at his side, and all in the same coach. This last remark drove the King beyond all patience, and he redoubled his reproaches, so that presently both were shouting to one another at the top of their voices. The door of the room in which they wrangled was open, and only covered by a curtain, as was the custom at Marly, and the adjoining room was full of courtiers, waiting to see the King go by to dinner. On the other side was a little salon, devoted to very private purposes, and filled with valets, who could hear distinctly every word of what passed. The attendant without, upon hearing this noise, entered, and told the King how many people were within hearing, and immediately retired. The conversation did not stop, however; it was simply carried on in a lower tone. *Monsieur* continued his reproaches; said that the King, in marrying his daughter to M. de Chartres, had promised marvels, and had done nothing; that for his part he had wished his son to serve, to keep him out of the way of these intrigues, but that his demands had been vain; that it was no wonder M. de Chartres amused himself, by way of consolation, for the neglect he had been treated with. *Monsieur* added, that he saw only too plainly the truth of what had been predicted, namely, that he would have all the shame and dishonour of the marriage without ever deriving any profit from it. The King, more and more carried away by anger, replied, that the war would soon oblige him to make some retrenchments, and that he would commence by cutting down the pensions of *Monsieur*, since he showed himself so little accommodating.

At this moment the King was informed that his dinner was ready, and both he and Monsieur left the room and went to table,—*Monsieur*, all fury, flushed, and with eyes inflamed by anger. His face thus crimsoned induced some ladies who were at table, and some courtiers behind—but more for the purpose of saying something than anything else—to make the remark, that *Monsieur*, by his appearance, had great need of bleeding. The same thing had been said some time before at Saint-Cloud; and, indeed, he had himself admitted that it was true. Even the King, in spite of their squabbles, had more than once pressed him to consent. But Tancrede, his head surgeon, was old, and an unskilful bleeder: he had missed fire once. *Monsieur* would not be bled by him; and not to vex him, was good enough to refuse being bled by another, and to die in consequence.

Upon hearing this observation about bleeding, the King spoke to him again on the subject; and said that he did not know what prevented him from having him at once taken to his room, and bled by force. The dinner passed in the ordinary manner; and *Monsieur* ate extremely, as he did at all his meals, to say nothing of an abundant supply of chocolate in the morning, and what he swallowed all day in the shape of fruit, pastry, preserves, and every kind of dainties, with which indeed the tables of his cabinets and his pockets were always filled.

In the evening, after supper, the King was in his cabinet, with *Monseigneur* and the Princesses, as at Versailles, when a messenger came from Saint-Cloud, and asked to see the King in the name of the Duc de Chartres. He was admitted into the cabinet, and said that *Monsieur* had been taken very ill while at supper; that he had been bled, that he was better, but that an emetic had been given to him. The fact was, *Monsieur* had supped as usual with the ladies, who were at Saint-Cloud. During the meal, as he poured out a glass of liqueur for Madame de Bouillon, it was perceived that he stammered, and pointed at something with his hand. As it was customary with him sometimes to speak Spanish, some of the ladies asked what he said, others cried aloud. All this was the work of an instant, and immediately afterwards *Monsieur* fell in a fit of apoplexy upon M. de Chartres, who supported him. He was taken into his room, shaken, moved about, bled considerably, and had strong emetics administered to him, but scarcely any signs of life did he show.

Upon hearing this news, the King, who had been accustomed to fly to visit *Monsieur* for a mere nothing, went to Madame de Maintenon's, and had her waked up. He passed a quarter of an hour with her, and then, towards midnight, returning to his room, ordered his coach to be got ready, and sent the Marquis de Gesvres to Saint-Cloud, to see if *Monsieur* was worse, in which case he was to return and wake him; and they went quietly to bed.

A moment after the King had got into bed, a page came to say that *Monsieur* was better, and that he had just asked for some Schaffhausen water, which is excellent for apoplexy. An hour and a half later, another messenger came, awakened the King, and told him that the emetic had no effect, and that *Monsieur* was very ill. At this the King rose and set out at once. On the way he met the Marquis de Gesvres, who was coming to fetch him, and brought similar news. It may be imagined what a hubbub and disorder there was this night at Marly, and what horror at Saint-Cloud, that palace of delight! Everybody who was at Marly hastened as he was best able to Saint-Cloud. Whoever was first ready started together. Men and women jostled each other, and then threw themselves into the coaches without order and without regard to etiquette.

The King arrived at Saint-Cloud before three o'clock in the morning. *Monsieur* had not had a moment's consciousness since his attack. A ray of intelligence came to him for an instant, while his confessor, Père du Trévoux, went to say mass, but it returned no more.

The King appeared much moved; naturally he wept with great facility; he was, therefore, all tears. He had never had cause not to love his brother tenderly; although on bad terms with him for the last two months, these sad moments recalled all his tenderness; perhaps too, he reproached himself for having hastened death by the scene of the morning. The King heard mass at Saint-Cloud; and, towards eight o'clock in the morning, *Monsieur* being past all hope, Madame de Maintenon and Madame la Duchesse de Bourgogne persuaded the King to stay no longer, and accordingly returned with him in his carriage to Marly. As he was going out and was showing some sign of affection to M. de Chartres—both weeping very much—that young Prince did not fail to take advantage of the opportunity. 'Oh Sire!' he exclaimed, embracing the King's thighs, 'what will become of me? I lose *Monsieur*, and I know that you do not like me.' The King, surprised and much touched, embraced him, and said all the tender things he could.

On arriving at Marly, the King went with the Duchesse de Bourgogne to Madame de Maintenon. Three hours after came M. Fagon, who had been ordered not to leave *Monsieur* until he was dead or better—which could not be but by miracle. The King said, as soon as he saw him: 'Well! M. Fagon, my brother is dead?' 'Yes, Sire,' said Fagon, 'no remedy has taken effect.'

The King wept a good deal. He was pressed to dine with Madame de Maintenon; but he would not do so, and had his dinner, as usual, with the ladies. The tears often ran down his cheek, during the meal, which was short. After this, he shut himself up in Madame de Maintenon's rooms until seven o'clock, and then took a turn in his garden. Afterwards he worked with Chamillart and Pontchartrain; and arranged all the funeral

Louis XIV

From a wax relief by Antoine Benoist, 1706

ceremonies of *Monsieur*. He supped an hour before his customary time, and went to bed soon afterwards.

At the departure from Saint-Cloud of the King, all the crowd assembled there little by little withdrew, so that *Monsieur* dying, stretched upon a couch in his cabinet, remained exposed to the scullions and the lower officers of the household, the majority of whom, either by affection or interest, were much afflicted. The chief officers and others who lost posts and pensions filled the air with their cries; whilst all the women who were at Saint-Cloud, and who lost their consideration and their amusement, ran here and there, crying, with dishevelled hair, like Bacchantes.

Madame, who had never had great affection or great esteem for *Monsieur*, but who felt her loss and her fall, meanwhile remained in her cabinet, and in the midst of her grief cried out, with all her might, 'No convent! Let no one talk of a convent! I will have nothing to do with a convent!' The good Princess had not lost her judgment. She knew that, by her compact of marriage, she had to choose, on becoming a widow, between a convent and the château of Montargis. She liked neither alternative; but she had greater fear of the convent than of Montargis; and perhaps thought it would be easier to escape from the latter than the former.

Next morning, Friday, M. de Chartres came to the King, who was still in bed, and who spoke to him in a very friendly manner. He said that the Duc must for the future regard him as his father; that he would take care of his position and his interests; that he had forgotten all the little causes of anger he had had against him; that he hoped the Duc would also forget them; that he begged that the advances of friendship he made him might serve to attach him to him, and make their two hearts belong to one another again. It may easily be conceived how well M. de Chartres answered all this.

The bulk of the Court regretted *Monsieur*, for it was he who set all pleasure a-going; and when he left it, life and merriment seemed to have disappeared likewise. Setting aside this obstinacy with regard to the Princes, he loved the order of rank, preferences, and distinctions: he caused them to be observed as much as possible, and himself set the example. He loved great people; and was so affable and polite, that crowds came to him. The difference which he knew how to make, and which he never failed to make, between every one according to his position, contributed greatly to his popularity. In his receptions, by his greater or less, or more neglectful attention, and by his words, he always marked in a flattering manner the differences made by birth and dignity, by age and merit, and by profession; and all this with a dignity natural to him, and a constant facility which he had

'Le Salon de Musique'

eft to right: standing, the Duc de Bourgogne; seated, Madame, *the Duchesse* *Chartres, the Duchesse du Maine, the Princesse de Conti; standing,* Mademoi-*lle, the Duc de Chartres.*

From an engraving by Antoine Trouvain, 1696

acquired. His familiarity obliged, and yet no rash people ever ventured to take advantage of it. He visited or sent exactly when it was proper; and under his roof he allowed a complete liberty, without injury to the respect shown him, or to a perfect court air. He had learned from the Queen, his mother, and well remembered this art. The crowd, therefore, constantly flocked towards the Palais Royal.

All this without any assistance from *Madame*, who dined and supped with the ladies and *Monsieur*, rode out sometimes in a calèche with one of them, often sulked with the company, made herself feared for her harsh and surly temper—frequently even for her words; and passed her days in a little cabinet she had chosen, where the windows were ten feet from the ground, gazing perpetually on the portraits of Paladins and other German princes, with which she had tapestried the walls; and writing every day with her own hand whole volumes of letters, of which she always kept autograph copies. *Monsieur* had never been able to bend her to a more human way of life; and lived decently with her, without caring for her person in any way.

Monsieur was a little round-bellied man, who wore such high-heeled shoes that he seemed mounted always upon stilts; was always decked out like a woman, covered everywhere with rings, bracelets, jewels; with a long black wig, powdered, and curled in front; with ribbons wherever he could put them; steeped in perfumes, and in fine a model of cleanliness. He was accused of putting on an imperceptible touch of rouge. He had a long nose, good eyes and mouth, a full but very long face. All his portraits resembled him. I was piqued to see that his features recalled those of Louis XIII, to whom, except in matters of courage, he was so completely dissimilar.

M. le Duc de Chartres was prodigiously well treated. The King gave him all the pensions *Monsieur* had enjoyed, besides allowing him to retain his own; so that he had one million, eight hundred thousand livres a year; added to the Palais Royal, St. Cloud, and other mansions. He had a Swiss guard, which none but the sons of France had ever had before, in fact he retained all the privileges his father had enjoyed, and he took the name of Duc d'Orléans. The pensions of Madame de Chartres were augmented. All these honours so great and so unheard of bestowed on M. de Chartres, and an income of a hundred thousand crowns more than his father, were due solely to the quarrel which had recently taken place between *Monsieur* and the King, as to the marriage M. de Chartres had made. People accustom themselves to everything, but this prodigious good fortune infinitely surprised everybody. The Princes of the Blood were extremely mortified. To console them, the King immediately gave to *M. le Prince* all the advantages of a first Prince of the Blood, and added ten thousand crowns to his pension.

The health of the King of England (James II), which had for some time been very languishing, grew weaker towards the middle of August of this year, and by the 8th of September completely gave way. There was no longer any hope. The King, Madame de Maintenon, and all the royal persons, visited him often. He received the last sacrament with a piety in keeping with his past life, and his death was expected every instant. In this conjuncture the King made a resolve more worthy of Louis XII, or Francis I, than of his own wisdom. On Tuesday, the 13th of September, he went from Marly to St. Germain. The King of England was so ill that, when the King was announced to him he scarcely opened his eyes for an instant. The King told him that he might die in peace respecting the Prince of Wales, whom he would recognise as King of England, Scotland, and Ireland. The few English who were there, threw themselves upon their knees, but the King of England gave no signs of life. The gratitude of the Prince of Wales and of his mother, when they heard what the King had said, may be imagined. On his return to Marly, the King repeated to all the Court what he had said. Nothing was heard but praises and applause.

Yet reflections did not fail to be made promptly, if not publicly. It was seen, that to recognise the Prince of Wales was to act in direct opposition to the recognition of the Prince of Orange as King of England, that the King had declared at the peace of Ryswick. It was to wound the Prince of Orange in the tenderest point, and to invite England and Holland to become allies of the Emperor against France. As for the Prince of Wales, this recognition was no solid advantage to him, but was calculated to make the party opposed to him in England only more bitter and vigilant in their opposition.

The King of England, in the few intervals of intelligence he had, appeared much impressed by what the King had done. He died about three o'clock in the afternoon of the 16th September of this year, 1701. He had requested that there might be no display at his funeral, and his wish was faithfully observed. He was buried on the Saturday, at seven o'clock in the evening in the church of the English Benedictines at Paris, Rue St. Jacques, without pomp, and attended by but few mourners. His body rests in the chapel, like that of the simplest private person, until the time, apparently very distant, when it shall be transported to England. His heart is at the Filles de Saint Marie, of Chaillot.

Immediately afterwards, the Prince of Wales was received by the King as King of England, with all the formalities and state with which his father before him had been received. Soon afterwards he was recognized by the new King of Spain.

The Earl of Manchester, English ambassador in France, ceased to appear at Versailles after this recognition of the Prince of Wales by the King, and immediately quitted his post and left the country without any leave-taking. King William heard, while in Holland, of the death of James II and of this recognition. He was at table with some German princes and other lords when the news arrived; did not utter a word, except to announce the death; but blushed, pulled down his hat, and could not keep his countenance. He sent orders to London, to drive out Poussin, acting as French ambassador immediately; and Poussin crossed the sea directly and arrived at Calais.

This event was itself followed by the signing of the great treaty of alliance offensive and defensive, against France and Spain, by Austria, England, and Holland; in which they afterwards succeeded in engaging other powers, which compelled the King to increase the number of his troops.

1702

The year 1702 commenced with balls at Versailles, many of which were masquerades. Madame du Maine gave several in her chamber, always keeping her bed because she was in the family-way; which made rather a singular spectacle. There were several balls at Marly, but the majority were not masquerades. The King often witnessed, but in strict privacy, and always in the apartments of Madame de Maintenon, sacred dramas such as 'Absolon,' 'Athalie,' &c. Madame la Duchesse de Bourgogne, M. le Duc d'Orléans, the young Comte de Noailles, Mademoiselle de Melun, urged by the Noailes, played the principal characters in very magnificent stage dresses. Baron, the excellent old actor, instructed them and played with them. M. de Noailles and his clever wife, backed by their relationship to Mme. de Maintenon, were the inventors and promoters of these interior pleasures, for the purpose of intruding themselves more and more into the society of the King.

Only forty spectators were admitted to the representations. *Madame* was sometimes invited by the King, because she liked plays. This favour was much sought after.

The changes which took place in the army after the peace of Ryswick, were very great and very strange. The excellence of the regiments, the merits of the officers, those who commanded, all were forgotten by Barbezieux, young and impetuous, whom the King allowed to act as he liked. My regiment was disbanded, and I resolved then to leave the service.

I wrote a short letter to the King, in which, without making any complaints, I said that as my health was not good (it had given me some trouble on different occasions) I begged to be allowed to quit his service, and said that I hoped I should be permitted to console myself for leaving the army by assiduously attending upon him at the Court. After despatching this letter I went away immediately to Paris.

I learnt afterwards from my friends, that upon receiving my letter the King called Chamillart to him, and said with emotion: 'Well! Monsieur, here is another man who quits us!' and he read my letter word for word. I did not learn that anything else escaped him.

As for me, I did not return to Versailles for a whole week, or see the King again until Easter Monday.

In the early part of this year (1702), King William (of England), worn out before his time with labours and business, in which he had been engaged all his life, and which he had carried on with a capacity, an address, a superiority of genius that acquired for him supreme authority in Holland, the crown of England, the confidence, and, to speak the truth, the complete dictatorship of all Europe—except France;—King William, I say, had fallen into a wasting of strength and of health which, without attacking or diminishing his intellect, or causing him to relax the infinite labours of his cabinet, was accompanied by a deficiency of breath, which aggravated the asthma he had had for several years. He felt his condition, and his powerful genius did not disavow it. Under assumed names he consulted the most eminent physicians of Europe, among others, Fagon; who, having to do, as he thought, with a curé, replied in all sincerity, and without dissimulation, that he must prepare for a speedy death. His illness increasing, William consulted Fagon anew, but this time openly. The physician recognised the malady of the *curé*—he did not change his opinion, but expressed it in a less decided manner, and prescribed the remedies most likely if not to cure, at least to prolong. These remedies were followed and gave relief; but at last the time had arrived when William was to feel that the greatest men finish like the humblest—and to see the nothingness of what the world calls great destinies.

He rode out as often as he could; but no longer having the strength to hold himself on horseback, received a fall, which hastened his end by the shock it gave him. He occupied himself with religion as little as he had all his life. He ordered everything, and spoke to his ministers and his familiars with a surprising tranquillity, which did not abandon him until the last moment. Although crushed with pain, he had the satisfaction of thinking that he had consummated a great alliance, which would last after his death, and that it would strike the great blow against France, which he had projected. This thought, which flattered him even in the hour of death, stood in place of all other consolation,—a consolation frivolous and cruelly deceitful, which left him soon the prey to eternal truths! For two days he was sustained by strong waters and spirituous liquors. His last nourishment was a cup of chocolate. He died the 19th March, 1702, at ten o'clock in the morning.

The Princess Anne, his sister-in-law, wife of Prince George of Denmark, was at the same time proclaimed queen.

The King was silent upon the news, except to *Monseigneur* and to Madame de Maintenon. On the next day confirmation of the intelligence arrived from all parts. The King no longer made a secret of it, but spoke little on the subject, and affected much indifference respecting it.

To maintain his own precedence whilst encroaching on the privileges of his superiors was the ceaseless preoccupation of every Frenchman from a Prince of the Blood down to the peasant office bearer in a village guild. The affaire Coislin *which follows is typical of the almost daily precedence squabbles which so keenly interested Saint-Simon.*

M. de Coislin went to the Sorbonne to listen to a thesis sustained by the second son of M. de Bouillon. When persons of distinction gave these discourses, it was customary for the Princes of the Blood, and for many of the Court, to go and hear them. M. de Coislin was at that time almost last in order of precedence among the Dukes. When he took his seat, therefore, knowing that a number of them would probably arrive, he left several rows of vacant places in front of him, and sat himself down. Immediately afterwards, Novion, Chief-President of the Parliament arrived, and seated himself in front of M. de Coislin. Astonished *at this act of madness*, M. de Coislin said not a word, but took an arm-chair, and, while Novion turned his head to speak to Cardinal de Bouillon, placed that arm-chair right in front of the chief president, in such a manner, that he was as it were imprisoned, and unable to stir. M. de Coislin then sat down. This was done so rapidly, that nobody saw it until it was finished. When once it was observed, a great stir arose. Cardinal de Bouillon tried to intervene. M. de Coislin replied, that since the chief-president had forgotten his position he must be taught it, and would not budge. The other presidents were in a fright, and Novion, enraged by the offence put on him, knew not what to do. It was in vain that Cardinal de Bouillon on one side, and his brother on the other, tried to persuade M. de Coislin to give way. He would not listen to them. They sent a message to him to say that somebody wanted to see him at the door on most important business. But this had no effect. 'There is no business so important,' replied M. de Coislin, 'as that of teaching M. le Premier Président what he owes me, and nothing will make me go from this place unless M. le Président, whom you see behind me, goes away first.'

At last *M. le Prince* was sent for, and he with much persuasion endeavoured to induce M. de Coislin to release the chief president from his prison. But for some time M. de Coislin would listen as little to *M. le Prince* as he had listened to the others, and threatened to keep Novion thus shut up during all the thesis. At length, he consented to set the Chief President free, but only on condition that he left the building immediately; that *M. le Prince* should guarantee this; and that no 'juggling tricks' (that was the term he made use of), should be played off to defeat the agreement. *M. le Prince* at once gave his word that everything should be as he required, and M. de Coislin then rose, moved away his arm-chair, and said to the Chief-President, 'Go away, sir! go away, sir!' Novion did on the instant go away, in the utmost confusion, and jumped into his coach. M. de Coislin thereupon took back his chair to its former position and composed himself to listen again.

On every side M. de Coislin was praised for the firmness he had shown. The Princes of the Blood called upon him the same evening, and complimented him for the course he had adopted; and so many other visitors came during the evening that his house was quite full until a late hour. On the morrow the King also praised him for his conduct, and severely blamed the Chief-President. Nay more, he commanded the latter to go to M. de Coislin, at his house, and beg pardon of him. It is easy to comprehend the shame and despair of Novion at being ordered to take so humiliating a step, especially after what had already happened to him. He prevailed upon M. de Coislin, through the mediation of friends, to spare him his pain, and M. de Coislin had the generosity to do so. He agreed therefore that when Novion called upon him he would pretend to be out, and this was done. The King, when he heard of it, praised very highly the forbearance of the Duc.

The Princesse d'Harcourt was a sort of personage whom it is good to make known, in order better to lay bare a Court which did not scruple to receive such as she. She had once been beautiful and gay; but though not old, all her grace and beauty had vanished. The rose had become an ugly thorn. At the time I speak of she was a tall, fat creature, mightily brisk in her movements, with a complexion like milk-porridge; great, ugly, thick lips, and hair like tow, always sticking out and hanging down in disorder, like all the rest of her fittings out. Dirty, slatternly, always intriguing, pretending, enterprising, quarrelling—always low as the grass or high as the rainbow, according to the person with whom she had to deal: she was a blonde Fury, nay more, a harpy: she had all the effrontery of one, and the deceit and violence; all the avarice and the audacity; moreover, all the gluttony, and all the promptitude to relieve herself from the effects thereof; so that she drove out of their wits those at whose house she dined; was often a victim of her confidence; and was many a time sent to the devil by the servants of M. du Maine and *M. le Grand*. She, however, was never in the least embarrassed, tucked up her petticoats and went her way; then returned, saying she had been unwell. People were accustomed to it.

Whenever money was to be made by scheming and bribery, she was there to make it. At play she always cheated, and if found out stormed and raged; but pocketed what she had won. People looked upon her as they would have looked upon a fishfag, and did not like to commit themselves by quarrelling with her.

Sometimes the Duchesse de Bourgogne used to send about twenty Swiss guards, with drums, into her chamber, who roused her from her first sleep by their horrid din. Another time—and these scenes were always at Marly —they waited until very late for her to go to bed and sleep. She lodged not far from the post of the Captain of the Guards, who was at that time the Maréchal de Lorges. It had snowed very hard, and had frozen. Madame la Duchesse de Bourgogne and her suite gathered snow from the terrace which is on a level with their lodgings; and, in order to be better supplied, waked up to assist them, the Maréchal's people, who did not let them want for ammunition. Then, with a false key, and lights, they gently slipped into the chamber of the Princesse d'Harcourt; and, suddenly drawing the curtains of her bed, pelted her amain with snowballs. The filthy creature, waking up with a start, bruised and stifled in snow, with which even her ears were filled, with dishevelled hair, yelling at the top of her voice, and wriggling like an eel, without knowing where to hide, formed a spectacle that diverted people more than half an hour: so that at last the nymph swam in her bed, from which the water flowed everywhere, slushing all the chamber. It was enough to make one die of laughter.

She was very violent with her servants, beat them, and changed them every day. Upon one occasion, she took into her service a strong and robust chambermaid, to whom, from the first day of her arrival, she gave many slaps and boxes on the ear. The chambermaid said nothing, but after submitting to this treatment for five or six days, conferred with the other servants; and one morning, while in her mistress's room, locked the door without being perceived, said something to bring down punishment upon her, and at the first box on the ear she received, flew upon the Princesse d'Harcourt, gave her no end of thumps and slaps, knocked her down, kicked her, mauled her from her head to her feet, and when she was tired of this exercise, left her on the ground, all torn and dishevelled, howling like a devil.

1703

In a previous page I have alluded to the Princesse des Ursins, when she was appointed Camerera Mayor to the Queen of Spain on her marriage.

From the first moment on which she entered the service of the Queen of Spain, it became her desire to govern not only the Queen, but the King; and by this means the realm itself. Such a grand project had need of support from our King, who, at the commencement, ruled the Court of Spain as much as his own Court, with entire influence over all matters.

The young Queen of Spain had been not less carefully educated than her sister, the Duchesse de Bourgogne. According to everything I have heard said in France and in Spain, she possessed all qualities that were necessary to make her adored. Indeed she became a divinity among the Spaniards, and to their affection for her, Philip V was more than once indebted for his crown.

Madame des Ursins soon managed to obtain the entire confidence of this Queen; and during the absence of Philip V in Italy, assisted her in the administration of all public offices. She even accompanied her to the Junta, it not being thought proper that the Queen should be alone amid such an assemblage of men. In this way she became acquainted with everything that was passing, and knew all the affairs of the Government.

This step gained, it will be imagined that the Princesse des Ursins did not forget to pay her court most assiduously to our King and to Madame de Maintenon. She continually sent them an exact account of everything relating to the Queen—making her appear in the most favourable light possible. Little by little she introduced into her letters details respecting public events, without, however, conveying a suspicion of her own ambition, or that she wished to meddle in these matters. Anchored in this way, she next began to flatter Madame de Maintenon, and by degrees to hint that she might rule over Spain, even more firmly than she ruled over France, if she would entrust her commands to Madame des Ursins. Madame des Ursins offered, in fact, to be the instrument of Madame de Maintenon; representing how much better it would be to rule affairs in this manner, than through the instrumentality of the ministers of either country.

Madame de Maintenon, whose passion it was to know everthing, to mix herself in everything, and to govern everything, was enchanted by the siren. This method of governing Spain without Ministers appeared to her an admirable idea. She embraced it with avidity, without reflecting that she would govern only in appearance, since she would know nothing except through the Princesse des Ursins, see nothing except in the light in which she presented it. From that time dates the intimate union which existed between these two important women, the unbounded authority of Madame des Ursins, the fall of all those who had placed Philip V upon the throne, and of all our ministers in Spain who stood in the way of the new power.

Such an alliance being made between the two women, it was necessary to draw the King of Spain into the same net. This was not a very arduous task. Nature and art indeed had combined to make it easy. Younger brother of an excitable, violent, and robust Prince, Philip V had been bred up in a submission and dependance that were necessary for the repose of the Royal family. Until the testament of Charles II, the Duc d'Anjou was necessarily regarded as destined to be a subject all his life; and therefore could not be too much abased by education, and trained to patience and obedience. That supreme law, the reason of state, demanded this preference, for the safety and happiness of the kingdom, of the elder over the younger brother. His mind for this reason was purposely narrowed and beaten down, and his natural docility and gentleness greatly assisted in the process. He was quite formed to be led, although he had enough judgment left to choose the better of two courses proposed to him, and even to express himself well, when the slowness, not to say the laziness of his mind did not prevent him from speaking at all. His great piety contributed to weaken his mind; and, being joined to very lively passions, made it disagreeable and even dangerous for him to be separated from his Queen. It may easily be conceived, therefore, how he loved her, and that he allowed himself to be guided by her in all things. As the Queen herself was guided in all things by Madame des Ursins, the influence of this latter was all powerful.

Soon, indeed, the Junta became a mere show. Everything was brought before the King in private, and he gave no decision until the Queen and Madame des Ursins had passed theirs. This conduct met with no opposition from our Court, but our ministers at the Court of Spain and the Spanish ministers here soon began to complain of it. The first to do so were Cardinals d'Estrées and Portocarrero. Disagreements continued, so that at last, feeling her position perfectly secure, the Princesse des Ursins begged permission to retire into Italy, knowing full well that she would not be taken at her word, and hoping by this means to deliver herself of these stumbling-blocks in her path.

Our ministers, who felt they would lose all control over Spanish affairs if Madame des Ursins was allowed to remain mistress, did all in their power to support the d'Estrées. But Madame de Maintenon pleaded so well with the King, representing the good policy of allowing a woman so much attached to him, and to the Spanish Queen, as was Madame des Ursins, to remain where she was, that he entirely swallowed the bait; the d'Estrées were left without support; the French ambassador at Madrid was virtually deprived of all power; the Spanish ministers were fettered in their every movement, and the authority of Madame des Ursins became stronger than ever. All public affairs passed through her hands. The King decided nothing without conferring with the Queen and her.

At length, Cardinal d'Estrées, continually in arms against Madame des Ursins, and continually defeated, could not bear his position any longer, but asked to be immediately recalled. All that the ministry could do was to obtain permission for the Abbé d'Estrées (nephew of the Cardinal) to remain as ambassador of France at Madrid. As for Portocarrero, seeing the step his associate had taken, he resolved to quit public business also, and resigned his place accordingly. Several others who stood in the way of the Princesse des Ursins were got rid of at the same time, so that she was now left mistress of the field.

In the mean time the Archduke was declared King of Spain by the Emperor, who made no mystery of his intention of attacking Spain by way of Portugal. The Archduke soon afterwards was recognised by Holland, England, Portugal, Brandenburg, Savoy, and Hanover, as King of Spain, under the title of Charles III, and soon after by the other powers of Europe. The Duke of Savoy had been treacherous to us, had shown that he was in league with the Emperor. The King accordingly had broken off all relations with him, and sent an army to invade his territory. It need be no cause of surprise, therefore, that the Archduke was recognised by Savoy.

Some little time previously it had been thought necessary to send an army to the frontiers of Portugal to oppose the Archduke. A French general was wanted to command this army. Madame des Ursins, who had been very intimate with the King of England (James II) and his Queen, thought she would please them if she gave this post to the Duke of Berwick, illegitimate son of King James. She proposed this therefore; and our King, out of regard for his brother monarch, and from a natural affection for bastards, consented to the appointment; but as the Duke of Berwick had never before commanded an army, he stipulated that Puységur, known to be a skilful officer, should go with him and assist him with his councils and advice.

Puységur set out before the Duke of Berwick. From the Pyrenees as far as Madrid, he found every provision made for the subsistence of the French troops, and sent a very advantageous account to the King of this circumstance. Arrived at Madrid, he had interviews with Orry (who, as I have already mentioned, had the finances under his control, and who was a mere instrument in the hands of Madame des Ursins), and was assured by the minister that all the magazines along the line of route to the frontiers of Portugal were abundantly filled with supplies for the French troops, that all the money necessary was ready, and that nothing, in fact, should fail in the course of the campaign. Puységur, who had found nothing wanting up to that time, never doubted but that these statements were perfectly correct; and had no suspicion that a minister would have the effrontery to show him in detail all these precautions if he had taken none. Pleased, then, to the utmost degree, he wrote to the King in praise of Orry, and consequently of Madame des Ursins and her wise government. Full of these ideas, he set out for the frontier of Portugal to reconnoitre the ground himself, and arrange everything for the arrival of the army and its general. What was his surprise, when he found that from Madrid to the frontier not a single preparation had been made for the troops, and that in consequence all that Orry had shown him, drawn out upon paper, was utterly fictitious. His vexation upon finding that nothing upon which he had reckoned was provided, may be imagined. He at once wrote to the King, in order to contradict all that he had recently written.

Our ministers, who, step by step, had been deprived of all control over the affairs of Spain, profited by the discontent of the King to reclaim their functions. Harcourt and Madame de Maintenon did all they could to ward off the blow from Madame des Ursins, but without effect. The King determined to banish her to Rome and to dismiss Orry from his post.

It was felt, however, that these steps must be taken cautiously, to avoid offending too deeply the King and Queen of Spain who supported their favourite through every emergency.

The King wrote to Philip, recommending him to head in person the army for the frontiers of Portugal, which, in spite of Orry's deception, it was still determined to send. No sooner was Philip fairly away, separated from the Queen and Madame des Ursins, and no longer under their influence, than the King wrote to the Queen of Spain, requesting her, in terms that could not be disputed, to dismiss at once and for ever her favourite Camerera Mayor. The Queen, in despair at the idea of losing a friend and adviser to whom she had been so much attached, believed herself lost. At the same time that the King wrote to the Queen of Spain, he also wrote to the Princesse des Ursins, ordering her to quit Madrid immediately, to leave Spain, and to retire into Italy.

At this conjuncture of affairs, when the Queen was in despair, Madame des Ursins did not lose her composure. She felt at once that for the present all was lost, that her only hope was to be allowed to remain in France. She made all her arrangements, therefore, so that affairs might proceed in her absence as much as possible as though she were present, and then prepared to set out. Dawdling day by day, she put off her departure as long as could be, and when at length she left Madrid only went to Alcala, a few leagues distant. She stopped there under various pretexts, and at length, after five weeks of delay, set out for Bayonne, journeying as slowly as she could and stopping as often as she dared.

She lost no opportunity of demanding an audience at Versailles, in order to clear herself of the charge which weighed upon her, and her importunities at length were not without effect. The King (Louis XIV) was satisfied with the success of his plans. He had been revenged in every way, and had humbled the pride of the Princesse des Ursins. It was not necessary to excite the anger of the Queen and King of Spain by too great harshness against their fallen friend. Madame de Maintenon took advantage of this change in the temper of the King, and by dint of persuasion and scheming succeeded in obtaining from him the permission for Madame des Ursins to remain in France. Toulouse was fixed upon for her residence. It was a place that just suited her, and from which communication with Spain was easy.

In the mean time, the King and Queen of Spain, distressed beyond measure at the loss of their favourite, thought only of the best means of obtaining her recall. They plotted with such ministers as were favourable to her; they openly quarrelled with and thwarted those who were her opponents, so that the most important matters perished in their hands. Nay more, upon the King of Spain's return, the Queen persuaded him to oppose in all things the wishes of the king (Louis XIV), his grandfather, and to neglect his counsels with studied care. Our King complained of this with bitterness. The aim of it was to tire him out, and to make him understand that it was only Madame des Ursins, well treated and sent back, who could restore Spanish affairs to their original state, and cause his authority to be respected. Madame de Maintenon, on her side, neglected no opportunity of pressing the King to allow Madame des Ursins, not to return into Spain—that would have been to spoil all by asking too much—but simply to come to Versailles in order to have the opportunity of justifying herself for her past conduct. From other quarters the King was similarly importuned. Tired at last of the obstinate opposition he met with in Spain from the Queen, who governed her husband completely, he gave permission to Madame des Ursins to come to Versailles to plead her own cause.

She reached Paris on Sunday the 4th of January, 1705. Torcy had orders from the King to go and see her: he did so; and from that moment Madame des Ursins changed her tone. Until then her manner had been modest, supplicating, nearly timid. She now saw and heard so much that from defendant, which she had intended to be, she thought herself in a condition to become accuser; and to demand justice of those, who, abusing the confidence of the King, had drawn upon her such a long and cruel punishment, and made her a show for the two kingdoms. All that happened to her surpassed her hopes.

On the morrow, she dressed herself in grand style, and went to the King, with whom she remained alone two hours and a half conversing in his cabinet. From there she went to the Duchesse de Bourgogne, with whom she also conversed a long time alone. In the evening, the King said, while in Madame de Maintenon's apartments, that there were still many things upon which he had not yet spoken to Madame des Ursins. The next day she saw Madame de Maintenon in private for a long time, and much at her ease. She had an interview soon after with the King and Madame de Maintenon, which was also very long.

A month after this a special courier arrived from the King and Queen of Spain, to thank the King (Louis XIV) for his conduct towards the Princesse des Ursins. From that moment it was announced that she would remain at Court until the month of April, in order to attend to her affairs and her health.

Whilst triumphant beyond all her hopes in Paris, she was at work in Spain, and with equal success. Rivas, who had drawn up the will of the late King Charles II, was disgraced, and never afterwards rose to favour.

The Duc de Gramont, our ambassador at Madrid, was so overwhelmed with annoyance, that he asked for his recall. Amelot, whom Madame des Ursins favoured, was appointed in his place, and many who had been disgraced were reinstated in office; everything was ordered according to her wishes.

At all the balls which Madame des Ursins attended, she was treated with much distinction. At every moment the King turned round to speak to her and Madame de Maintenon, who came for half an hour or so to these balls, and on her account displaced the Grand Chamberlain, who put himself behind her. In this manner she joined Madame des Ursins, and was close to the King—the conversation between the three being continual. What appeared extremely singular was to see Madame des Ursins in the *salon* with a little spaniel in her arms, as though she had been in her own house. People could not sufficiently express their astonishment at a familiarity upon which even Madame la Duchesse de Bourgogne would not have dared to venture; still less could they do so when they saw the King caress this little dog over and over again.

In relating what happened to Madame des Ursins up to her return to Spain, I have carried the narrative into the year 1705. It is now necessary to retrace our steps to 1703.

Here we leave Saint-Simon, the watch-dog of the Dukes, in a characteristic fit of indignation. It is not difficult to understand the impatience with which the King regarded his activities, or the dislike felt for him by the King's wife.

The year finished with an affair in which I was not a little interested. During the year there were several grand fêtes, at which the King went to High Mass and vespers. On these occasions a lady of the Court, named by the Queen, or when there was none, by the Dauphiness, made a collection for the poor. The house of Lorraine, always anxious to increase its importance, shirked impudently this duty, in order thereby to give itself a new distinction, and assimilate its rank to that of the princes of the blood. It was a long time before this was perceived. At last the Duchesse de Noailles, the Duchesse de Guiche, her daughter, the Maréchal de Boufflers, and others, took notice of it; and I was soon after informed of it. I determined that the matter should be arranged, and that justice should be done.

The Duchesse de Lude was first spoken to on the subject: she, weak and timid, did not dare to do anything; but at last was induced to speak to Madame la Duchesse de Bourgogne, who, wishing to judge for herself as to the truth of the matter, ordered Madame de Montbazon to make the collection for the poor at the next fête that took place. Although very well, Madame de Montbazon pretended to be ill, stopped in bed half a day, and excused herself on this ground from performing the duty. Madame de Bourgogne was annoyed, but she did not dare to push matters farther; and, in consequence of this refusal, none of the Duchesses would make the collection. Other ladies of quality soon perceived this, and they also refused to serve; so that the collection fell into all sorts of hands, and sometimes was not made at all. Matters went on so far, indeed, that the King at last grew angry, and threatened to make Madame de Bourgogne herself take this office. But refusals still followed upon refusals, and the bomb thus at length was ready to burst!

1704

The King, who at last ordered the daughter of M. le Grand to take the plate on New Year's Day, 1704, had, it seems, got wind of the part I was taking in this matter, and expressed himself to Madame de Maintenon, as I learnt, as very discontented with me and one or two other Ducs. He said that the Ducs were much less obedient to him than the Princes; and that although many Duchesses had refused to make the collection, the moment he had proposed that the daughter of M. le Grand should take it, M. le Grand consented. On the next day, early in the morning, I saw Chamillart, who related to me that on the previous evening, before he had had time to open his business, the King had burst out in anger against me, saying it was very strange, but that since I had quitted the army I did nothing but meddle in matters of rank and bring actions against everybody; finishing, by declaring that if he acted rightly he should send me so far away that I should be unable to importune him any more. Chamillart added, that he had done all in his power to appease the King, but with little effect.

After consulting with my friends, I determined to go up to the King and boldly ask to speak to him in his cabinet, believing that to be the wisest course I could pursue. He was not yet so reconciled to me as he afterwards became, and, in fact, was sorely out of humour with me. This step did not seem, therefore, altogether unattended with danger; but, as I have said,

The Duc de Saint-Simon

From an engraving by L. F. Mariage
after a portrait by Vanloo

The Duc de Vendôme

From an engraving by P. Dupin

Louis XIV playing billiards

Left to right: Monsieur, the Duc de Chartres, the Comte de Toulouse, Chamillart, the King, d'Armagnac; far right, the Duc de Vendôme: From an engraving by A. Trouvain, 1694

Madame de Maintenon

Detail from a group portrait by N. de Largillière

Philippe de France (*Monsieur*)

From an engraving by J. Gole

I resolved to take it. As he passed, therefore, from his dinner that same day, I asked permission to follow him into his cabinet. Without replying to me, he made a sign that I might enter, and went into the embrasure of the window.

When we were quite alone I explained, at considerable length, my reasons for acting in this matter, declaring that it was from no disrespect to his Majesty that I had requested Madame de Saint-Simon and the other Duchesses to refuse to collect for the poor, but simply to bring those to account, who had claimed without reason to be exempt from this duty. I added, keeping my eyes fixed upon the King all the time, that I begged him to believe that none of his subjects were more submissive to his will or more willing to acknowledge the supremacy of his authority in all things than the Ducs. Until this his tone and manner had been very severe; but now they both softened, and he said, with much goodness and familiarity, that 'that was how it was proper to speak and think,' and other remarks equally gracious. After I had finished the King remained still a moment, as if ready to hear if I had anything more to say, and then quitted me with a bow, slight but very gracious, saying it was well, and that he was pleased with me.

On Wednesday, the 25th of June, Monseigneur le Duc de Bourgogne had a son born to him. This event caused great joy to the King and the Court. But even while these rejoicings were being celebrated, news reached us which spread consternation in every family, and cast a gloom over the whole city.

I have already said that a grand alliance, with the Emperor at its head, had been formed against France, and that our troops were opposing the allies in various parts of Europe. The Elector of Bavaria had joined his forces to ours, and had already done us some service. On the 12th of August he led his men into the plain of Hochstedt, where, during the previous year, he had gained a victory over the Imperialists. In this plain he was joined by our troops, who took up positions right and left of him, under the command of Tallard and Marsin. The Elector himself had command of all.[1] Soon after their arrival at Hochstedt, they received intelligence that Prince Eugène, with the Imperialist forces, and the Duke of Marlborough with the English were coming to meet them. Our generals had, however, all the day before them to choose their ground, and to make their dispositions. It would have been difficult to succeed worse, both with the one and the other. A brook, by no means of a miry kind, ran parallel

---

[1] This is incorrect. The fact is that the Elector, Tallard, and Marsin each held an independent command, and the consequence was the disaster of Blenheim.

to our army; and in front of it a spring, which formed a long and large quagmire, nearly separated the two lines of Marshal Tallard. It was a strange situation for a general to take up, who is master of a vast plain; and it became, as will be seen, a very sad one. At his extreme right was the large village of Blenheim, in which, by a blindness without example, he had placed twenty-six battalions of infantry, six regiments of dragoons, and a brigade of cavalry. One of two courses was open, either to take up a position behind the brook, and parallel to it, so as to dispute its passage with the enemies, or to take advantage of the disorder they would be thrown into in crossing it by attacking them then. Both these plans were good; the second was the better; but neither were adopted. What was done was, to leave a large space between our troops and the brook, that the enemy might pass at their ease, and be overthrown afterwards, as we said. With such dispositions it is impossible to doubt but that our chiefs were struck with blindness. The Danube flowed near enough to Blenheim to be of sufficient support to our right, better indeed than that village, which consequently there was no necessity to hold.

The enemies arrived on the 13th of August at the dawn, and at once took up their positions on the banks of the brook. Their surprise must have been great to see our army so far off, drawn up in battle array. They profited by the extent of ground left to them, crossed the brook at nearly every point, formed themselves in several lines on the side to which they crossed, and then extended themselves at their ease, without receiving the slightest opposition. This is exact truth, but posterity will with difficulty believe it. It was nearly eight o'clock before all these dispositions, which our troops saw made without moving, were completed. Prince Eugène with his army had the right; the Duke of Marlborough the left. The latter thus opposed to the forces of Tallard, and Prince Eugène to those of Marsin.

The battle commenced; and in one part was so far favourable to us that the attack of Prince Eugène was repulsed by Marsin, who might have profited by this circumstance but for the unfortunate position of our right. Two things contributed to place us at a disadvantage. The second line, separated by the quagmire I have alluded to from the first line, could not sustain it properly; and in consequence of the long bend it was necessary to make round this quagmire, neither line, after receiving or making a charge, could retire quickly to rally and return again to the attack. As for the infantry, the twenty-six battalions shut up in Blenheim left a gap in it that could not fail to be felt. The English, who soon perceived the advantage they might obtain from this want of infantry, and from the difficulty with which our cavalry of the right was rallied, profited by these circumstances with the readiness of people who have plenty of ground at their disposal. They redoubled their charges, and to say all in one word, they defeated at their first attack all this army, notwithstanding the efforts of our general officers and of several regiments to repel them. The army of the Elector, entirely unsupported, and taken in flank by the English, wavered in its turn. All the valour of the Bavarians, all the prodigies of the Elector, were unable to remedy the effects of this wavering. Thus was seen, at one and the same time, the army of Tallard beaten and thrown into the utmost disorder; that of the Elector sustaining itself with great intrepidity, but already in retreat; and that of Marsin charging and gaining ground upon Prince Eugène. It was not until Marsin learnt of the defeat of Tallard and of the Elector, that he ceased to pursue his advantages, and commenced his retreat. This retreat he was able to make without being pursued.

In the meantime the troops in Blenheim had been twice attacked, and had twice repulsed the enemy. Tallard had given orders to these troops on no account to leave their positions, nor to allow a single man even to quit them. Now, seeing his army defeated and in flight, he wished to countermand these orders. He was riding in hot haste to Blenheim to do so, with only two attendants, when all three were surrounded, recognised, and taken prisoners.

These troops shut up in Blenheim had been left under the command of Blansac, major-general, and Clérembault, lieutenant-general. During the battle this latter was missed, and could nowhere be found. Blansac, thus left alone in command, was much troubled by the disorders he saw and heard, and by the want which he felt of fresh orders. He sent a messenger to Tallard for instructions how to act, but his messenger was stopped on the road, and taken prisoner.

While Blansac was in this trouble, he saw Denonville, one of our officers who had been taken prisoner, coming towards the village, accompanied by an officer who waved a handkerchief in the air and demanded a parley. Instead of speaking in private to Blansac and the other principal officers— since he had undertaken so strange a mission—Denonville, who had some intellect, plenty of fine talk, and a mighty opinion of himself, set to work haranguing the troops, trying to persuade them to surrender themselves prisoners of war, so that they might preserve themselves for the service of the King. Blansac, who saw the wavering this caused among the troops, sharply told Denonville to hold his tongue, and began himself to harangue the troops in a contrary spirit. But it was too late. The mischief was done. Only one regiment, that of Navarre, applauded him, all the rest maintained a dull silence.

Soon after Denonville and his companion had returned to the enemy, an English lord came, demanding a parley with the commandant. He was admitted to Blansac, to whom he said that the Duke of Marlborough had sent him to say, that he had forty battalions and sixty pieces of cannon at his disposal, with reinforcements to any extent at command; that he should surround the village on all sides; that the army of Tallard was in flight, and the remains of that of the Elector in retreat; that Tallard and many general officers were prisoners; that Blansac could hope for no reinforcements; and that, therefore, he had better at once make an honourable capitulation, and surrender himself with all his men prisoners of war, than attempt a struggle in which he was sure to be worsted with great loss. Blansac wanted to dismiss this messenger at once, but the Englishman pressed him to advance a few steps out of the village, and see with his own eyes the defeat of the Electoral army, and the preparations that were made on the other side to continue the battle. Blansac accordingly, attended by one of his officers, followed this lord, and was astounded to see with his own eyes that all he had just heard was true. Returned into Blenheim, Blansac assembled all his principal officers, made them acquainted with the proposition that had been made, and told them what he had himself seen. Every one comprehended what a frightful shock it would be for the country when it learnt that they had surrendered themselves prisoners of war; but all things well considered, it was thought best to accept these terms.

The King received the cruel news of this battle on the 21st of August. By this courier the King learnt that a battle had taken place on the 13th; had lasted from eight o'clock in the morning until evening; that the entire army of Tallard was killed or taken prisoners; that it was not known what had become of Tallard himself, or whether the Elector and Marsin had been at the action. The private letters that arrived were all opened to see what news they contained, but no fresh information could be got from them. For six days the King remained in this uncertainty as to the real losses that had been sustained. Everybody was afraid to write bad news; all the letters which from time to time arrived, gave, therefore, but an unsatisfactory account of what had taken place. The King used every means in his power to obtain some news. Every post that came in was examined by him, but there was little found to satisfy him. Neither the King nor anybody else could understand, from what had reached them, how it was that an entire army had been placed inside a village, and had surrendered itself by a signed capitulation. It puzzled every brain. At last the details, that had oozed out little by little, augmented to a perfect stream, by the arrival of one of our officers, who, taken prisoner, had been allowed by the Duke of Marlborough to go to Paris to relate to the King the misfortune that had happened to him.

We were not accustomed to misfortunes. This one, very reasonably, was utterly unexpected. It seemed in every way the result of bad generalship, of an unjustifiable disposition of troops, and of a series of gross and incredible errors. The commotion was general. There was scarcely an illustrious family that had not had one of its members killed, wounded, or taken prisoner. Other families were in the same case. The public sorrow and indignation burst out without restraint. Nobody who had taken part in this humiliation was spared; the generals and the private soldiers alike came in for blame. Denonville was ignominiously broken for the speech he had made at Blenheim. The generals, however, were entirely let off. All the punishment fell upon certain regiments, which were broken, and upon certain unimportant officers—the guilty and innocent mixed together. The outcry was universal. The grief of the King at this ignomiy and this loss, at the moment when he imagined that the fate of the Emperor was in his hands, may be imagined. At a time when he might have counted upon striking a decisive blow, he saw himself reduced to act simply on the defensive, in order to preserve his troops; and had to repair the loss of an entire army, killed or taken prisoners. The sequel showed not less that the hand of God was weighty upon us. All judgment was lost. We trembled even in the midst of Alsace.

The King did not long remain without some consolation for the loss of the battle of Hochstedt (Blenheim). The Comte de Toulouse was wearied with cruising in the Mediterranean, without daring to attack enemies that were too strong for him. He had, therefore, obtained reinforcements this year, so that he was in a state to measure his forces with any opponent. The English fleet was under the command of Admiral Rooke. The Comte de Toulouse wished above all things to attack. He asked permission to do so, and, the permission being granted, he set about his enterprise. He met the fleet of Admiral Rooke near Malaga, on the 24th of September of this year, and fought with it from ten o'clock in the morning until eight o'clock in the evening. The fleets, as far as the number of vessels was concerned, were nearly equal. So furious or so obstinate a sea-fight had not been seen for a long time. They had always the wind upon our fleet, yet all the advantage was on the side of the Comte de Toulouse, who could boast that he had obtained the victory, and whose vessel fought that of Rooke, dismasted it, and pursued it all next day towards the coast of Barbary, where the Admiral retired. The enemy lost six thousand men; the ship of the Dutch Vice-Admiral was blown up; several others were sunk, and some dismasted. Our fleet lost neither ship nor mast, but the victory cost the lives of many distinguished people, in addition to those of fifteen hundred soldiers or sailors killed or wounded.

The Secretary of State for the Navy became so unendurable, that the Comte de Toulouse, at the end of his cruise in the Mediterranean, returned to Court and determined to expose the doings of Pontchartrain to the King.

The very day he had made up his mind to do this, and just before he intended to have his interview with the King, Madame Pontchartrain, casting aside her natural timidity and modesty, came to him, and with tears in her eyes begged him not to bring about the ruin of her husband. The Comte de Toulouse was softened. He admitted afterwards that he could not resist the sweetness and sorrow of Madame de Pontchartrain, and that all his resolutions, his weapons, fell from his hands at the thought of the sorrow which the poor woman would undergo, after the fall of her brutal husband, left entirely in the hands of such a furious Cyclops. In this manner Pontchartrain was saved, but it cost dear to the State.

It was not long before Madame de Maintenon began to feel impatient at the long-delayed departure of Madame des Ursins. She spoke at last upon the subject, and pressed Madame des Ursins to set out for Spain. This was just what the other wanted. She said that as she had been driven out of Spain like a criminal, she must go back with honour, if Madame de Maintenon wished her to gain the confidence and esteem of the Spaniards. That although she had been treated by the King with every consideration and goodness, many people in Spain were, and would be, ignorant of it, and that, therefore, her return to favour ought to be made known in as public and convincing a manner as was her disgrace.

The favours she obtained were prodigious. Twenty thousand livres by way of annual pension, and thirty thousand for her journey. One of her brothers, M. de Noirmoutiers, blind since the age of eighteen or twenty, was made hereditary duke; another, the Abbé de la Trémoille, was made cardinal. Pleased and loaded with favour as never subject was before, Madame des Ursins set out towards the middle of July, and was nearly a month on the road. It may be imagined what sort of a reception awaited her in Spain. The King and the Queen went a day's journey out of Madrid to meet her.

The war, as I have said, still continued, but without bringing us any advantages. I saw quite plainly towards what rock we were drifting. We had met losses at Hochstedt, Gibraltar, and Barcelona; Catalonia and the neighbouring countries were in revolt; Italy yielding us nothing but miserable successes; Spain exhausted; France, failing in men and money, and with incapable generals, protected by the Court against their faults. I saw all these things so plainly that I could not avoid making reflections, or reporting them to my friends in office. I thought that it was time to finish the war before we sank still lower, and that it might be finished by giving to the Archduke what we could not defend, and making a division of the rest. My plan was to leave Philip V possession of all Italy, except those parts which belonged to the Grand Duke, the republics of Venice and Genoa, and the ecclesiastical states of Naples and Sicily; our King to have Lorraine and some other slight additions of territory; and to place elsewhere the Dukes of Savoy, of Lorraine, of Parma, and of Modena. I related this plan to the Chancellor and to Chamillart, amongst others. The contrast between their replies was striking. The Chancellor, after having listened to me very attentively, said, if my plan were adopted, he would most willingly kiss my toe for joy. Chamillart, with gravity replied, that the King would not give up a single mill of all the Spanish succession. Then I felt the blindness which had fallen upon us, and how much the results of it were to be dreaded.

1706

Nevertheless, the King, as if to mock at misfortune and to show his enemies the little uneasiness he felt, determined, at the commencement of the new year, 1706, that the Court should be gayer than ever. He announced that there would be balls at Marly every time he was there this winter, and he named those who were to dance there; and said he should be very glad to see balls given to Madame de Bourgogne at Versailles. Accordingly, many took place there, and also at Marly, and from time to time there were masquerades.

Since the departure of Maréchal de Villeroy for Flanders, the King had more than once pressed him to engage the enemy. The Maréchal, piqued with these reiterated orders, which he considered as reflections upon his courage, determined to risk anything in order to satisfy the desire of the King. But the King did not wish this. At the same time that he wished for a battle in Flanders, he wished to place Villeroy in a state to fight it. He sent orders, therefore, to Marsin to take eighteen battalions and twenty squadrons of his army, to proceed to the Moselle, where he would find twenty others, and then to march with the whole into Flanders, and join Maréchal de Villeroy. At the same time he prohibited the latter from doing anything until this reinforcement reached him. Four couriers, one after the other, carried this prohibition to the Maréchal; but he had determined to give battle without assistance, and he did so, with what result will be seen.

On the 24th of May he posted himself between the villages of Taviers and Ramillies. He was superior in force to the Duke of Marlborough who was opposed to him, and this fact gave him confidence. Yet the position which he had taken up was one which was well known to be bad. The late M. de Luxembourg had declared it so, and had avoided it. M. de Villeroy had been a witness of this, but it was his destiny and that of France that he should forget it. Before he took up this position he announced that it was his intention to do so to M. d'Orléans. M. d'Orléans said publicly to all who came to listen, that if M. de Villeroy did so he would be beaten. M. d'Orléans proved to be only too good a prophet.

It was about two hours after midday when the enemy arrived within range, and came under our fire from Ramillies. It forced them to halt until their cannon could be brought into play, which was soon done. The cannonade lasted a good hour. At the end of that time they marched to Taviers, where a part of our army was posted, found but little resistance, and made themselves masters of that place. From that moment they brought their cavalry to bear. They perceived that there was a marsh which covered our left, but which hindered our two wings from joining. They made good use of the advantage this gave them. We were taken in the rear at more than one point, and Taviers being no longer able to assist us, Ramillies itself fell, after a prodigious fire and an obstinate resistance. All this time our left had been utterly useless with its nose in the marsh, no enemy in front of it, and with strict orders not to budge from its position.

Our retreat commenced in good order, but soon the night came and threw us into confusion. The defile of Judoigne became so gorged with baggage and with the wrecks of the artillery we had been able to save, that everything was taken from us there. Nevertheless, we arrived at Louvain, and then not feeling in safety, passed the canal of Wilworde without being very closely followed by the enemy.

We lost in this battle four thousand men, and many prisoners of rank, all of whom were treated with much politeness by Marlborough. Brussels was one of the first-fruits he gathered of this victory, which had such grave and important results.

The King did not learn this disaster until Wednesday, the 26th of May, at his waking. I was at Versailles. Never was such trouble or such consternation. The worst was, that only the broad fact was known; for six days we were without a courier to give us details. Even the post was stopped. Days seemed like years in the ignorance of everybody as to details, and in the inquietude of everybody for relatives and friends. The King was forced to ask one and another for news; but nobody could tell him any. Worn out at last by the silence, he determined to despatch Chamillart to Flanders to ascertain the real state of affairs. Chamillart accordingly left Versailles on Sunday, the 30th of May, to the astonishment of all the Court, at seeing a man charged with the war and the finance department sent on such an errand. He astonished the army no less, when he arrived at Courtrai, where it had stationed itself. Having gained all the information he sought, Chamillart returned to Versailles on Friday, the 4th of June, at about eight o'clock in the evening, and at once went to the King, who was in the apartments of Madame de Maintenon. It was known then that the army, after several hasty marches, finding itself at Ghent, the Elector of Bavaria had insisted that it ought at least to remain there. A council of war was held, the Maréchal de Villeroy, who was quite discouraged by the loss he had sustained, opposed the advice of the Elector. Ghent was abandoned, so was the open country. The army was separated and distributed here and there, under the command of the general officers. In this way, with the exception of Namur, Mons, and a very few other places, all the Spanish Low Countries were lost, and a part of ours, even. Never was rapidity equal to this. The enemies were as much astonished as we.

However tranquilly the King sustained in appearance this misfortune, he felt it to the quick.

Villeroy who, since his defeat, had quite lost his head, received several strong hints from the King that he ought to give up his command. But he either could not or would not understand them, and so tired out the King's patience, at length. But he was informed in language which admitted of no misapprehension that he must return. Even then, the King was so kindly disposed towards him, that he said the Maréchal had begged to be recalled with such obstinacy that he could not refuse him. But M. de Villeroy was absurd enough to reject this salve for his honour; which led to his disgrace. M. de Vendôme had orders to leave Italy, and succeed to the command in Flanders, where the enemies had very promptly taken Ostend and Nieuport.

The siege of Barcelona made no progress. It was raised accordingly on the night between the 10th and 11th of May, after fourteen days' bombardment. As Catalonia was in revolt, it was felt that retreat could not take place in that direction; it was determined, therefore, to retire by the way of the French frontier. For eight days, however, our troops were harassed in flank and rear by Miquelets, who followed us from mountain to mountain. The army stopped at Roussillon, and the King of Spain, escorted by two regiments of dragoons, made the best of his way to Madrid. That city was itself in danger from the Portuguese, and, indeed, fell into their hands soon after. The Queen, who, with her children, had left it in time to avoid capture, felt matters to be in such extremity, that she despatched all the jewels belonging to herself and her husband to France. They were placed in the custody of the King.

The King of Spain effected a junction with the army of Berwick, and both set to work to reconquer the places the Portuguese had taken from them. In this they were successful. The Portuguese, much harassed by the people of Castille, were forced to abandon all they had gained; and the King of Spain was enabled to enter Madrid towards the end of September, where he was received with much rejoicing.

In Italy we experienced the most disastrous misfortunes. M. de Vendôme, having been called from the command to go into Flanders, M. d'Orléans, after some deliberation, was appointed to take his place. La Feuillade was besieging Turin. M. d'Orléans went to the siege. He found everything defective. La Feuillade was very young, and very inexperienced. Inflated by the importance of his position, and by the support of Chamillart, he would listen to no advice from any one.

Marsin wished to keep in the good graces of La Feuillade, son-in-law of the all-powerful minister, and would not adopt the views of M. d'Orléans.

When M. d'Orléans was convinced, soon after his arrival, that the enemy was approaching to succour Turin, he suggested that they should be opposed as they attempted the passage of the Dora. But this advice was not listened to. He found the siege works bad, imperfect, very wet, and very ill-guarded. He tried to remedy all these defects, but he was opposed at every step. A council of war was held. M. d'Orléans stated his views, but all the officers present, with one honourable exception, servilely chimed in with the views of Marsin and La Feuillade, and things remained as they were. M. Orléans, thereupon, protested that he washed his hands of all the misfortunes that might happen in consequence of his advice being neglected. He declared that as he was no longer master over anything, it was not just that he should bear any part of the blame which would entail to those in command. He asked, therefore, for his postchaise, and wished immediately to quit the army. La Feuillade and Marsin, however, begged him to remain, and upon second thoughts he thought it better to do so.

After the council of war, M. d'Orléans ceased to take any share in the command, walked about or stopped at home, like a man who had nothing to do with what was passing around him. On the night of the 6th to the 7th of September, he rose from his bed alarmed by information sent to him in a letter, that Prince Eugène was about to attack. He hastened at once to Marsin, and showed him the letter. Marsin would listen to none of the arguments of M. d'Orléans. The Prince, more piqued and more disgusted than ever, retired to his quarters fully resolved to abandon everything to the blind and deaf, who would neither see nor hear.

Soon after entering his chamber the news spread from all parts of the arrival of Prince Eugène. He did not stir. Some general officers came, and forced him to mount his horse. He went forth negligently at a walking pace. What had taken place during the previous days had made so much noise that even the common soldiers were ashamed of it. They liked him, and murmured because he would no longer command them. One of them called him by his name, and asked him if he refused them his sword. This question did more than all that the general officers had been able to do. M. d'Orléans replied to the soldier, that he would not refuse to serve them, and at once resolved to lend all his aid to Marsin and La Feuillade.

But the enemy was in sight, and advanced so diligently, that there was no time to make arrangements. Marsin more dead than alive, was incapable of giving any order or any advice. But La Feuillade still persevered in his obstinacy.

The attack commenced about ten o'clock in the morning, was pushed with incredible vigour, and sustained, at first, in the same manner. Prince Eugène poured his troops into those places which the smallness of our forces had compelled us to leave open. Marsin, towards the middle of the battle, received a wound, which incapacitated him from further service, and was taken prisoner immediately after. La Feuillade ran about like a madman, tearing his hair, and incapable of giving any order. The Duc d'Orléans preserved his coolness, and did wonders to save the day. Finding our men beginning to waver, he called the officers by their name, aroused the soldiers by his voice, and himself led the squadrons and battalions to

77

the charge. Vanquished at last by pain, and weakened by the blood he had lost, he was constrained to retire a little, to have his wounds dressed.

This was the last moment of the little order that there had been at this battle. All that followed was only trouble, confusion, disorder, flight, discomfiture. The most terrible thing is, that the general officers, with but very few exceptions, more intent upon their equipage and upon what they had saved by pillage, added to the confusion instead of diminishing it, and were worse than useless.

M. d'Orléans, convinced at last that it was impossible to re-establish the day, thought only how to retire as advantageously as possible. Gathering round him all the officers he could collect, he explained to them that nothing but retreat was open to them, and that the road to Italy was that which they ought to pursue. By this means they would leave the victorious army of the enemy in a country entirely ruined and desolate, and hinder it from returning into Italy, where the army of the King, on the contrary, would have abundance, and where it would cut off all succour from the others.

This proposition dismayed to the last degree our officers, who hoped at least to reap the fruit of this disaster by returning to France with the money with which they were gorged. La Feuillade opposed it with so much impatience, that the Prince, exasperated by an effrontery so sustained, told him to hold his peace and let others speak. Others did speak, but only one was for following the counsel of M. d'Orléans. Feeling himself now, however, the master, he stopped all further discussion, and gave orders that the retreat to Italy should commence. This was all he could do. His body and his brain were equally exhausted.

The officers obeyed his orders most unwillingly. They murmured amongst each other so loudly that the Duc d'Orléans, justly irritated by so much opposition to his will, made them hold their peace. The retreat continued. But it was decreed that the spirit of error and vertigo should ruin us and save the allies. As the army were about to cross the bridge over the Ticino, and march into Italy, information was brought to M. d'Orléans, that the enemy occupied the roads by which it was indispensable to pass. M. d'Orléans, not believing this intelligence, persisted in going forward. Our officers, thus foiled, for it was known afterwards that the story was their invention, and that the passes were entirely free, hit upon another expedient. They declared there was no more provisions or ammunition, and that it was accordingly impossible to go into Italy. M. d'Orléans, worn out by so much criminal disobedience, and weakened by his wound, could hold out no longer. He threw himself back in the chaise, and said they might go where they would. The army therefore turned about, and directed itself towards Pignerol.

After the victory, M. de Savoie and Prince Eugène lost no time in idle rejoicings. They thought only how to profit by a success so unheard of and so unexpected. They retook rapidly all the places in Piedmont and Lombardy that we occupied, and we had no power to prevent them.

Never battle cost fewer soldiers than that of Turin; never was retreat more undisturbed than ours; yet never were results more frightful or more rapid. Ramillies, with a light loss, cost the Spanish Low Countries and part of ours: Turin cost all Italy by the ambition of La Feuillade, the incapacity of Marsin, the avarice, the trickery, the disobedience of the general officers opposed to M. d'Orléans. So complete was the rout of our army, that it was found impossible to restore it sufficiently to send it back to Italy, not at least before the following spring. M. d'Orléans returned therefore to Versailles, on Monday, the 8th of November, and was well received by the King. La Feuillade arrived on Monday the 13th of December, having remained several days at Paris without daring to go to Versailles. He was taken to the King by Chamillart. As soon as the King saw them enter he rose, went to the door, and without giving them time to utter a word, said to La Feuillade, 'Monsieur, we are both very unfortunate!' and instantly turned his back upon him. La Feuillade, on the threshold of the door that he had not had time to cross, left the place immediately, without having dared to say a single word. The King always afterwards turned his eyes from La Feuillade, and would never speak to him.

Such was our military history of the year 1706—a history of losses and dishonour. It may be imagined in what condition was the exchequer with so many demands upon its treasures.

The necessity for money had now become so great, that all sorts of means were adopted to obtain it. Amongst other things, a tax was established upon baptisms and marriages. This tax was extremely onerous and odious. The result of it was a strange confusion. Poor people, and many of humble means, baptised their children themselves, without carrying them to the church, and were married at home by reciprocal consent and before witnesses, when they could find no priest who would marry them without formality. In consequence of this there were no longer any baptismal extracts; no longer any certainty as to baptisms or births. From public cries and murmurs the people in some places passed to sedition. In the end it was found necessary to drop this tax upon baptism and marriages, to the great regret of the tax-gatherers, who, by all manner of vexations and rogueries, had enriched themselves cruelly.

1707

On Thursday, the 7th of March, 1707, a strange event troubled the King and filled the Court and the town with rumours. Beringhen, First Equerry, left Versailles at seven o'clock in the evening of that day, to go to Paris, alone in one of the King's coaches, two of the royal footmen behind, and a groom carrying a torch before him on the seventh horse. The carriage had reached the plain of Bissancourt, and was passing between a farm on the road near Sèvres bridge and a cabaret, called the 'Dawn of Day,' when it was stopped by fifteen or sixteen men on horseback, who seized on Beringhen, hurried him into a post-chaise in waiting, and drove off with him. The King's carriage, with the coachman, footmen, and groom, was allowed to go back to Versailles. As soon as it reached Versailles the King was informed of what had taken place. He sent immediately to his four Secretaries of State, ordering them to send couriers everywhere to the frontiers, with instructions to the governors to guard all the passages, so that if these horsemen were foreign enemies, as was suspected, they would be caught in attempting to pass out of the kingdom. It was known that a party of the enemy had entered Artois, that they had committed no disorders, but that they were there still. Although people found it difficult, at first, to believe that Beringhen had been carried off by a party such as this, yet as it was known that he had no enemies, that he was not reputed sufficiently rich to afford hope of a large ransom, and that not one of our wealthiest financiers had been seized in this manner, this explanation was at last accepted as the right one.

So in fact it proved. A certain Guetem, a fiddler of the Elector of Bavaria, had entered the service of Holland, had taken part in the war against France, and had become a colonel. Chatting one evening with his comrades, he laid a wager that he would carry off some one of mark between Paris and Versailles. He obtained a passport, and thirty chosen men, nearly all of whom were officers. They passed the rivers disguised as traders, by which means they were enabled to post their relays [of horses]. Several of them had remained seven or eight days at Sèvres, Saint Cloud, and Boulogne, from which they had the hardihood to go to Versailles and see the King sup. One of these was caught on the day after the disappearance of Beringhen, and when interrogated by Chamillart, replied with a tolerable amount of impudence. Another was caught in the forest of Chantilly by one of the servants of *M. le Prince*. From him it became known that relays of horses and a post-chaise had been provided at Morlière for the prisoner when he should arrive there, and that he had already passed the Oise.

Notwithstanding the diligence used, the horsemen had traversed the Somme and had gone four leagues beyond Ham, when the party was stopped.

The grand fault they had committed was to allow the King's carriage and the footmen to go back to Versailles so soon after the abduction. Had they led away the coach under cover of the night, and so kept the King in ignorance of their doings until the next day, they would have had more time for their retreat. Instead of doing this they fatigued themselves by too much haste. They had grown tired of waiting for a carriage that seemed likely to contain somebody of mark. The Chancellor had passed, but in broad daylight, and they were afraid in consequence to stop him. M. le Duc d'Orléans had passed, but in a post-chaise, which they mistrusted. At last Beringhen appeared in one of the King's coaches, attended by servants in the King's livery, and wearing his *cordon bleu*, as was his custom. They thought they had found a prize indeed. They soon learnt with whom they had to deal, and told him also who they were. Guetem bestowed upon Beringhen all kinds of attention, and testified a great desire to spare him as much as possible all fatigue.

On Tuesday, the 29th of March, Beringhen arrived at Versailles, about eight o'clock in the evening, and went at once to the King, who was in the apartments of Madame de Maintenon, and who received him well, and made him relate all his adventures.

Guetem and his officers, while waiting the pleasure of the King, were lodged in Beringhen's house in Paris, where they were treated above their deserts. Beringhen obtained permission for Guetem to see the King. He did more; he presented Guetem to the King, who praised him for having so well treated his prisoner, and said that war always ought to be conducted properly. Guetem, who was not without wit, replied, that he was so astonished to find himself before the greatest King in the world, and to find that King doing him the honour of speaking to him, that he had not power enough to answer. He remained ten or twelve days in Beringhen's house to see Paris, the Opera and the Comedy, and became the talk of the town. Beringhen regaled him, furnished him with carriages and servants to accompany him, and, at parting, with money and considerable presents. Guetem went on his parole to Rheims to rejoin his comrades until exchanged, and had the town for prison. Nearly all the others had escaped.

On Wednesday, the 27th of May, 1707, at three o'clock in the morning, Madame de Montespan, aged sixty, died very suddenly at the waters of Bourbon. Her death made much stir, although she had long retired from the Court and from the world, and preserved no trace of the commanding influence she had so long possessed. I need not go back beyond my own experience, and to the time of her reign as mistress of the King. I will simply say, because the anecdote is little known, that her conduct was more the fault of her husband than her own. She warned him as soon as she suspected the King to be in love with her; and told him when there was no longer any doubt upon her mind. She assured him that a great entertainment that the King gave was in her honour. She pressed him, she entreated him in the most eloquent manner, to take her away to his estates of Guyenne, and leave her there until the King had forgotten her or chosen another mistress. It was all to no purpose; and Montespan was not long before repentance seized him; for his torment was that he loved her all his life, and died still in love with her—although he would never consent to see her again after the first scandal.

At last God touched her. Her sin had never been accompanied by forgetfulness; she used often to leave the King to go and pray in her cabinet; nothing could ever make her evade any fast-day or meagre day; her austerity in fasting continued amidst all her dissipation. She gave alms, was esteemed by good people, never gave way to doubt or impiety; but she was imperious, haughty and overbearing, full of mockery, and of all the qualities by which beauty with the power it bestows is naturally accompanied. Being resolved at last to take advantage of an opportunity which had been given her against her will, she put herself in the hands of Père de la Tour, that famous General of the Oratory. From that moment to the time of her death her conversion continued steadily, and her penitence augmented.

Little by little she gave almost all she had to the poor. She worked for them several hours a day, making stout shirts and such things for them. Her table, that she had loved to excess, became the most frugal; her fasts multiplied; she would interrupt her meals in order to go and pray. Her mortifications were continued; her chemises and her sheets were of rough linen, of the hardest and thickest kind, but hidden under others of ordinary kind. She unceasingly wore bracelets, garters, and a girdle, all armed with iron points, which oftentimes inflicted wounds upon her; and her tongue, formerly so dangerous, had also its peculiar penance imposed on it.

She received the last sacrament with an ardent piety. The fear of death which all her life had so continually troubled her, disappeared suddenly, and disturbed her no more. She died, without regret, occupied only with thoughts of eternity, and with a sweetness and tranquillity that accompanied all her actions.

Madame de Montespan was bitterly regretted by all the poor of the province, amongst whom she spread an infinity of alms, as well as amongst others of different degree.

The armies assembled this year towards the end of May, and the campaign commenced. The Duc de Vendôme was in command in Flanders, under the Elector of Bavaria, and by his slothfulness and inattention, allowed Marlborough to steal a march upon him, which, but for the failure of some of the arrangements, might have caused serious loss to our troops. The enemy was content to keep simply on the defensive after this, having projects of attack in hand elsewhere to which I shall soon allude.

On the Rhine, the Maréchal de Villars was in command, and, was opposed by the Marquis of Bayreuth, and afterwards by the Duke of Hanover, since King of England. Villars was so far successful, that finding himself feebly opposed by the Imperials, he penetrated into Germany, after having made himself master of Heidelberg, Mannheim, and all the Palatinate, and seized upon a number of cannons, provisions, and munitions of war. He did not forget to tax the enemy wherever he went. He gathered immense sums—treasures beyond all his hopes. Thus gorged, he could not hope that his brigandage would remain unknown. He put on a bold face and wrote to the King, that the army would cost him nothing this year. His booty clutched, he thought of withdrawing from the enemy's country, and passing the Rhine.

He crossed it tranquilly, with his army and his immense booty, despite the attempts of the Duke of Hanover to prevent him, and as soon as he was on this side, had no care but how to terminate the campaign in repose. Thus finished a campaign, tolerably brilliant, if the sordid and prodigious gain of the general had not soiled it.

The little effort made by the enemy in Flanders and Germany, had a cause, which began to be perceived towards the middle of July. We had been forced to abandon Italy. By a shameful treaty that was made, all our troops had retired from that country into Savoy. We had given up everything. Prince Eugène, who had had the glory of driving us out of Italy, remained there some time, and then entered the county of Nice.

Forty of the enemy's vessels arrived at Nice shortly afterwards, and landed artillery. M. de Savoie arrived there also, with six or seven thousand men. It was now no longer hidden that the siege of Toulon was determined on. Every preparation was at once made to defend the place. Tessé was in command. The delay of a day on the part of the enemy saved Toulon, and it may be said, France. M. de Savoie had been promised money by the English. They disputed a whole day about the payment, and so retarded the departure of the fleet from Nice. In the end, seeing M. de Savoie firm, they paid him a million, which he received himself. But in the mean time twenty-one of our battalions had had time to arrive at Toulon. They decided the fortune of the siege. After several unsuccessful attempts to take the place, the enemy gave up the siege and retired in the night, between the 22nd and 23rd of August, in good order, and without being disturbed. Our troops could obtain no sort of assistance from the people of Provence, so as to harass M. de Savoie in his passage of the Var. They refused money, militia, and provisions bluntly, saying that it was no matter to them who came, and that M. de Savoie could not torment them more than they were tormented already.

The important news of a deliverance so desired arrived at Marly on Friday, the 26th of August, and overwhelmed all the Court with joy.

1708

I went this summer to Forges, to try, by means of the waters there, to get rid of a tertian fever that quinquina only suspended.

For a long time a most important project had knocked at every door, without being able to obtain a hearing anywhere. The project was a French-financed Jacobite invasion of England via Scotland. Preparations for the invasion of Scotland were commenced.

The expedition turned out a complete fiasco and 'James III' was lucky to fight his way back to France.

Great care was taken that no movement should be seen at Saint Germain. The affair, however, began in time to get noised abroad. A prodigious quantity of arms and clothing for the Scotch had been embarked; the movements by sea and land became only too visible upon the coast. At last, on Wednesday the 6th of March, the King of England set out from Saint Germain. But his departure had been postponed too long. At the moment when all were ready to start, people learned with surprise that the English fleet had appeared in sight, and was blockading Dunkerque. Our troops, who were already on board ship, were at once landed. The King of England cried out so loudly against this, and proposed so eagerly that an attempt should be made to pass the enemy at all risks, that a fleet was sent out to reconnoitre the enemy, and the troops were re-embarked. But then a fresh mischance happened. The Princess of England had had the measles, and was barely growing convalescent at the time of the departure of the King, her brother. She had been prevented from seeing him, lest he should be attacked by the same complaint. In spite of this precaution, however, it declared itself upon him at Dunkerque, just as the troops were re-embarked. He was in despair, and wished to be wrapped up in blankets and carried on board. The doctors said that it would kill him; and he was obliged to remain. The worst of it was, that two of five Scotch deputies who had been hidden at Montrouge, near Paris, had been sent into Scotland a fortnight before, to announce the immediate arrival of the King with arms and troops. The movement which it was felt this announcement would create, increased the impatience for departure. At last, on Saturday the 19th of March, the King of England, half cured and very weak, determined to embark in spite of his physicians, and did so. The enemy's vessels had retired; so, at six o'clock in the morning, our ships set sail with a good breeze, and in the midst of a mist, which hid them from view in about an hour.

Forty-eight hours after the departure of our squadron, twenty-seven English ships of war appeared before Dunkerque. But our fleet was away. The very first night it experienced a furious tempest. The ship in which was the King of England, took shelter afterwards behind the works of Ostend. During the storm, another ship was separated from the squadron, and was obliged to take refuge on the coast of Picardy. This vessel, a frigate, was commanded by Rambures, a lieutenant. As soon as he was able he sailed after the squadron that he believed already in Scotland. He directed his course towards Edinburgh, and found no vessel during all the voyage. As he approached the mouth of the river, he saw around him a number of barques and small vessels that he could not avoid, and that he determined in consequence to approach with as good a grace as possible. The masters of these ships told him that the King was expected with impatience, but that they had no news of him, that they had come out to meet him, and that they would send pilots to Rambures, to conduct him up the river to Edinburgh, where all was hope and joy. Rambures, equally surprised that the squadron which bore the King of England, had not appeared, and of the publicity of his forthcoming arrival, went up towards Edinburgh more and more surrounded by barques, which addressed to him the same language. A gentleman of the country passed from one of these barques upon the frigate. He told Rambures that the principal noblemen of Scotland had resolved to act together, that these noblemen could count upon more than twenty thousand men ready to take up arms, and that all the towns awaited only the arrival of the King to proclaim him.

More and more troubled that the squadron did not appear, Rambures, after a time, turned back and went in search of it. As he approached the mouth of the river, he distinguished our squadron, chased by twenty-six large ships of war and a number of other vessels, all of which he soon lost sight of, so much was our squadron in advance. He continued on his course in order to join them; but he could not do so until all had passed by the mouth of the river. Then steering clear of the rear-guard of the English ships, he remarked that the English fleet was hotly chasing the ship of the King of England, which ran along the coast, however, amid the fire of cannon and oftentimes of musketry. Rambures tried, for a long time, to profit by the lightness of his frigate to get a-head; but, always cut off by the enemy's vessels, and continually in danger of being taken, he returned to Dunkerque, where he immediately despatched to the Court this sad and disturbing news. He was followed, five or six days after, by the King of England, who returned to Dunkerque on the 7th of April, with his vessels badly knocked about.

The war this year proceeded much as before. M. d'Orléans went to Spain again. Before taking the field he stopped at Madrid to arrange matters. There he found nothing prepared, and everything in disorder. He was compelled to work day after day, for many hours, in order to obtain the most necessary supplies. This is what accounted for a delay which was maliciously interpreted at Paris into love for the Queen. M. le Duc was angry at the idleness in which he was kept; even Madame la Duchesse, who hated him, because she had formerly loved him too well, industriously circulated this report, which was believed at Court, in the city, even in foreign countries, everywhere, save in Spain, where the truth was too well known. It was while he was thus engaged that he gave utterance to a pleasantry that made Madame de Maintenon and Madame des Ursins his two most bitter enemies for ever afterwards.

One evening he was at table with several French and Spanish gentlemen, all occupied with his vexation against Madame des Ursins, who governed everything, and who had not thought of even the smallest thing for the campaign. The supper and the wine somewhat affected M. d'Orléans. Still full of his vexation, he took a glass, and, looking at the company, made an allusion in a toast to the two women, one the captain, the other the lieutenant, who governed France and Spain, and that in so coarse and yet humorous a manner, that it struck at once the imagination of the guests. No comment was made, but everybody burst out laughing, sense of drollery overcoming prudence, for it was well known that the she-captain was Madame de Maintenon, and the she-lieutenant Madame des Ursins. The health was drunk, although the words were not repeated, and the scandal was strange.

Half an hour at most after this, Madame des Ursins was informed of what had taken place. She knew well who were meant by the toast, and was transported with rage. She at once wrote an account of the circumstances to Madame de Maintenon, who, for her part, was quite as furious. *Inde iræ.* They never pardoned M. d'Orléans.

Early in July, we took Ghent and Bruges.

Here follows Saint-Simon's account of the Oudenarde disaster. It is a battle impossible to follow without a large-scale map, especially in an account designed to denigrate Vendôme and exalt the Duke of Burgundy. Its chief domestic result was to split the Court into contesting groups each supporting one of these generals.

Our disasters at Oudenarde were very great. We had many men and officers taken prisoners, and a prodigious quantity missing and dispersed. All these losses were, as I have shown, entirely due to the laziness and inattention of M. de Vendôme. Yet the friends of that General—and he had many at the Court and in the army—actually had the audacity to lay the blame upon Monseigneur le Duc de Bourgogne.

A powerful cabal was in fact got up against him. Vaudevilles, verses, atrocious songs against him, ran all over Paris and the provinces with a licence and a rapidity that no one checked; while at the Court, the libertines and the fashionables applauded; so that in six days it was thought disgraceful to speak with any measure of this Prince, even in his father's house.

Madame de Bourgogne was cruelly wounded by the insults of Vendôme to her husband, and by all the atrocities and falsehoods his emissaries published. She gained Madame de Maintenon, and the first result of this step was, that the King censured Chamillart for not speaking of the letters in circulation, and ordered him to write to Albéroni and D'Evreux (Campistron, strangely enough, was forgotten), commanding them to keep silence for the future.

The cabal was amazed to see Madame de Maintenon on the side of Madame de Bourgogne, while M. du Maine (who was generally in accord with Madame de Maintenon) was for M. de Vendôme. They concluded that the King had been led away, but that if they held firm, his partiality for M. de Vendôme, for M. du Maine, and for bastardy in general, would bring him round to them. In point of fact, the King was led now one way, and now another, with a leaning always towards M. de Vendôme.

Soon after this, Chamillart, who was completely of the party of M. de Vendôme, thought fit to write a letter to Monseigneur le Duc de Bourgogne, in which he counselled him to live on good terms with his general. Madame de Bourgogne never forgave Chamillart this letter, and was always annoyed with her husband that he acted upon it. His religious sentiments induced him to do so. She wrote to her husband that for M. de Vendôme she had more aversion and contempt than for any one else in the world, and that nothing would make her forget what he had done.

Some anxiety was felt just about this time for Lille, to which it was feared the enemy would lay siege. Boufflers went to command there, at his own request, and found the place very ill-garrisoned with raw troops, many of whom had never smelt powder. M. de Vendôme, however, laughed at the idea of the siege of Lille, as something mad and ridiculous. Nevertheless, the town was invested on the 12th of August. They drove out the besiegers from the projecting angles of the counterscarp, which they had kept possession of for eight days. They twice repulsed seven thousand men who attacked their covered way and an outwork; at the third attack they lost an angle of the outwork, but remained masters of all the rest.

So many attacks and engagements terribly weakened the garrison. On the 28th of September some assistance was sent to the besieged by the daring of the Chevalier de Luxembourg. But all was in vain. The enemy returned again and again to the attack. Every attempt to cut off their supplies failed. Finally, on the 23rd of October, a capitulation was signed. Maréchal Boufflers obtained all he asked, and retired into the citadel with all the prisoners of war, after two months of resistance.

The position of Monseigneur le Duc de Bourgogne at the army continued to be equivocal. He was constantly in collision with M. de Vendôme. The latter, after the loss of Lille, wished to defend the Escaut, without any regard to its extent of forty miles. The Duc de Bourgogne, as far as he dared, took the part of Berwick, who maintained that the defence was impossible. The King, hearing of all these disputes, actually sent Chamillart to the army to compose them. Chamillart continued to admire Vendôme, and treated the Duc de Bourgogne with little respect, both at the army, and, after his return, in conversation with the King. His report was given in presence of Madame de Maintenon, who listened without daring to say a word, and repeated everything to the Duchesse de Bourgogne. We may imagine what passed between them, and the anger of the Princess against the minister.

M. de Vendôme arrived at Versailles on the morning of December 15th, and saluted the King as he left table. The King embraced him with a sort of enthusiasm that made his cabal triumph. He monopolised all conversation during the dinner, but only trifles were talked of. The King said he would talk to him next day at Madame de Maintenon's. This delay, which was new to him, did not seem of good augury. He went to pay his respects to M. de Bourgogne, who received him well in spite of all that had passed.

1709

The winter was terrible; the memory of man could find no parallel to it. The frost came suddenly on Twelfth Night, and lasted nearly two months, beyond all recollection. In four days the Seine and all the other rivers were frozen, and, what had never been seen before, the sea froze all along the coasts, so as to bear carts, even heavily laden, upon it. The violence of the cold was such, that the strongest elixirs and the most spirituous liquors broke their bottles in cupboards of rooms with fires in them. There were no walnut-trees, no olive-trees, no apple-trees, no vines left. The other trees died in great numbers; the gardens perished, and all the grain in the earth. It is impossible to imagine the desolation of this general ruin.

In several places large stores of corn were collected by the government authorities, but with the greatest possible secrecy. Private people were expressly forbidden to do this. The Parliament assembled to debate upon these disorders. It came to the resolution of submitting various proposals to the King, which it deemed likely to improve the condition of the country. As soon as the King heard of this, he flew into a strange passion, and his first intention was to send a harsh message to the Parliament to attend to law trials, and not to mix with matters that did not concern it. The chancellor did not dare to represent to the King that what the Parliament wished to do belonged to its province, but calmed him by representing the respect and affection with which the Parliament regarded him, and that he was master either to accept or refuse its offers. No reprimand was given, therefore, to the Parliament, but it was informed that the King prohibited it from meddling with the corn question.

Payments, hitherto most strictly made, began to cease. Those of the customs, those of the divers loans, the dividends upon the Hôtel de Ville—in all times so sacred—all were suspended; these last alone continued, but with delays, then with retrenchments, which desolated nearly all the families of Paris and many others. At the same time the taxes—increased, multiplied, and exacted with the most extreme rigour—completed the devastation of France. Everything rose incredibly in price, while nothing was left to buy with, even at the cheapest rate. A great number of people who, in preceding years, used to relieve the poor, found themselves so reduced as to be able to subsist only with great difficulty, and many of them received alms in secret.

People never ceased wondering what had become of all the money of the realm. Nobody could any longer pay, because nobody was paid: the country-people, overwhelmed with exactions and with valueless property, had become insolvent: trade no longer yielded anything—good faith and confidence were at an end. All was perishing step by step; the realm was entirely exhausted; the troops, even, were not paid. This was the frightful state to which we were reduced, when envoys were sent into Holland to try and bring about peace.

It was shortly after this, when the news of the arrogant demands of the allies, and the vain attempts of the King to obtain an honourable peace became known, that the Duchesse de Gramont conceived the idea of offering her plate to the King, to replenish his impoverished exchequer. The project made a great hubbub at the Court. Nobody dared to refuse to offer his plate, yet each offered it with much regret. Some had been keeping it as a last resource, which they were very sorry to deprive themselves of; others feared the dirtiness of copper and earthenware.

Summer came. The dearness of all things, and of bread in particular, continued to cause frequent commotions all over the realm. The King himself from his windows heard the people of Versailles crying aloud in the street.

For some time past, Chamillart, with the knowledge of the King, had sent people to Holland and elsewhere to negotiate for peace, although he had no right to do so, Torcy being the minister to whose department this business belonged. Torcy likewise sent people to Holland and elsewhere with a similar object, and these ambassadors of the two ministers, instead of working in common, did all in their power to thwart each other. They succeeded so well that it was said they seemed in foreign countries ministers of different powers, whose interests were quite opposed. Those who sincerely wished to treat with us, found themselves so embarrassed between the rival factions, that they did not know what to do; and others made our disagreements a plausible pretext for not listening to our propositions.

At last Torcy was so annoyed with the interference of Chamillart, that he called the latter to account for it, and made him sign an agreement by which he bound himself to enter into no negotiations for peace and to mix himself in no foreign affairs; and so this absurdity came to an end.

In Italy, early this year, we received a check of no small importance. I have mentioned that we were invited to join in an Italian league, having for its object to oppose the Emperor. We joined this league, but not before its existence had been noised abroad, and put the allies on their guard as to the danger they ran of losing Italy. Therefore the Imperialists entered the Papal States, laid them under contribution, ravaged them, lived there in true Tartar style, and snapped their fingers at the Pope, who cried aloud as he could obtain no redress and no assistance. Pushed at last to extremity by the military occupation which desolated his States, he yielded to all the wishes of the Emperor, and recognised the Archduke as King of Spain. Philip V immediately ceased all intercourse with Rome, and dismissed the nuncio from Madrid.

In Spain, everything went wrong, and people began to think it would be best to give up that country to the house of Austria, in the hope that by this means the war would be terminated. It was therefore seriously resolved to recall all our troops from Spain, and to give orders to Madame des Ursins to quit the country. Instructions were accordingly sent to this effect. The King and Queen of Spain, in the greatest alarm at such a violent determination, cried aloud against it, and begged that the execution of it might at least be suspended for a while.

At this, our King paused and called a Council to discuss the subject. It was ultimately agreed to leave sixty-six battalions of our troops to the King of Spain, but to withdraw all the rest. This compromise satisfied nobody. Those who wished to support Spain said this assistance was not enough. The other party said it was too much.

This determination being arrived at, it seemed as though the only thing to be done was to send M. d'Orléans to Spain to take command there.

But now will be seen the effect of that mischievous pleasantry of his upon Madame de Maintenon and Madame des Ursins, the 'she-captain,' and the 'she-lieutenant'—as he called them, in the gross language to which I have before alluded. Those two ladies had not forgiven him his witticism, and had determined to accomplish his disgrace. His own thoughtless conduct assisted them in bringing about this result.

The King one day asked him if he had much desire to return into Spain. He replied in a manner evidencing his willingness to serve, marking no eagerness. In a few days it was publicly known that he would not go. At the same time the King gave orders to M. d'Orléans to send for his equipages from Spain, M. d'Orléans chose for this errand a man named Flotte, very skilful in intrigue, in which he had, so to speak, been always brought up. Flotte stayed some time in Madrid, and then went to the army which was still in quarters. He remained there three weeks, idling from quarter to quarter, saluting the Maréchal in command, who was much surprised at his long stay, and who pressed him to return into France. At last Flotte took leave of the Maréchal, asking him for an escort for himself and a commissary, with whom he meant to go in company across the Pyrenees. Twenty dragoons were given him as escort, and he and the commissary set out in a chaise.

They had not proceeded far before Flotte perceived that they were followed by other troops besides those guarding them. Flotte fearing that something was meant by this, slipped a pocket-book into the hands of the commissary, requesting him to take care of it. Shortly afterwards the chaise was surrounded by troops, and stopped; the two travellers were made to alight. The commissary was ordered to give up the pocket-book, an order that he complied with very rapidly, and Flotte was made prisoner, and escorted back to the spot he had just left.

The news of this occurrence reached the King on the 12th of July, by the ordinary courier from Madrid. The King informed M. d'Orléans of it, who, having learnt it by a private courier six days before, affected nevertheless surprise, and said it was strange that one of his people should have been thus arrested, and that as his Majesty was concerned, it was for him to demand the reason. The King replied, that in fact the injury regarded him more than M. d'Orléans, and that he would give orders to Torcy to write as was necessary to Spain.

It is not difficult to believe that such an explosion made a great noise, both in France and Spain; but the noise it made at first was nothing to that which followed. A cabal was formed against Monsieur le Duc d'Orléans. It was said that he had plotted to place himself upon the Spanish throne, by driving out Philip V. The King and *Monseigneur* treated M. d'Orléans with a coldness which made him sorely ill at ease; the majority of the courtiers, following this example, withdrew from him.

I learnt at last from M. d'Orléans how far he was deserving of public censure, and what had given colouring to the reports spread against him. He admitted to me, that several of the Spanish grandees had persuaded him that it was not possible the King of Spain could stand, and had proposed to him to hasten his fall, and take his place; that he had rejected this proposition with indignation, but had been induced to promise, that if Philip V fell of himself, without hope of rising, he would not object to mount the vacant throne, believing that by so doing he would be doing good to our King, by preserving Spain to his house.

As soon as I heard this, I advised him to make a clean breast of it to the King, but the King would not listen to anything in favour of his nephew. The whole Court cried out against M. d'Orléans; never was such an uproar heard.

Madame des Ursins and Madame de Maintenon had so far triumphed, that M. d'Orléans found himself plunged in the deepest disgrace. He was universally shunned. Whenever he appeared, people flew away, so that they might not be seen in communication with him. His solitude was so great, that for a whole month only one friend entered his house. In the midst of this desertion, he had no resource but debauchery, and the society of his mistress, Madame d'Argenton. The disorder and scandal of his life had for a long time offended the King, the Court, and the public. They now unhappily confirmed everybody in the bad opinion they had formed of him. That the long disgrace he suffered continued to confirm him in his bad habits, and that it explains to some extent his after-conduct, there can be no doubt. But I must leave him now, and return to other matters.

There rose in the Court, I know not what confused murmurs, the origin of which could not be pointed out, publishing that either the State or Chamillart must perish; that already his ignorance had brought the kingdom within an ace of destruction; that it was a miracle this destruction had not yet come to pass; and that it would be madness to tempt Providence any longer. All admitted his rectitude, but maintained that a successor of some kind or other was absolutely necessary.

On Sunday morning, November 9th, the King, on entering the Council of State, called the Duc de Beauvilliers to him, and requested him to go in the afternoon and tell Chamillart that he was obliged, for motives of public interest, to ask him to resign his office; but that, in order to give him a mark of his esteem and satisfaction with his services, he continued his pension of minister—that is to say, twenty thousand francs, and added as much more, with one to his son of twenty thousand francs likewise.

Next day after the fall of Chamillart, it became known that the triumph of Madame de Maintenon was completed, and that Voysin, her creature, was the succeeding Secretary of State. This Voysin had the one indispensable quality for admission into the counsels of Louis XIV—not a drop of noble blood in his veins.

He was perfectly ignorant of everything but the duties of an Intendant. He was, moreover, rough and uncivil, as the courtiers soon found. He was never unjust for the sake of being so, nor was he bad naturally; blind obedience to the King and to regulations was the only principle which he respected in others or in himself.

Flanders, ever since the opening of the campaign, had been the principal object of attention. Prince Eugène and Marlborough, joined together, continued their vast designs, and disdained to hide them. Their prodigious preparations spoke of sieges. Shall I say that we desired them, and that we thought of nothing but how to preserve, not use our army?

Tournai was the first place towards which the enemies directed their arms. After a short resistance it fell into their hands. Villars was commander in Flanders. Boufflers feeling that, in the position of affairs, such a post must weigh very heavily upon one man, and that in case of his death there was no one to take his place, offered to go to assist him. The King, after some little hesitation, accepted this magnanimous offer, and Boufflers set out.

Villars received him with an air of joy and respect, and at once showed every willingness to act in concert with him. The two generals accordingly worked harmoniously together.

After the fall of Tournai, our army took up position at Malplaquet, the right and the left supported by two woods, with hedges and woods before the centre, so that the plain was, as it were, cut in two. Marlborough and Prince Eugène marched in their turn, fearing lest Villars should embarrass them as they went towards Mons, which place they had resolved to besiege. They sent on a large detachment of their army, under the command of the Prince of Hesse, to watch ours. He arrived in sight of the camp at Malplaquet at the same time that we entered it, and was quickly warned of our existence by three cannon shots that Villars, out of braggadocio, fired by way of challenge to Marlborough and Prince Eugène. Some little firing took place this day and the next, the 10th of September, but without doing much harm on either side.

Marlborough and Prince Eugène, warned of the perilous state in which the Prince of Hesse was placed—he would have been lost if attacked—hastened at once to join him, and arrived in the middle of the morning of the 10th.

It was decided that evening to give us battle on the morrow, and on the following morning the battle began.

The struggle lasted many hours. But our position had been badly chosen, and, in spite of every effort, we were unable to maintain it. Villars, in the early part of the action, received a wound which incapacitated him from duty. All the burden of command fell upon Boufflers. He bore it well; but after a time finding his army dispersed, his infantry overwhelmed, the ground slipping from under his feet, he thought only of beating a good and honourable retreat. He led away his army in such good order, that the enemy were unable to interfere with it in the slightest degree. The enemy frankly admitted that in men killed and wounded, in general officers and privates, in flags and standard, they had lost more than we.

Saint-Simon's account of Malplaquet is glaringly unjust to Villars. It ignores the near miracle whereby Villars had to turn the starving demoralized wreckage of Villeroi's Army of Flanders into an efficient fighting force in under six months; and that largely by his own conduct in the first field of battle he destroyed the French belief that Marlborough was invincible. French morale after Malplaquet was higher than it had been since the spring of 1704. Saint-Simon's detestation of Villars makes him consistently unjust to the greatest French soldier of the day. The reason for Saint-Simon's attitude is not far to seek. Even had he nursed no grievance against Villars, this plump, jovial, hail-fellow-well-met Gascon was not a man with whom the punctilious Saint-Simon would have had much in common. But natural antipathy was exacerbated by grievances. Saint-Simon was shocked at Villars' open contempt for etiquette and precedence; disgusted at the Marshal's friendship with Mme. de Maintenon and the Duc du Maine; and when the saviour of France was created a Duke and given the St. Esprit, Saint-Simon was furious at having to recognize as an equal a man who was 'hardly a gentleman'.

Why the Maréchal Villars waited ten days to be attacked in a position so disadvantageous, instead of at once marching upon the enemies and overcoming, as he might at first easily have done, it is difficult to understand. He threw all the blame upon his wound, although it was well known that the fate of the day was decided long before he was hurt.

Although forced to retire, our men burned with eagerness to engage the enemies again. Mons had been laid siege to. Boufflers tried to make the besiegers give up the undertaking. But his men were without bread and without pay. The common soldiers were reduced to herbs and roots for all sustenance. Under these circumstances it was found impossible to persevere in trying to save Mons. Nothing but subsistence could be thought of.

The Court had now become so accustomed to defeats that a battle lost as was Malplaquet seemed half a victory. Boufflers sent a courier to the King with an account of the event, and spoke so favourably of Villars that all the blame of the defeat fell upon himself. Villars was everywhere pitied and applauded, although he had lost an important battle.

1710

On Saturday, the 15th of February, the King was waked up at seven o'clock in the morning, an hour earlier than usual, because Madame la Duchesse de Bourgogne was in the pains of labour. He dressed himself diligently in order to go to her. She did not keep him waiting long. At three minutes and three seconds after eight o'clock, she brought into the world a Duc d'Anjou, who is the King Louis XV, at present reigning.

This year Villars was chosen for Flanders, as before. He set forth for the frontier, therefore, in his coach, and travelling easy stages, on account of his wound, arrived in due time at the army. Neither Prince Eugène nor the Duke of Marlborough wished for peace, whilst the King wished passionately for nothing so much as a victory, which should disturb the plans of the enemies, and deliver him from the necessity of continuing the sad and shameful negotiations for peace he had set on foot at Gertruydemberg.

Douai, Saint Venant, and Aire fell into the hands of the enemy during this campaign, while we did little or nothing. This was the last campaign in Flanders of the Duke of Marlborough. On the Rhine our troops observed and subsisted: nothing more; but in Spain there was more movement.

Towards the end of March the King of Spain set out from Madrid to put himself at the head of his army in Aragon. He crossed the Sègre on the 14th of May, and advanced towards Balaguier, designing to lay siege to it. But heavy rains falling and causing the waters to rise, he was obliged to abandon his project. Joined a month afterwards by troops arrived from Flanders, he sought to attack the enemy, but was obliged to content himself for the moment by scouring the country, and taking some little towns where the Archduke had established stores. All this time the Count of Staremberg, who commanded the forces of the Archduke, was ill, this circumstance the King of Spain was profiting by. But the Count grew well again quicker than was expected; promptly assembled his forces; marched against the army of the King of Spain; engaged it, and obliged it, all astonished, to retire under Saragossa. This ill-success fell entirely on Villadarias, who was accused of imprudence and negligence. He was desperately in want of generals, and M. de Vendôme knowing this, and sick to death of banishment, had asked some little time before to be allowed to offer his services. At first he was snubbed. But the King of Spain, who eagerly wished for M. de Vendôme, despatched a courier begging the King to allow him to come and take command. The King held out no longer.

I omit Saint-Simon's account of the 1710 campaign in Spain because his hatred of Vendôme transforms it into a sermon on the text that the rain falls alike upon the just and the unjust. What really happened was that Vendôme, at the top of his form, defeated greatly superior allied forces at Villaviciosa on 9th December. The Franco-Spanish victory provided Louis with what was to prove an irreversible decision—Philippe of Bourbon, not Charles of Hapsburg, was to be King of Spain.

The impossibility of obtaining peace, and the exhaustion of the realm, threw the King into the most cruel anguish, and Desmarets into the saddest embarrassment. The paper of all kinds with which trade was inundated, and which had all more or less lost credit, made a chaos for which no remedy could be perceived. State-bills, bank-bills, receiver-general's-bills, title-bills, utensil-bills, were the ruin of private people, who were forced by the King to take them in payment, and who lost half, two-thirds, and sometimes more by the transaction. This depreciation enriched the financiers, at the expense of the public; and the circulation of money ceased, because there was no longer any money.

The capitation tax was doubled and trebled, at the will of the Intendants of the Provinces, merchandise and all kinds of provision were taxed to the amount of four times their value; new taxes of all kinds and upon all sorts of things were exacted; all this crushed nobles and roturiers, lords and clergy, and yet did not bring enough to the King, who drew the blood of all his subjects, squeezed out their very marrow, without distinction, and who enriched an army of tax-gatherers and officials of all kinds, in whose hands the best part of what was collected remained.

Desmarets, in whom the King had been forced to put all his confidence in finance matters, conceived the idea of establishing, in addition to so many taxes, that Royal Tithe upon all the property of each community and of each private person of the realm, that the Maréchal de Vauban, on the one hand, and Boisguilbert on the other, had formerly proposed; but, as I have already described, as a simple and sole tax which would suffice for all, which would all enter the coffers of the King, and by means of which every other impost would be abolished.

We have seen what success this proposition met with; how the financiers trembled at it; how the ministers blushed at it, with what anathemas it was rejected, and to what extent these two excellent and skilful citizens were disgraced. All this must be recollected here, since Desmarets, who had not lost sight of this system, now had recourse to it.

Desmarets thereupon proposed it to the King, who, accustomed as he was to the most ruinous imposts, could not avoid being terrified at this. For a long while he had heard nothing talked of but the most extreme misery: this increase saddened him in a manner so evident, that his valets perceived it several days running, and were so disturbed at it, that the Maréchal made bold to speak to the King upon this sadness, fearing for his health. Eight or ten days after, the King regained his usual calmness, and called the Maréchal to explain the cause of his trouble.

The King related to the Maréchal that the extremity of his affairs had forced him to put on furious imposts; that setting aside compassion, scruples had much tormented him for taking thus the wealth of his subjects; that at last he had unbosomed himself to the Père Tellier, who had asked for a few days to think upon the matter, and that he had returned after having had a consultation with some of the most skilful doctors of the Sorbonne, who had decided that *all the wealth of his subjects was his, and that when he took it he only took what belonged to him!* The King added, that this decision had taken away all his scruples, and had restored to him the calm and tranquillity he had lost.

After the King had been thus satisfied by his confessor, no time was lost in establishing the tax. On Tuesday, the 30th of September, Desmarets entered the Finance Council with the necessary edict in his bag.

For some days everybody had known of this bomb-shell in the air, and had trembled with that remnant of hope which is founded only upon desire; all the Court as well as all Paris waited in a dejected sadness to see what would happen. People whispered to each other, and even when the project was rendered public, no one dared to talk of it aloud.

On the day above-named, the King brought forward this measure in the Council, by saying, that the impossibility of obtaining peace, and the extreme difficulty of sustaining the war, had caused Desmarets to look about in order to discover extraordinary means of raising further revenue; that he had pitched upon this tax; that he (the King), although sorry to adopt such a resource, approved it, and had no doubt the Council would do so likewise, when it was explained to them. Desmarets, in a pathetic discourse, then dwelt upon the reasons which had induced him to propose this tax, and afterwards read the edict through from beginning to end without interruption.

Thus was settled this bloody business, and immediately after signed, sealed, and registered, amid the bitter, but suppressed complaints of the public. The product of this tax was nothing like so much as had been imagined in this bureau of Cannibals; and the King did not pay a single farthing more to any one than he had previously done. Thus all the fine relief expected by this tax ended in smoke.

Monseigneur le Duc de Bourgogne spoke openly against this tax, and against the financiers, who lived upon the very marrow of the people; spoke with a just and holy anger that recalled the memory of Saint Louis, of Louis XII, father of the People, and of Louis the Just. *Monseigneur*, too, moved by this indignation, so unusual, of his son, sided with him, and showed anger at so many exactions as injurious as barbarous, and at so many insignificant men so monstrously enriched with the nation's blood. Both father and son infinitely surprised those who heard them, and made themselves looked upon in some sort, as resources from which something might hereafter be hoped for. But the edict was issued, and though there might be some hope in the future, there was none in the present. And no one knew who was to be the real successor of Louis XIV, and how under the next government we were to be still more overwhelmed than under this one.

One result of this tax was, that it enabled the King to augment all his infantry with five men per company.

A tax was also levied upon the usurers, who had much gained by trafficking in the paper of the King, that is to say, had taken advantage of the need of those to whom the King gave this paper in payment. These usurers are called *agioteurs*. Their mode was, ordinarily, to give, for example, according as the holder of paper was more or less pressed, three or four hundred francs (the greater part often in provisions), for a bill of a thousand francs! This game was called *agio*. It was said that thirty millions were obtained from this tax. Many people gained much by it; I know not if the King was the better treated.

Soon after this the coin was re-coined, by which great profit was made for the King, and much wrong done to private people and to trade. In all times it has been regarded as a very great misfortune to meddle with corn and money. Desmarets has accustomed us to tricks with the money; M. le Duc and Cardinal Fleury to interfere with corn and to fictitious famine.

At the commencement of December, the King declared that he wished there should be, contrary to custom, plays and "apartments" at Versailles even when *Monseigneur* should be at Meudon. He thought apparently he must keep his Court full of amusements, to hide, if it was possible, abroad and at home, the disorder and the extremity of affairs. For the same reason, the carnival was opened early this season, and all through the winter there were many balls of all kinds at the Court, where the wives of the ministers gave very magnificent displays, like fêtes, to Madame la Duchesse de Bourgogne and to all the Court.

But Paris did not remain less wretched or the provinces less desolated.

1711

On Thursday, the 9th of April, *Monseigneur* rose, and meant to go out wolf-hunting; but as he was dressing, such a fit of weakness seized him, that he fell into his chair. Boudin made him get into bed again; but all the day his pulse was in an alarming state. The King, only half informed by Fagon of what had taken place, believed there was nothing the matter, and went out walking at Marly after dinner, receiving news from time to time. Monseigneur le Duc de Bourgogne and Madame de Bourgogne dined at Meudon, and they would not quit *Monseigneur* for one moment. The Princess performed the duties of a daughter-in-law with the grace which she showed in everything that she did; she could not feel much real grief at the thought of the event which might possibly be impending; but she was assiduous in her attentions, though quite natural and unaffected. The Duc de Bourgogne, simple and holy as he was, and full of the idea of his duty, exaggerated his attentions; and although there was a strong suspicion of the small pox, neither quitted *Monseigneur*, except for the King's supper.

The next day, Friday, the 10th, in reply to his express demands, the King was informed of the extremely dangerous state of *Monseigneur*. He had said on the previous evening that he would go on the following morning to Meudon, and remain there during all the illness of *Monseigneur* whatever its nature might be. He was now as good as his word. Immediately after mass he set out for Meudon. Before doing so, he forbade his children, and all who had not had the small pox, to go there. The King held his Council, and worked in the evening with his ministers as usual. He saw *Monseigneur* morning and evening, oftentimes in the afternoon, and always remained long by the bedside.

Versailles presented another scene. Monseigneur le Duc and Madame la Duchesse de Bourgogne held their Court openly there; and this Court resembled the first gleamings of the dawn. When the Prince and Princess rose, when they went to bed, when they dined and supped with the ladies,— all public conversations—all meals—all assemblies—were opportunities of paying court to them. The apartments could not contain the crowd.

On Tuesday, the 14th of April, I went to see the Chancellor, and asked for information upon the state of *Monseigneur*. He assured me it was good, and repeated to me the words Fagon had spoken to him, 'that things were going on according to their wishes, and beyond their hopes.'

As I was going home, I saw the Duchesse d'Orléans walking on a terrace. She called to me; but I pretended not to notice her, because La Montauban was with her, and hastened home, my mind filled with this news, and withdrew to my cabinet. Almost immediately afterwards Madame la Duchesse d'Orléans joined me there. To speak frankly and to our shame, she and I lamented together to see *Monseigneur*, in spite of his age and his fat, escape from so dangerous an illness. She reflected seriously but wittily, that after an illness of this sort, apoplexy was not to be looked for; that an attack of indigestion was equally unlikely to arise, considering the care *Monseigneur* had taken not to over-gorge himself since his recent danger; and we concluded more than dolefully, that henceforth we must make up our minds that the Prince would live and reign for a long time. Thus two hours passed, seemingly very short.

While thus all was tranquillity at Versailles, everything had changed its aspect in the sick room. Towards four o'clock *Monseigneur* grew worse, but nobody dared to open his mouth before Fagon, and the King was actually allowed to go to supper and to finish it without interruption, believing on the faith of Fagon that *Monseigneur* was going on well.

As the King rose from the supper-table, he well nigh fell backward when Fagon, coming forward, cried in great trouble that all was lost. It may be imagined what terror seized all the company at this abrupt passage from perfect security to hopeless despair. The King, scarcely master of himself, at once began to go towards the apartment of *Monseigneur*, and repelled very stiffly the indiscreet eagerness of some courtiers who wished to prevent him, saying that he would see his son again, and be quite certain that nothing could be done. The agony, without consciousness, of *Monseigneur* lasted more than an hour after the King had come into the cabinet. At last the fatal moment arrived. Fagon came out, and allowed so much to be understood.

Monseigneur was no more: it was known: it was spoken of: constraint with respect to him no longer existed. Madame la Duchesse de Bourgogne consoled her husband with less trouble than she had to appear herself in want of consolation. Without attempting to play a part, it was evident that she did her best to acquit herself of a pressing duty of decorum. But she found extreme difficulty in keeping up appearances. I tried not to be glad. I know not if I succeeded well, but at least it is certain, that neither joy nor sorrow blunted my curiosity, and that while taking due care to preserve all decorum, I did not consider myself in any way forced to play the doleful.

He was a good horseman, and looked well when mounted; but he was not a bold rider.

My joy at *Monseigneur's* death may be imagined. In a few days all my causes of disquietude had been removed, and I saw a future opening before me full of light and promise. Monseigneur le Duc de Bourgogne become Dauphin, heir to the throne of France; what favour might I not hope for? I could not conceal or control my satisfaction.

M. le Dauphin, for, as I have said, it is by that title I shall now name Monseigneur le Duc de Bourgogne—M. le Dauphin, I say, soon gained all hearts. Aided by his clever wife, who already had full possession of the King's heart and of that of Madame de Maintenon, M. le Dauphin re-doubled his attentions in order to possess them also. These attentions, addressed to Madame de Maintenon, produced their fruit. She was transported with pleasure at finding a Dauphin upon whom she could rely, instead of one whom she did not like, gave herself up to him accordingly, and by that means secured to him the King's favour. The first fortnight made evident to everybody at Marly the extraordinary change that had come over the King with respect to the Dauphin. His Majesty, generally severe beyond measure with his legitimate children, showed the most marked graciousness for this prince. The effect of this, and of the change that had taken place in his state, were soon most clearly visible in the Dauphin. Instead of being timid and retiring, diffident in speech and more fond of his study than of the salon, he became on a sudden easy and frank, showing himself in public on all occasions, conversing right and left in a gay, agreeable, and dignified manner.

The Court being changed by the death of *Monseigneur*, I soon began indeed to think of changing my conduct with regard to the new Dauphin. I joined him in the gardens at Marly, and profited by his gracious welcome to say to him, confidentially, that many reasons, of which he was not ignorant, had necessarily kept me until then removed from him, but that now I hoped to be able to follow with less constraint my attachment and my inclination, and that I flattered myself this would be agreeable to him. He replied in a low tone, that there were sometimes reasons which fettered people, but in our case such no longer existed; that he knew of my regard for him, and reckoned with pleasure that we should soon see each other more frequently than before. I am writing the exact words of his reply, on account of the singular politeness of the concluding ones. I regarded that reply as the successful result of a bait that had been taken as I wished. Little by little I became more assiduous at his promenades, but without following them when the crowd or any dangerous people do so; and I spoke more freely. I remained content with seeing the Dauphin in public, and I approached him in the Salon only when I saw a good opportunity.

A few days after this the Dauphin sent for me. For a full hour we talked upon the state of affairs.

His views, I found, were almost entirely in harmony with mine. He was sorry, and touchingly said so, for the ignorance of all things in which the King was kept by his ministers; he was anxious to see the power of those ministers restricted; he looked with dislike upon the incredible elevation of the illegitimate children; he wished to see the order to which I belonged restored to the position it deserved to occupy.

It is difficult to express what I felt in quitting the Dauphin. A magnificent and near future opened out before me. I saw a prince, pious, just, débonnaire, enlightened, and seeking to become more so; with principles completely in accord with my own, and capacity to carry out those principles when the time for doing so arrived. I relished deliciously a confidence so precious and so full, upon the most momentous matters, and at a first interview. I felt all the sweetness of this perspective, and of my deliverance from a servitude which, in spite of myself, I sometimes could not help showing myself impatient of. I felt, too, that I now had an opportunity of elevating myself, and of contributing to those grand works, for the happiness and advantage of the state I so much wished to see accomplished.

There was need of great circumspection in carrying on even private intercourse with the Dauphin. From this time I continually saw him in his cabinet, talking with him in all liberty upon the various persons of the Court, and upon the various subjects relating to the state; but always with the same secrecy as at first. This was absolutely necessary; as I have just said, I was still in a sort of half disgrace: the King did not regard me with the eyes of favour; Madame de Maintenon was absolutely averse to me. If they two had suspected my strict intimacy with the heir to the throne, I should have been assuredly lost.

Every time I went to see the Dauphin I garnished all my pockets with papers, and I often smiled within myself passing through the Salon, at seeing there many people who at that moment were in my pockets, and who were far indeed from suspecting the important discussion that was going to take place.

No sooner did I feel myself pretty firmly established on this footing of delicious intimacy with the Dauphin than I conceived the desire to unite him with M. le Duc d'Orléans. M. d'Orléans, on his side, saw without difficulty the advantage to him of union with the Dauphin. To bring it about I laid before him two conditions. One, that when in the presence of the Prince he should suppress that detestable heroism of impiety he affected more than he felt, and allow no licentious expressions to escape him. The second was to go less often into evil company. He promised obedience, and was faithful to his promise. The Dauphin perceived and approved the change; little by little the object of my desire was gained.

1712

Domestically speaking this is the most tragic year of Louis XIV's reign. Between 12th February and 8th March three of the royal family—the Dauphine, the Dauphin, and their elder son—all died suddenly of an undiagnosed complaint. In the seventeenth century it was unusual for a prominent person to die without rumours circulating that the deceased had been poisoned; and these three tragic deaths produced the worst poisoning panic of the reign, unchecked by the fact that the post-mortems disclosed no symptoms of poison. In these deaths the Duc d'Orléans, as we shall see, was made the scapegoat by the public, although his innocence was strenuously upheld by Saint-Simon. The memoirist's own choice of a poisoner was the hated Duc du Maine, but this is too absurd to call for any refutation. In point of fact the cause of death in all three cases seems to have been malignant scarlet fever, and, for me at any rate, the poisoning theory is demolished by the fact that in February 1712 there were over five hundred deaths in Paris with symptoms identical with those of the royal victims.

On Saturday, the 6th of February, the Dauphine, who had had fever all night, did not fail to rise at her ordinary hour, and to pass the day as usual; but in the evening the fever returned. She was but middling all that night, a little worse the next day.

On Thursday, the 11th of February, at nine o'clock in the morning, the King entered the Dauphine's chamber, which Madame de Maintenon scarcely ever left, except when he was in her apartments. The Princess was so ill it was resolved to speak to her of receiving the sacrament. Prostrated though she was she was surprised at this. She put some questions as to her state; replies as little terrifying as possible were given to her, and little by little she was warned against delay.

Meanwhile the Dauphin had given way. He had hidden his own illness as long as he could, so as not to leave the pillow of his Dauphine. Now the fever he had was too strong to be dissimulated; and the doctors who wished to spare him the sight of the horrors they foresaw, forgot nothing to induce him to stay in his chamber, where, to sustain him, false news was, from time to time, brought him of the state of his wife. The confession of the Dauphine was long. Extreme unction was administered immediately afterwards; and the holy viaticum directly. On Friday 12th, she died.

Monseigneur le Dauphin, ill and agitated by the most bitter grief, kept his chamber; but on Saturday morning the 13th, being pressed to go to Marly to avoid the horror of the noise overhead where the Dauphine was lying dead, he set out for that place at seven o'clock in the morning. The Dauphin reached the chamber of the King, full just then of company. As soon as he appeared the King called him and embraced him tenderly again and again. These first moments, so touching, passed in words broken by sobs and tears.

Shortly afterwards the King looking at the Dauphin was terrified by the same things that had previously struck me with affright. Everybody around was so, the doctors more than the others. The King ordered them to feel his pulse; that they found bad, so they said afterwards; for the time they contented themselves with saying it was not regular, and that the Dauphin would be wise to go to bed. The King embraced him again, recommended him very tenderly to take care of himself, and ordered him to go to bed. He obeyed and rose no more!

On the morrow, Sunday, the uneasiness felt on account of the Dauphin augmented. He himself did not conceal his belief that he should never rise again. On Tuesday the 16th, the Dauphin was worse. He felt himself devoured by a consuming fire, which the external fever did not seem to justify; but the pulse was very extraordinary and exceedingly menacing. On Wednesday the 17th, the malady considerably increased. On Thursday morning, the 18th of February, I learned that the Dauphin, who had waited for midnight with impatience, had heard mass immediately after the communion, had passed two hours in devout communication with God, and that his reason then became embarrassed. Madame de Saint-Simon told me afterwards that he had received extreme unction: in fine, that he died at half-past eight.

The youth of this prince made every one tremble. But God worked a miracle on this prince between his eighteenth and twentieth years. From this abyss he came out affable, gentle, humane, moderate, patient, modest, penitent, and humble; and austere, even more than harmonised with his position. But for a long time he behaved not like a prince but like a novice. In due time, however, he comprehended that the faithful performance of the duties proper to the state in which he had been placed, would be the conduct most agreeable to God. A volume would not describe sufficiently my private interviews with this prince,—what love of good! what forgetfulness of self! what researches! what fruit! what purity of purpose!

It was he who was not afraid to say publicly, in the Salon of Marly, 'that a king is made for his subjects, and not the subjects for him'; a remark that, except under his own reign, which God did not permit, would have been the most frightful blasphemy.

Great God! what a spectacle you gave to us in him. What tender but tranquil views he had! What submission and love of God! What a consciousness of his own nothingness, and of his sins! What a magnificent idea of the infinite mercy! What religious and humble fear! What tempered confidence! What patience! What constant goodness for all who approached him! France fell, in fine, under this last chastisement. God showed to her a prince she merited not. The earth was not worthy of him; he was ripe already for the blessed eternity!

On Tuesday, the 8th of March, Monseigneur le Duc de Bretagne, eldest son of Monsieur le Dauphin, who had succeeded to the name and rank of his father, being then only five years and some months old, and who had been seized with measles within a few days, expired, in spite of all the remedies given him. His brother, M. le Duc d'Anjou, who still sucked, was taken ill at the same time, but thanks to the care of the Duchesse de

Ventadour, whom in after life he never forgot, and who administered an antidote, escaped, and is now King.

That the cause of the Dauphin's and the Dauphine's death was poison, soon spread like wildfire over the Court and the city. Public indignation fell upon M. d'Orléans, who was at once pointed out as the poisoner. In effect M. du Maine did all in his power to circulate this odious report. M. d'Orléans was, however, already in such bad odour, that people were ready to believe anything to his discredit. I was the only person, I say distinctly, the only person, who spoke to M. d'Orléans as before. Whether in his own house or in the palace I conversed with him, seated myself by his side in a corner of the *salon*, where assuredly we had no third person to fear, and walked with him in the gardens under the very windows of the King and of Madame de Maintenon.

Nevertheless, all my friends warned me that if I pursued this conduct so opposite to that in vogue, I should assuredly fall into disgrace. I held firm. I thought that when we did not believe our friends guilty we ought not to desert them, but, on the contrary, to draw closer to them.

I have said little of the grief I felt at the loss of the prince whom everybody so deeply regretted. As will be believed, it was bitter and profound. The truth is, I was in despair.

In the casket of the Dauphin there were several papers he had asked me for. I had drawn them up in all confidence; he had preserved them in the same manner. There was one, very large, in my hand, which if seen by the King, would have robbed me of his favour for ever; ruined me without hope of return. We do not think in time of such catastrophes. The King knew my handwriting; he did not know my mode of thought, but might pretty well have guessed it. I had sometimes supplied him with means to do so; my good friends of the Court had done the rest. The King when he discovered my paper would also discover on what close terms of intimacy I had been with the Dauphin, of which he had no suspicion. My anguish was then cruel, and there seemed every reason to believe that if my secret was found out, I should be disgraced and exiled during all the rest of the King's reign.

On Tuesday, the 1st of March, M. de Beauvilliers carried the casket to the King. He came to me shortly after, and before sitting down, indicated by signs that there was no further occasion for fear. He then related to me that he had found the casket full of a mass of documents, finance projects, reports from the provinces, papers of all kinds, that he had read some of them to the King on purpose to weary him, and had succeeded so well that the King soon was satisfied by hearing only the titles; and, at last, tired out by not finding anything important, said it was not worth while to read more, and that there was nothing to do but to throw everything into the fire. The Duc assured me that he did not wait to be told twice, being all the more anxious to comply, because at the bottom of the casket he had seen some of my handwriting, which he had promptly covered up in taking other papers to read their titles to the King; and that immediately the word 'fire' was uttered, he confusedly threw all the papers into the casket, and then emptied it near the fire, between the King and Madame de Maintenon, taking good care, as he did so that my documents should not be seen,— even cautiously using the tongs in order to prevent any piece flying away, and not quitting the fireplace until he had seen every page consumed. We embraced each other, in the relief we reciprocally felt, relief proportioned to the danger we had run.

Vendôme was one of the few to whom the death of the Dauphin and the Dauphine brought hope and joy. He had deemed himself expatriated for the rest of his life. He saw, now, good chances before him of returning to our Court, and of playing a part there again. He had obtained some honour in Spain; he aimed at others even higher, and hoped to return to France with all the honours of a Prince of the Blood. His idleness, his free living, his debauchery had prolonged his stay upon the frontier, where he had more facilities for gratifying his tastes than at Madrid.

In order to be more at liberty he separated from the general officers, and established himself with his valets and two or three of his most familiar friends, cherished companions everywhere, at Vignarez, a little isolated hamlet, almost deserted, on the sea-shore and in the kingdom of Valencia. His object was to eat fish there to his heart's content. He carried out that object, and filled himself to repletion for nearly a month. He became unwell —his diet, as may be believed, was enough to cause this—but his illness increased so rapidly, that the few around him suspected poison, and sent on all sides for assistance. But the malady would not wait; it augmented rapidly with strange symptoms. Everybody near flew from him and abandoned him, so that he remained in the hands of three or four of the meanest valets, whilst the rest robbed him of everything and decamped. He passed thus, the last two or three days of his life, without a priest,—no mention even had been made of one,—without other help than that of a single surgeon. Thus died on Friday, the 10th of June, 1712, the haughtiest of men; and the happiest, except in the latter years of his life.

On the 17th of July, a truce between France and England, was published in Flanders, at the head of the troops of the two crowns. The Emperor, however, was not yet inclined for peace and his forces under Prince

Eugène continued to oppose us in Flanders, where, however, the tide at last turned in our favour.

1713

Peace was now all but concluded between France and England. There was, however, one great obstacle still in its way. Queen Anne and her Council, were stopped by the consideration, that the King of Spain would claim to succeed to the Crown of France, if the little Dauphin should die. Neither England nor any of the other powers at war, would consent to see the two principal crowns of Europe upon the same head. It was a long time before we could get over the difficulty. The King would accord nothing except promises. Absolute without reply, as he had become, he had extinguished and absorbed even the minutest trace, idea, and recollection, of all other authority, all other power in France except that which emanated from himself alone. The English, little accustomed to such maxims, proposed that the States-General should assemble in order to give weight to the renunciations to be made. The effect of this upon the mind of a Prince almost deified in his own eyes, and habituated to the most unlimited despotism cannot be expressed. The English were made to understand the weakness and the uselessness of what they asked; for the powerlessness of our States-General was explained to them, and they saw at once how vain their help would be, even if accorded.

For a long time nothing was done. But the renunciations were ready towards the middle of March and were agreed upon. The King of Spain had made his renunciations with all the solidity and solemnity which could be desired. It only remained for France to imitate him. For the ceremony that was to take place, all that could be obtained in order to render it more solemn was the presence of the peers. We all received written invitations, and Wednesday, the 18th of May, was fixed for the ceremony.

The renunciations were read; and by these the King of Spain and his posterity gave up all claim to the throne of France, and M. le Duc d'Orléans, and M. le Duc de Berry to succeed to that of Spain. These and other forms occupied a long time. Let me say here that, the ceremony over, peace was signed at Utrecht on the 10th of April, 1713, at a late hour of the night. It was published in Paris with great solemnity on the 22nd. On the 25th a

Te Deum was sung at Notre Dame, and in the evening there was a grand display of fireworks at the Grève, which was followed by a superb banquet given at the Hôtel de Ville by the Duc de Tresmes, the Governor of Paris.

A new and assuredly a very original History of France, in three large folio volumes, appeared under the name of Father Daniel, evidently composed in order to persuade people that the majority of the Kings of the first race, several of the second, some, even of the third, were bastards, whom this defect did not exclude from the throne, or affect in any way.

The effect of the book was great; its vogue such, that everybody, even women, asked for it. The King spoke of it to several of his Court, asked if they had read it; it was the sole historical book the King and Madame de Maintenon had ever spoken of. Thus the work appeared at Versailles upon every table, nothing else was talked about, marvellous eulogies were lavished upon it. Father Daniel obtained two thousand francs' pension for his history—a prodigious recompense—with a title of Historiographer of France.

1714

Towards the close of 1713, peace with the Emperor seemed certain. Negotiations were set on foot, and on the 6th of March of the following year, 1714, after much debate, they ended successfully. On that day, in fact, peace was signed at Rastadt.

The Queen of Spain, for a long time violently attacked with the king's evil around the face and neck, was just now at the point of death. Obtaining no relief from the Spanish doctors, she wished to have Helvetius, and begged the King by an express command to send him to her. Helvetius much inconvenienced, and knowing besides the condition of the princess, did not wish to go, but the King expressly commanded him. He set out then in a post chaise, followed by another in case his own should break down, and arrived thus at Madrid on the 11th of February, 1714. As soon as he had seen the Queen, he said there was nothing but a miracle could save her. On the 14th she died, with much courage, consciousness, and piety. Despair was general in Spain, where this queen was universally adored.

It has been seen with what art Madame des Ursins had unceasingly isolated the King of Spain; in what manner she had shut him up with the

Queen, and rendered him inaccessible. At the death of the Queen this solitude continued. But the Princesse des Ursins, judging that this inter-regnum in the Palace of Medina-Celi could not last for ever, resolved to assure herself of the King by a Queen who should owe to her such a grand marriage, and who, having no other support, would throw herself into her arms by gratitude and necessity. With this view she explained herself to Alberoni. The King of Spain was devout, he absolutely wanted a wife, the Princesse des Ursins set Alberoni to work, and it may be believed she was not scrupulous as to her means as soon as they were persuaded at Parma that she was serious and not joking.

It was not until the 27th of June that our King was made acquainted by the King of Spain with his approaching marriage. He could not hinder it; but from this moment he was determined upon vengeance against her who had arranged and brought it about in this manner. The disgrace of Madame des Ursins was in fact determined on between the King and Madame de Maintenon, but in a manner so secret before and since, that I know nobody who has found out by whom or how it was carried out.

A short time after this, the Princesse des Ursins conceived such strong suspicion of the lofty and enterprising spirit of the Princess of Parma that she repented having made this marriage, and wished to break it off. The marriage, which was to have been celebrated on the 25th of August, took place on the 15th of September. Immediately after the ceremony the new queen set out for Spain.

The Queen of Spain was to be met by the King of Spain at Guadalaxara. He arrived there, accompanied by the attendants that the Princesse des Ursins had placed near him, to keep him company, and to allow no one else to approach him. She followed in her coach, so as to arrive at the same time. This was on the 22nd of December. The next day the Princesse des Ursins set out with a small suite for a little place, seven leagues further, called Quadraqué, where the Queen was to sleep that night. Madame des Ursins counted upon enjoying all the gratitude that the Queen would feel for the unhoped-for grandeur she had obtained by her means; counted upon passing the evening with her, and upon accompanying her next day to Guadalaxara. She found, upon arriving at Quadraqué, that the Queen had already reached there. She at once entered into a lodging that had been prepared for her, opposite that of the Queen. She was in a full Court dress. After adjusting it in a hurried manner, she went to the Queen. The cold-ness and stiffness of her reception surprised her extremely. She attributed it in the first place to the embarrassment of the Queen, and tried to melt this ice. Everybody withdrew, in order to leave the two alone.

Then the conversation commenced. The Queen would not long allow Madame des Ursins to continue it; but burst out into reproaches against her for her manners, and for appearing there in a dress that showed want of respect for the company she was in. Madame des Ursins, whose dress was proper, and who, on account of her respectful manners and her discourse, calculated to win the Queen, believed herself to be far from meriting this treatment, was strangely surprised, and wished to excuse herself; but the Queen immediately began to utter offensive words, to cry out, to call aloud, to demand the officers of the guard, and sharply to command Madame des Ursins to leave her presence. The latter wished to speak and defend herself against the reproaches she heard; but the Queen, increasing her fury and her menaces, cried out to her people to drive this mad woman from her presence and from the house; and absolutely had her turned out by the shoulders. Immediately afterwards, she called Amenzago, lieutenant of the bodyguard, and at the same time the écuyer who had the control of her equipages. She ordered the first to arrest Madame des Ursins, and not quit her until he had placed her in a coach, with two sure officers of the guard and fifteen soldiers as sentinels over her; the second she commanded to provide instantly a coach and six, with two or three footmen, and send off in it the Princesse des Ursins towards Burgos and Bayonne, without once stopping on the road.

Soon, too, the Princesse des Ursins found that the assistance she expected from the King did not arrive. No rest, no provisions, nothing to put on, until St. Jean de Luz was reached. It was not until she arrived at Saint Jean de Luz, on the 14th of January, 1715, she found at last her corporeal ills at an end. She obtained a bed, change of dress, food, and her liberty.

1715

In due time the Princesse des Ursins arrived in Paris but found times had changed. *Monseigneur* was dead, the Meudon cabal annihilated; Madame de Maintenon had turned her back upon her.

Her journey to Versailles did not pass off very pleasantly. She dined with the Duchesse de Lude, and then visited Madame de Maintenon; waited with her for the King, but when he came did not stop long, withdrawing to Madame Adam's, where she passed the night. The next day she dined with the Duchesse de Ventadour, and returned to Paris. She was allowed to give up the pension she received from the King, and in exchange to have her Hôtel de Ville stock increased, so that it yielded forty thousand livres a year. Her income, besides being doubled, was thus much more sure than would have been a pension from the King which she doubted not M. d'Orléans, as soon as he became master, would take from her. She thought of retiring into Holland, but the States-General would have nothing to do with her, either at the Hague, or at Amsterdam. She had reckoned upon the Hague. She next thought of Utrecht, but was soon out of conceit with it, and turned her regards towards Italy.

The health of the King, meanwhile, visibly declining, Madame des Ursins feared lest she should fall entirely into the clutches of M. d'Orléans. She fully resolved, therefore, to make off, without knowing, however, where to fix herself. Genoa determined on, she went there. She was well received, hoped to fix her tabernacle there, and indeed stayed some years. But at last *ennui* seized her. She turned her thoughts, therefore, towards Rome. Then, on sounding, found her course clear, quitted Genoa and returned to her nest.

She was not long there before she attached herself to the King and Queen of England (the Pretender and his wife), and soon governed them openly. What a poor resource! But it was courtly and had a flavour of occupation for a woman who could not exist without movement.

This is the famous episode of the elevation of the bastards and Saint-Simon's fury at it was fully justified; though his account of the machinations which induced the King to act as he did must be received with caution.

About midday on Sunday, the 29th of July, I found a lackey of Maisons with a note from him, in which he conjured me to quit all business and come immediately to his house at Paris, where he would wait for me alone, and where I should find that something was in question, that could not suffer the slightest delay, that could not even be named in writing, and which was of the most extreme importance.

I found Maisons alone with the Duc de Noailles. At the first glance I saw two dismayed men, who said to me in an exhausted manner, but after a heated though short preface, that the King had declared his two bastards and their male posterity to all eternity, real princes of the blood, with full liberty to assume all their dignities, honours, and rank, and capacity to succeed to the throne in default of the others.

At this news, which I did not expect, and the secret of which had hitherto been preserved, without a particle of it transpiring, my arms fell. I

lòwered my head and remained profoundly silent, absorbed in my reflections. They were soon disturbed by cries which aroused me. These two men
commenced pacing the chamber; stamped with their feet; pushed and
struck at the furniture; raged as though each wished to be louder than the
other, and made the house echo with their noise. I avow that so much
hubbub seemed suspicious to me.

I asked them if they had gone mad, and if instead of this tempest it
would not be better to reason, and see whether something could not be
done. They declared it was precisely because nothing could be done against
a thing not only resolved on, but executed, declared, and sent to the
Parliament, that they were so furious. I argued with them and said, that
after all I preferred to see the bastards princes of the blood, capable of
succeeding to the throne, than to see them in the intermediary rank they
occupied. And it is true that as soon as I had cooled myself, I felt thus.

Our talk led to nothing, and I regained Marly in all haste, in order that
my absence might not be remarked. I went straight to the salon, and found
it very dejected. People looked, but scarcely dared to approach each other;
at the most, a sign or a whisper in the ear, as the courtiers brushed by one
another, was ventured on. I saw the King sit down to table; he seemed to
me more haughty than usual, and continually looked all around. As soon
as the King was seated (he had looked very hard at me in passing) I went
straight to M. du Maine's, who received me with joyful surprise. I said
that I came to offer him a sincere compliment, that we (the Dukes) claimed
no precedence over the princes of the blood; but what we claimed was,
that there should be nobody between the princes of the blood and us; that
as this intermediary rank no longer existed, we had nothing more to say,
but to rejoice that we had no longer to support what was insupportable.
The joy of M. du Maine burst forth at my compliments, and he startled me
with a politeness inspired by the transport of triumph.

I will content myself with but few reflections upon this most monstrous,
astounding, and frightful determination of the King. I will simply say, that
it is impossible not to see in it an attack upon the Crown; contempt for the
entire nation, whose rights are trodden under foot by it; insult to all the
princes of the blood; in fact the crime of high treason in its most rash
and most criminal extent. Yes! to overthrow the most holy laws, that have
existed ever since the establishment of monarchy; to extinguish a right the
most sacred—the most important—the most inherent in the nation: to
make succession to the throne, purely, supremely, and despotically arbitrary;
in a word, to make of a bastard a crown prince,—is a crime more black,

more vast, more terrible, than that of high treason against the chief of the state.

But let me now explain by what means the King was induced to arrive at, and publish this terrible document.

He was growing old, all his children had disappeared before him, and left him abandoned to the most fatal reflections. At every moment he himself expected the same kind of death. M. du Maine, and Madame de Maintenon had much interest to maintain him in this fear, and by their art filled him with horror against M. d'Orléans, whom they named as the author of these crimes, so that the King with this prince before his eyes every day, was in a perpetual state of alarm.

With his children the King had lost, a princess, who in addition to being the soul and ornament of his court, was, moreover, all his amusement, all his joy, all his affection, in the hours when he was not in public. Never, since he entered the world, had he become really familiar with any one but her. This unfortunate state made him seek relief everywhere in abandoning himself more and more to Madame de Maintenon and M. du Maine.

They soon managed to obtain possession of him, as it were, entirely; leaving no art unexhausted in order to flatter, to amuse, to please, and to interest him.

Established thus in the mind and heart of the King, the opportunity seemed ripe for profiting by precious time that could not last long. Everybody smiled upon the project of M. du Maine and Madame de Maintenon. They had rendered M. d'Orléans odious in the eyes of the King and of the whole country, by the most execrable calumnies. M. du Maine wished not only to be made prince of the blood, but to be made guardian of the heir to the throne, so as to dwarf the power of the Regent as much as possible.

But the schemers had tough work before they obtained this success. They found that the King would not consent to their wishes without much opposition. They hit upon a devilish plan to overpower his resistance. Hitherto, they had only been occupied in pleasing him, in amusing him, in anticipating his wishes, in praising him—let me say the word—in adoring him. They had redoubled their attention, since, by the Dauphine's death, they had become his sole resource. Not being able now to lead him as they wished, but determined to do so at all cost, they adopted another system, certain as they were that they could do so with impunity. Both became serious, oftentimes dejected, silent, furnishing nothing to the conversation, letting pass what the King forced himself to say, sometimes not even replying, if it was not a direct interrogation. In this manner all the leisure hours of the King were rendered dull and empty.

Time ran on, and the dejection of M. du Maine and Madame de Maintenon increased. I cannot go farther, or pierce deeper into the density of these dark mysteries. What is certain is, that cheerfulness came back all at once, with the same surprise to the witnesses of it, as the long-continued dejection had caused them, simply because they understood no more of the end than of the commencement.

On Sunday, the 27th of August, the Chief-President and the Attorney-General were sent for by the King. He was at Versailles. As soon as they were alone with him, he took from a drawer, which he unlocked, a large and thick packet, sealed with seven seals. In handing it to them, the King said: 'Gentlemen, this is my will. No one but myself knows its contents. I commit it to you to keep in the Parliament. The example of the Kings my predecessors, and that of the will of the King, my father, do not allow me to be ignorant of what may become of this; but they would have it; they have tormented me; they have left me no repose, whatever I might say. Very well! I have bought my repose. Here is the will; take it away: come what may of it, at least, I shall have rest, and shall hear no more about it.'

Notwithstanding all this secrecy, the terms of the will were pretty generally guessed, and as I have said, the consternation was general. This consternation was very natural, and is precisely why the Duc du Maine found himself deceived and troubled by it. He believed he had prepared everything, smoothed everything, in rendering M. d'Orléans so suspected and so odious; he had succeeded, but not so much as he imagined. His desires and his emissaries had exaggerated everything; and he found him-self overwhelmed with astonishment, when instead of the public acclama-tions with which he had flattered himself, the will would be accompanied, it was precisely the opposite.

It was seen very clearly that the will assuredly could not have been made in favour of M. d'Orléans, and although public feeling against him had in no way changed, no one was so blind as not to see that he must be Regent by the incontestable right of his birth. M. d'Orléans was stunned by the blow; he felt that it fell directly upon him, but during the lifetime of the King he saw no remedy for it.

The commencement of the new year, 1715, was marked by the death of Fénelon, at Cambrai, where he had lived in disgrace so many years. His life at Cambrai was remarkable for the assiduity with which he attended to the spiritual and temporal wants of his flock. He was indefatigable in the discharge of his functions, and in endeavouring to gain all hearts. Cambrai is a place much frequented; through which many people pass. During the war the number of wounded soldiers he had received into his house or attended to in the hospitals passes all belief. His manners, to high and low, were most affable, yet everywhere he was the prelate, the gentleman, the author of 'Telemachus'. He ruled his diocese with a gentle hand. Take him for all in all, he had a bright genius and was a great man.

The reign of Louis XIV is approaching its conclusion, so this is the place to give a portrait of his successor the Regent.

M. le Duc d'Orléans was, at the most, of mediocre stature, full-bodied without being fat; his manner and his deportment were easy and very noble; his face was broad and very agreeable, high in colour; his hair black, and wig the same. Although he danced very badly, and had but ill succeeded at the riding-school, he had in his face, in his gestures, in all his movements, infinite grace, and so natural that it adorned even his most ordinary commonplace actions. With much ease when nothing constrained him. He was gentle, affable, open, of facile and charming access; the tone of his voice was agreeable, and he had a surprisingly easy flow of words upon all subjects which nothing ever disturbed, and which never failed to surprise; his eloquence was natural and extended even to his most familiar discourse, while it equally entered into his observations upon the most abstract sciences, on which he talked most perspicuously; the affairs of government, politics, finance, justice, war, the court, ordinary conversation, the arts, and mechanics. He could speak as well too upon history and memoirs, and was well acquainted with pedigrees. He excelled in unpremeditated discourse, which, whether in the shape of repartee or jest, was always appropriate and vivacious. Besides having infinite ability and of various kinds, the singular perspicuity of his mind was joined to so much exactness, that he would never have made a mistake in anything if he had followed the first suggestions of his judgment. With all this he had no presumption, no trace of superiority natural or acquired; he reasoned with you as with his equal, and struck the most able with surprise. Although he never forgot his own position, nor allowed others to forget it, he carried no constraint with him but put everybody at his ease, and placed himself upon the level of all others.

M. d'Orléans loved liberty, and as much for others as for himself. He extolled England to me one day on this account, as a country where there are no banishments, no 'lettres de cachet,' and where the king may close the door of his palace to anybody, but can keep no one in prison. The Grand Prieur, young and amiable in those days, driven out of France for some folly, had gone to England to pass his exile and had been well received by the King. By way of thanks, he seduced one of those mistresses, by whom the King was then so smitten, that he sued for mercy, offered money to the Grand Prieur, and undertook to obtain his reconciliation in France. The Grand Prieur held firm. Charles prohibited him the palace. He laughed at this, and went every day to the theatre with his conquest, and placed himself opposite the King. At last, Charles not knowing what to do to deliver himself from his tormentor, begged our King to recall him, and this was done. But the Grand Prieur said he was very comfortable in England and continued his game. Charles outraged, confided to the King (Louis XIV), the state he was thrown into by the Grand Prieur, and obtained a command so absolute and so prompt, that his tormentor was afterwards obliged to go back into France.

M. d'Orléans admired this; and I know not if he would not have wished to be the Grand Prieur. He always related this story with delight. Of ambition for reigning or governing, he had none. If he made a false move in Spain it was because he had been misdirected. What he would have liked best would have been to command armies while war lasted, and divert himself the rest of the time without constraint to himself or to others. He was, in fact, very fit for this.

M. d'Orléans was not fortunate in his teachers. Saint Laurent, to whom he was first confided, was, it is true, the man in all Europe best fitted to act as the instructor of kings, but he died before his pupil was beyond the birch, and the young Prince, as I have related, fell entirely into the hands of the Abbé Dubois. The Abbé Dubois was a little, pitiful, wizened, herring-gutted man, in a flaxen-wig, with a weazel's face, brightened by some intellect. All the vices unceasingly fought within him for supremacy, so that a continual uproar filled his mind. Avarice, debauchery, ambition, were his gods; perfidy, flattery, foot-licking his means of action; complete impiety was his repose; and he held the opinion as a great principle, that probity and honesty are chimeras, with which people deck themselves, but which have no existence. In consequence, all means were good to him.

Dubois led M. le Duc d'Orléans into debauchery, made him despise all duty and all decency, and persuaded him that he had too much mind to be the dupe of religion, which he said was a politic invention to frighten ordinary intellects, and keep the people in subjection. He filled him too with his favourite principle, that probity in man and virtue in woman, are mere chimeras, without existence in anybody except a few poor slaves of early training.

Unfortunately all conspired in M. d'Orléans to open his heart and his mind to this execrable poison: a fresh and early youth, much strength and health, joy at escaping from the yoke as well as vexation at his marriage, the wearisomeness produced by idleness, the impulse of his passions, the example of other young men, whose vanity and whose interest it was to make him live like them. Thus he grew accustomed to debauchery, above all to the uproar of it, so that he could not do without it, and could only divert himself by dint of noise, tumult, and excess. It is this which led him often into such strange and such scandalous debauches, and as he wished to surpass all his companions, to mix up with his parties of pleasure the most impious discourses, and as a precious refinement, to hold the most outrageous orgies on the most holy days, as he did several times during his Regency on Good Friday, by choice, and on other similar days. The more debauched a man was, the more he esteemed him; and I have unceasingly seen him in admiration, that reached almost to veneration for the Grand Prieur,—because for forty years he had always gone to bed drunk, and had never ceased to keep mistresses in the most public manner, and to hold the most impious and irreligious discourses. With these principles, and the conduct that resulted from them, it is not surprising that M. le Duc d'Orléans was false to such an extent, that he boasted of his falsehood, and plumed himself upon being the most skilful deceiver in the world.

M. le Duc d'Orléans, following out the traditions of the Palais Royal, had acquired the detestable taste and habit of embroiling people one with the other, so as to profit by their divisions. This was one of his principal occupations during all the time he was at the head of affairs, and one that he liked the best; but which, as soon as discovered, rendered him odious, and caused him a thousand annoyances. He was not wicked, far from it; but he could not quit the habits of impiety, debauchery, and deceit into which Dubois had led him.

It is surprising that with all his talents he was totally without honest resources for amusing himself. He was born bored; and he was so accustomed to live out of himself, that it was insufferable to him to return, incapable as he was of trying even to occupy himself. He began to languish as soon as he was without noise, excess, and tumult, the time painfully hanging upon his hands. He cast himself upon painting, when his great fancy for chemistry had passed or grown deadened, in consequence of what had been said upon it. He painted nearly all the afternoon at Versailles and at Marly. He was a good judge of pictures, liked them, and made a collection, which in number and excellence was not surpassed by those of the crown. He amused himself afterwards in making composition stones and seals over charcoal, the fumes of which often drove me away; and the strongest perfumes, which he was fond of all his life, but from which I turned him because the King was very much afraid of them, and soon sniffed them. In fact, never was man born with so many talents of all kinds, so much readiness and facility in making use of them, and yet never was man so idle, so given up to vacuity and weariness.

His constant mistrust of everything and everybody was disgusting, above all when he was at the head of affairs. The fault sprang from that unfortunate opinion which he held, that probity was a sham. He was, nevertheless, persuaded of my probity; and would often reproach me with it as a fault and prejudice of education which had cramped my mind and obscured my understanding.

His curiosity, joined to a false idea of firmness and courage, had early led him to try and raise the devil and make him speak. He left nothing untried, even the wildest reading, to persuade himself there was no God; and yet believed meanwhile in the devil, and hoped to see him and converse with him. He worked with all sorts of obscure people; and above all with Mirepoix, sub-lieutenant of the Black Musketeers, to find out Satan. They passed whole nights in the quarries of Vanvres and of Vaugirard uttering invocations. M. le Duc d'Orléans, however, admitted to me that he had never succeeded in hearing or seeing anything, and at last had given up this folly.

His passionate desire, like that of his companions in morals, was this, that it would turn out that there is no God; but he had too much enlightenment to be an atheist; who is a particular kind of fool much more rare than is thought. This enlightenment importuned him; he tried to extinguish it and could not. A mortal soul would have been to him a resource; but he could not convince himself of its existence.

Madame la Duchesse d'Orléans was another kind of person. She was tall, and in every way majestic. She had a good deal of intellect, and spoke with much ability. She said all she wished, and often conveyed her meaning to you without directly expressing it; saying, as it were, what she did not say. Her utterance was, however, slow and embarrassed, so that unaccustomed ears with difficulty followed her.

Every kind of decency and decorum centred themselves in her, and the most exquisite pride was there upon its throne. Astonishment will be felt at what I am going to say, and yet, however, nothing is more strictly true: it is, that at the bottom of her soul she believed that she, bastard of the King, had much honoured M. d'Orléans in marrying him! M. le Duc d'Orléans often laughed at her pride, called her Madame Lucifer, in speaking to her, and she admitted that the name did not displease her. She was a princess to the backbone, at all hours, and in all places. Yet, at the same time, her timidity was extreme. The King could have made her feel ill with a single severe look.

M. le Duc and Madame la Duchesse d'Orléans lived an idle, languishing, shameful, indecent, and despised life, abandoned by all the Court. This, I felt, was one of the first things that must be remedied. Accordingly, I induced Madame la Duchesse d'Orléans to make an effort to attract people to her table. She did so, persevering against the coldness and aversion she met with, and in time succeeded in drawing a tolerably numerous company to her dinners. They were of exquisite quality, and people soon got over their first hesitation, when they found everything orderly, free, and unobjectionable. At these dinners, M. d'Orléans kept within bounds, not only in his discourse, but in his behaviour.

As the King became weaker in health, and evidently drew near his end, I had continued interviews with Madame d'Orléans upon the subject of the regency, the plan of government to be adopted, and the policy he should follow. Hundreds of times before we had reasoned together upon the faults of the Government, and the misfortunes that resulted from them. What we had to do was to avoid those faults, educate the young King in good and national maxims, so that when he succeeded to power he might continue what the Regency had not had time to finish. This, at least, was my idea, and I laboured hard to make it the idea of M. le Duc d'Orléans.

What I considered the most important thing to be done, was to overthrow entirely the system of government in which Cardinal Mazarin had imprisoned the King and the realm. A foreigner, risen from the dregs of the people, who thinks of nothing but his own power and his own greatness, cares nothing for the state, except in its relation to himself. He despises its laws, its genius, its advantages: he is ignorant of its rules and its forms; he thinks only of subjugating all, of confounding all, of bringing all down to one level. Richelieu and his successor, Mazarin, succeeded so well in this policy that the nobility, by degrees, became annihilated, as we now see them. The pen and the robe people, on the other hand, were exalted; so that now things have reached such a pretty pass that the greatest lord is without power, and in a thousand different manners is dependent upon the meanest plebeian. It is in this manner that things hasten from one extreme to the other.

My design was to commence by introducing the nobility into the ministry, with the dignity and authority due to them, and by degrees to dismiss the pen and robe people from all employ not purely judicial. In this manner the administration of public affairs would be entirely in the hands of the aristocracy. I proposed to abolish the two offices of secretary of state for the war department, and for foreign affairs, and to supply their place by councils; also, that the offices of the navy should be managed by a council. I insisted upon the distinct and perfect separation of these councils, so that their authority should never be confounded, and the public should never have the slightest trouble in finding out where to address itself for any kind of business.

M. le Duc d'Orléans exceedingly relished my project, which we much discussed. This point arrived at, it became necessary to debate upon the persons who were to form these councils.

After some little debate, that between equals would have been called complimentary, he proposed to me the Presidency of the Council of Finance. But I had good reasons for shrinking from this office. I saw that disordered as the finances had become there was only one remedy by which improvement could be effected; and this was National Bankruptcy. Had I occupied the office, I should have been too strongly tempted to urge this view, and carry it out, but it was a responsibility I did not wish to take upon myself before God and man. Yet, I felt as I said, that to declare the State bankrupt would be the wisest course, and I am bold enough to think, that there is not a man, having no personal interest in the continuance of imposts, who of two evils, viz., vastly increased taxation, and national failure, would not prefer the latter.

I shrunk accordingly from the finances for the reason I have above given, and made M. le Duc d'Orléans so angry by my refusal to accept the office he had proposed to me, that for three weeks he sulked and would not speak to me, except upon unimportant matters.

At the end of that time, in the midst of a languishing conversation, he exclaimed, 'Very well, then. You stick to your text, you won't have the finances?'

I respectfully lowered my eyes and replied, in a gentle tone, that I thought that question was settled. He could not restrain some complaints, but they were not bitter, nor was he angry, and then rising and taking a few turns in the room, without saying a word, and his head bent, as was his custom when embarrassed, he suddenly spun round upon me, and exclaimed, 'But whom shall we put there?'

I suggested the Duc de Noailles, and although the suggestion at first met with much warm opposition from M. le Duc d'Orléans, it was ultimately accepted by him.

The moment after we had settled this point he said to me, 'And you! what will you be?' and he pressed me so much to explain myself that I said at last if he would put me in the council of affairs of the interior, I thought I should do better there than elsewhere.

'Chief, then,' replied he with vivacity.

'No, no! not that,' said I; 'simply a place in the council.'

We both insisted, he for, I against. 'A place in that council,' he said, 'would be ridiculous, and cannot be thought of. Since you will not be chief, there is only one post which suits you, and which suits me also. You must be in the council I shall be in—the Supreme Council.'

I accepted the post, and thanked him. From that moment this distinction remained fixed.

Louis XIV began, as I have before remarked, sensibly to decline, and even foreign countries became aware of this. Bets were laid in London that his life would not last beyond the first of September, that is to say, about three months, and although the King wished to know everything, it may be imagined that nobody was very eager to make him acquainted with the news.

On Friday, the 9th of August, 1715, the King hunted the stag after dinner in his *calèche*, that he drove himself as usual. It was for the last time. Upon his return he appeared much knocked up. There was a grand concert in the evening in Madame de Maintenon's apartment.

On Saturday, the 10th of August, he walked before dinner in his gardens at Marly; he returned to Versailles about six o'clock in the evening, and never again saw that strange work of his hands. In the evening he worked with the Chancellor in Madame de Maintenon's rooms, and appeared to everybody very ill. On Sunday, the 11th of August, he held the Council of State, walked after dinner to Trianon, never more to go out again during life.

On the morrow, the 12th of August, he took medicine as usual, and lived as usual the following days. It was known that he complained of sciatica in the leg and thigh. He had never before had sciatica, or rheumatism, or a cold; and for a long time no touch of gout. In the evening there was a little concert in Madame de Maintenon's rooms. This was the last time in his life that he walked alone.

On Tuesday, the 13th of August, he made a violent effort, and gave a farewell audience to a sham Persian ambassador whom Pontchartrain had imposed upon him. This was the last public action of his life. The audience, which was long, fatigued the King. He resisted the desire for sleep which came over him, held the finance council, dined, had himself carried to Madame de Maintenon's, where a little concert was given, and on leaving his cabinet stopped for the Duchesse de la Rochefoucauld, who presented to him the Duchesse de la Rocheguyon, her daughter-in-law, who was the last lady presented to him. She took her seat of honour that evening at the King's grand supper, which was the last he ever gave. On the morrow he sent some precious stones to the Persian ambassador just alluded to.

The gout of which the King had had long attacks, induced Fagon to swaddle him, so to say, every evening in a heap of feather pillows, which made him sweat all night to such an extent that it was necessary in the morning to rub him down and change his linen before the grand chamberlain and the first gentleman of the chamber could enter. For many years he had drunk nothing but Burgundy wine, half mixed with water. At no time had he ever drank pure wine, or made use in any way of spirits, or even tea, coffee, or chocolate. Upon rising, instead of a little bread and wine and water, he had taken for a long time two glasses of sage and veronica; often between his meals, and always on going to bed, glasses of water with a little orange-flower water in them, and always iced. Even on the days when he had medicine he drank this, and always also at his meals, between which he never ate anything except some cinnamon lozenges that he put into his pocket at his dessert, with a good many cracknels for the bitches he kept in his cabinet.

Normally he ate so prodigiously and so solidly morning and evening that no one could get accustomed to see it. So much water and so much fruit uncorrected by anything spirituous, turned his blood into gangrene; while those forced night sweats diminished its strength and impoverished it; and thus his death was caused, as was seen by the opening of his body. The organs were found in such good and healthy condition that there is reason to believe he would have lived beyond his hundredth year. His stomach above all astonished, and also his bowels by their volume and extent, double that of the ordinary, whence it came that he was such a great yet uniform eater.

On Wednesday the 14th of August, the King was carried to hear mass for the last time; held the council of state, ate a meat dinner, and had music in Madame de Maintenon's rooms. He supped in his chamber, where the court saw him as at his dinner; was with his family a short time in his cabinet, and went to bed a little after ten.

On Thursday, the Festival of the Assumption, he heard mass in his bed. The night had been disturbed and bad. He dined in his bed, the courtiers being present, rose at five and was carried to Madame de

Maintenon's, where music was played. He supped and went to bed as on the previous evening. As long as he could sit up he did the same.

On Friday, the 16th of August, the night had been no better; much thirst and drink. The King ordered no one to enter until ten. Mass and dinner in his bed as before; then he was carried to Madame de Maintenon's; he played with the ladies there, and afterwards there was a grand concert.

On Saturday, the 17th of August, the night as the preceding. He held the Finance Council, he being in bed; saw people at his dinner, rose immediately after; gave audience in his cabinet to the General of the order of Sainte-Croix de la Brétonnerie; passed to Madame de Maintenon's, where he worked with the Chancellor. At night, Fagon slept for the first time in his chamber.

Sunday, the 18th of August, passed like the preceding days. Fagon pretended there had been no fever. The King held a Council of State before and after his dinner; worked afterwards upon the fortifications with Pelletier; then passed to Madame de Maintenon's, where there was music.

Monday, the 19th, and Tuesday, the 20th of August, passed much as the previous days, excepting that on the latter the King supped in his dressing-gown, seated in an arm-chair; and that after this evening he never left his room or dressed himself again. That same day Madame de Saint-Simon, whom I had pressed to return, came back from the waters of Forges. The King, entering after supper into his cabinet, perceived her. Ordered his chair to be stopped; spoke to her very kindly upon her journey and her return; then had himself wheeled on by Bloin into the other cabinet. She was the last Court lady to whom he spoke.

On Thursday, the 22nd of August, the King was still worse. He saw four other physicians, who, like the first four, did nothing but admire the learned and admirable treatment of Fagon, who made him take towards evening some Jesuit bark and water and intended to give him at night, ass's milk.

Friday, the 23rd of August, the night was as usual, the morning also. The King worked with Père Tellier, who tried, but in vain, to make him fill up several benefices that were vacant; that is to say, Père Tellier wished to dispose of them himself, instead of leaving them to M. le Duc d'Orléans. The King declared to him that he had enough to render account of to God, without charging himself with this nomination, and forbade him to speak again upon the subject.

On Saturday evening, the 24th of August, he supped in his dressing-gown, in presence of the courtiers, for the last time. I noticed that he could only swallow liquids, and that he was troubled if looked at. He could not finish his supper, and begged the courtiers to pass on, that is to say, go away. He went to bed, where his leg, on which were several black marks, was examined. It had grown worse lately and had given him much pain. He sent for Père Tellier and made confession. Confusion spread among the doctors at this. Milk, and Jesuit bark and water had been tried and abandoned in turns; now, nobody knew what to try. The doctors admitted that they believed he had had a slow fever ever since Whitsuntide; and excused themselves for doing nothing on the ground that he did not wish for remedies.

On Sunday, the 25th of August, no more mystery was made of the King's danger. Nevertheless, he expressly commanded that nothing should be changed in the usual order of this day (the fête of St. Louis), that is to say, that the drums and the hautboys, assembled beneath his windows, should play their accustomed music as soon as he awoke, and that the twenty-four violins should play in the ante-chamber during his dinner. He worked afterwards with the Chancellor, who wrote under his dictation, a codicil to his will, Madame de Maintenon being present. She and M. du Maine, who thought incessantly of themselves, did not consider the King had done enough for them by his will; they wished to remedy this by a codicil, which equally showed how enormously they abused the King's weakness in this extremity, and to what an excess ambition may carry us. By this codicil the King submitted all the civil and military household of the young King to the Duc du Maine, and under his orders to Maréchal de Villeroy, who, by this disposition became the sole masters of the person and the dwelling place of the King, and of Paris, by the troops placed in their hands; so that the Regent had not the slightest shadow of authority and was at their mercy; certainly liable to be arrested or worse, any time it should please M. du Maine.

Soon after the Chancellor left the King, Madame de Maintenon who remained, sent for the ladies; and the musicians came at seven o'clock in the evening. But the King fell asleep during the conversation of the ladies. He awoke; his brain confused, which frightened them and made them call the doctors. They found his pulse so bad that they did not hesitate to propose to him, his senses having returned, to take the sacrament without delay. Père Tellier was sent for; the musicians who had just prepared their books and their instruments, were dismissed, the ladies also; and in a quarter of an hour from that time, the King made confession to Père Tellier, the Cardinal de Rohan, meanwhile, bringing the Holy Sacrament from the Chapel.

On Monday the 26th of August, the King called to him the Cardinals de Rohan and de Bissy, protested that he died in the faith, and in submission to the church, then added, looking at them, that he was sorry to leave the affairs of the church as they were; that they knew he had done nothing except what they wished; that it was therefore for them to answer before God for what he had done.

This same Monday, 26th of August, after the two Cardinals had left the room, the King dined in his bed in the presence of those who were privileged to enter. As the things were being cleared away, he made them approach and addressed to them these words, which were stored up in their memory:—'Gentlemen, I ask your pardon for the bad example I have given you. I have much to thank you for the manner in which you have served me, and for the attachment and fidelity you have always shown for me. I am very sorry I have not done for you all I should have wished to do; bad times have been the cause. I ask for my grandson the same application and the same fidelity you have had for me. He is a child who may experience many reverses. Let your example be one for all my other subjects. Follow the orders my nephew will give you; he is to govern the realm; I hope he will govern it well; I hope also that you will all contribute to keep up union, and that if any one falls away you will aid in bringing him back. I feel that I am moved, and that I move you also. I ask your pardon. Adieu, gentlemen, I hope you will sometimes remember me.'

Some time after the King requested the Duchesse de Ventadour to bring the little Dauphin to him. He made the child approach, and then said to him, before Madame de Maintenon and the few privileged people present, 'My child, you are going to be a great king; do not imitate me in the taste I have had for building, or in that I have had for war; try, on the contrary, to be at peace with your neighbours. Render to God what you owe Him; recognise the obligations you are under to Him; make Him honoured by your subjects. Always follow good counsels; try to comfort your people, which I unhappily have not done. Never forget the obligation you owe to Madame de Ventadour. Madame (*addressing her*), let me embrace him (*and while embracing him*), my dear child, I give you my benediction with my whole heart.'

On Tuesday, the 27th of August, the King said to Madame de Maintenon, that he had always heard, it was hard to resolve to die; but that as for him, seeing himself upon the point of death, he did not find this resolution so difficult to form. She replied that it was very hard when we had attachments to creatures, hatred in our hearts, or restitutions to make. 'Ah,' rejoined the King, 'as for restitutions, to nobody in particular do I owe any; but as for those I owe to the realm, I hope in the mercy of God.'

The night which followed was very agitated. The King was seen at all moments joining his hands, striking his breast, and was heard repeating the prayers he ordinarily employed.

About seven o'clock in the morning, he saw in the mirror two of his valets at the foot of the bed weeping, and said to them, 'Why do you weep? Is it because you thought me immortal? As for me, I have not thought myself so, and you ought, considering my age, to have been prepared to lose me.'

On Thursday, the 29th of August, he grew a little better; he even ate two little biscuits steeped in wine, with a certain appetite. The news immediately spread abroad that the King was recovering. I went that day to the apartments, of M. le Duc d'Orléans, where, during the previous eight days, there had been such a crowd that, speaking exactly, a pin would not have fallen to the ground. Not a soul was there! As soon as the Duc saw me he burst out laughing, and said, I was the first person who had been to see him all the day! And until the evening he was entirely deserted. Such is the world!

In the evening it was known that the King had only recovered for the moment. In giving orders during the day, he called the young Dauphin 'the young King'. Towards eight o'clock his brain appeared confused; he himself said he felt very ill. Towards eleven o'clock his leg was examined. The gangrene was found to be in the foot and the knee; the thigh much inflamed. He swooned during this examination.

Friday, the 30th of August, was a bad day preceded by a bad night. The King continually lost his reason. About five o'clock in the evening Madame de Maintenon left him, gave away her furniture to the domestics, and went to St. Cyr never to leave it.

On Saturday, the 31st of August, everything went from bad to worse. The gangrene had reached the knee and all the thigh. Towards eleven o'clock at night the King was found to be so ill that the prayers for the dying were said. This restored him to himself. He repeated the prayers in a voice so strong that it rose above all the other voices. At the end he recognised Cardinal de Rohan, and said to him, 'These are the last favours of the church.' This was the last man to whom he spoke. He repeated several times, *Nunc et in horâ mortis*, then said, 'Oh, my God, come to my aid: hasten to succour me.'

These were his last words. All the night he was without consciousness and in a long agony, which finished on Sunday, the 1st of September, 1715, at a quarter past eight in the morning, three days before he had accomplished his seventy-seventh year, and in the seventy-second of his reign.

He had survived all his sons and grandsons, except the King of Spain. Europe never saw so long a reign or France a King so old.

Louis XIV was made for a brilliant Court. In the midst of other men, his figure, his courage, his grace, his beauty, his grand mien, even the tone of his voice and the majestic and natural charm of all his person, distinguished him till his death. He reigned, indeed, in little things; the great he could never reach: even in the former, too, he was often governed. The superior ability of his early ministers and his early generals soon wearied him. He liked nobody to be in any way superior to him. Thus he chose his ministers, not for their knowledge, but for their ignorance; not for their capacity, but for their want of it. He liked to form them, as he said; liked to teach them even the most trifling things. It was the same with his generals. He took credit to himself for instructing them; wished it to be thought that from his cabinet he commanded and directed all his armies. Naturally fond of trifles, he unceasingly occupied himself with the most petty details of his troops, his household, his mansions. This vanity, this unmeasured and unreasonable love of admiration, was his ruin. His ministers, his generals, his mistresses, his courtiers, soon perceived his weakness. They praised him with emulation and spoiled him. Those whom he liked owed his affection for them, to their untiring flatteries. This is what gave his ministers so much authority, and the opportunities they had for adulating him, of attributing everything to him, and of pretending to learn everything from him. Suppleness, meanness, an admiring, dependent, cringing manner—above all, an air of nothingness—were the sole means of pleasing him.

Though his intellect, as I have said, was beneath mediocrity, it was capable of being formed. He loved glory, was fond of order and regularity; was by disposition prudent, moderate, discreet, master of his movements and his tongue. Will it be believed? He was also by disposition good and just! God had sufficiently gifted him to enable him to be a good King; perhaps even *a tolerably great King!* All the evil came to him from elsewhere. His early education was so neglected that nobody dared approach his apartment. He has often been heard to speak of those times with bitterness, and even to relate that, one evening he was found in the basin of the Palais Royal garden fountain, into which he had fallen! He was scarcely taught how to read or write, and remained so ignorant, that the most familiar historical and other facts were utterly unknown to him! He fell, accordingly, and sometimes even in public, into the grossest absurdities.

He was exceedingly jealous of the attention paid him. Not only did he notice the presence of the most distinguished courtiers, but those of inferior degree also. He looked to the right and to the left, not only upon rising but upon going to bed, at his meals, in passing through his apartments, or his gardens of Versailles, where alone the courtiers were allowed to follow him; he saw and noticed everybody; not one escaped him, not even those who hoped to remain unnoticed. He marked well all absentees from the court, found out the reason of their absence, and never lost an opportunity of acting towards them as the occasion might seem to justify. With some of the courtiers (the most distinguished), it was a demerit not to make the court their ordinary abode; with others 'twas a fault to come but rarely; for those who never or scarcely ever came it was certain disgrace. When their names were in any way mentioned, 'I do not know them,' the King would reply haughtily. Those who presented themselves but seldom were thus characterised: 'They are people I never see'; these decrees were irrevocable. He could not bear people who liked Paris.

Louis XIV took great pains to be well informed of all that passed everywhere; in the public places, in the private houses, in society and familiar intercourse. His spies and tell-tales were infinite. He had them of all species; many who were ignorant that their information reached him; others who knew it; others who wrote to him direct, sending their letters through channels he indicated; and all these letters were seen by him alone, and always before everything else; others who sometimes spoke to him secretly in his cabinet, entering by the back stairs. These unknown means ruined an infinite number of people of all classes, who never could discover the cause; often ruined them very unjustly; for the King, once prejudiced, never altered his opinion, or so rarely, that nothing was more rare. He had, too, another fault, very dangerous for others and often for himself, since it deprived him of good subjects. He had an excellent memory; in this way, that if he saw a man who, twenty years before, perhaps, had in some manner offended him, he did not forget the man, though he might forget the offence. This was enough, however, to exclude the person from all favour. The representations of a minister, of a general, of his confessor even, could not move the King. He would not yield.

The most cruel means by which the King was informed of what was passing—for many years before anybody knew it—was that of opening letters. The promptitude and dexterity with which they were opened passes understanding. He saw extracts from all the letters in which there were passages that the chiefs of the post-office, and then the minister who governed it, thought ought to go before him; entire letters, too, were sent

The Duchesse de
Bourgogne

*om an engraving after a
contemporary portrait*

The Duc de Bourgogne

*From an engraving after a
contemporary portrait*

The Duchesse du Maine

From an engraving after a contemporary portrait

The Duc du Maine

From an engraving by P. Drevet after a portrait by F. de Troy

to him, when their contents seemed to justify the sending. Thus the chiefs of the post, nay, the principal clerks were in a position to suppose what they pleased and against whom they pleased. A word of contempt against the King or the government, a joke, a detached phrase, was enough. It is incredible how many people, justly or unjustly, were more or less ruined, always without resource, without trial, and without knowing why. The secret was impenetrable; for nothing ever cost the King less than profound silence and dissimulation.

This last talent he pushed almost to falsehood, but never to deceit, pluming himself upon keeping his word,—therefore he scarcely ever gave it. The secrets of others he kept as religiously as his own. He was even flattered by certain confessions and certain confidences; and there was no mistress, minister, or favourite, who could have wormed them out, even though the secret regarded themselves.

Never did man give with better grace than Louis XIV, or augmented so much, in this way, the price of his benefits. Never did man sell to better profit his words, even his smiles,—nay, his looks. Never did disobliging words escape him; and if he had to blame, to reprimand, or correct, which was very rare, it was nearly always with goodness. Never was man so naturally polite, or of a politeness so measured, so graduated, so adapted to person, time, and place. Towards women his politeness was without parallel. Never did he pass the humblest petticoat without raising his hat; even to chambermaids, that he knew to be such, as often happened at Marly. For ladies he took his hat off completely, but to a greater or less extent; for titled people half off, holding it in his hand or against his ear some instants, more or less marked. For the nobility he contented himself by putting his hand to his hat. He took it off for the princes of the blood, as for the ladies. If he accosted ladies he did not cover himself until he had quitted them. All this was out of doors, for in the house he was never covered. His reverences, more or less marked, but always light, were incomparable for their grace and manner; even his mode of half raising himself at supper for each lady who arrived at table. Though at last this fatigued him, yet he never ceased it; the ladies who were to sit down, however, took care not to enter after supper had commenced.

If he was made to wait for anything while dressing, it was always with patience. He was exact to the hours that he gave for all his day, with a precision clear and brief in his orders. If in the bad weather of winter, when he could not go out, he went to Madame de Maintenon's a quarter of an hour earlier than he had arranged (which seldom happened), and the captain of the guards was not on duty, he did not fail afterwards to say that it was his own fault for anticipating the hour, not that of the captain of the guards for being absent. Thus, with this regularity which he never deviated from, he was served with the utmost exactitude.

He treated his valets well, above all those of the household. It was amongst them that he felt most at ease, and that he unbosomed himself the most familiarly, especially to the chiefs. Their friendship and their aversion have often had great results. They were unceasingly in a position to render good and bad offices. The ministers, even the most powerful, openly studied their caprices; and the princes of the blood,—nay, the bastards,—not to mention people of lower grade, did the same.

The King loved air and exercise very much, as long as he could make use of them. He had excelled in dancing, and at tennis and mall. On horseback he was admirable, even at a late age. He liked to see everything done with grace and address. To acquit yourself well or ill before him was a merit or a fault. He said that with things not necessary it was best not to meddle, unless they were done well. He was very fond of shooting, and there was not a better or more graceful shot than he. He had always in his cabinet seven or eight pointer bitches, and was fond of feeding them, to make himself known to them. He was very fond, too, of stag hunting; but in a calèche, since he broke his arm, while hunting at Fontainebleau, immediately after the death of the Queen. He rode alone in a species of 'box,' drawn by four little horses—with five or six relays, and drove himself with an address and accuracy unknown to the best coachmen. His postillions were children from ten to fifteen years of age, and he directed them.

He liked splendour, magnificence, and profusion in everything: you pleased him if you shone through the brilliancy of your houses, your clothes, your table, your equipages.

As for the King himself, nobody ever approached his magnificence. His buildings, who could number them? At the same time, who was there who did not deplore the pride, the caprice, the bad taste seen in them? St. Germains, a lovely spot, with a marvellous view, rich forest, terraces, gardens, and water he abandoned for Versailles; the dullest and most ungrateful of all places, without prospect, without wood, without water, without soil; for the ground is all shifting sand or swamp, the air accordingly bad.

But he liked to subjugate nature by art and money. He built at Versailles, on, on, without any general design, the beautiful and the ugly, the vast and the mean, all jumbled together. His own apartments and those of the Queen, are inconvenient to the last degree, dull, close, stinking. The gardens astonish by their magnificence, but cause regret by their bad taste. You are introduced to the freshness of the shade only by a vast torrid zone, at the end of which there is nothing for you but to mount or descend; and with the hill, which is very short, terminate the gardens. The violence everywhere done to nature repels and wearies us despite ourselves. The abundance of water, forced up and gathered together from all parts, is rendered green, thick, muddy; it disseminates humidity, unhealthy and evident; and an odour still more so.

At last, the King, tired of the cost and bustle, persuaded himself that he should like something little and solitary. He found behind Lucienne a deep narrow valley, completely shut in, inaccessible from its swamps, and with a wretched village called Marly upon the slope of one of its hills. The King was overjoyed at his discovery. The hermitage was made. At first, it was only for sleeping in three nights, from Wednesday to Saturday, two or three times a-year, with a dozen at the outside of courtiers, to fill the most indispensable posts.

By degrees, the hermitage was augmented, the hills were pared and cut down, to give at least the semblance of a prospect; in fine, what with buildings, gardens, waters, aqueducts, the curious and well known machine, statues, precious furniture, the park, the ornamental enclosed forest,— Marly has become what it is to-day, though it has been stripped since the death of the King. Great trees were unceasingly brought from Compiègne or farther, three-fourths of which died and were immediately after replaced; vast spaces covered with thick wood, or obscure alleys, were suddenly changed into immense pieces of water, on which people were rowed in gondolas; then they were changed again into forests (I speak of what I have seen in six weeks); basins were changed a hundred times; cascades the same; carp ponds adorned with the most exquisite painting, scarcely finished, were changed and differently arranged by the same hands; and this an infinite number of times; then there was that prodigious machine just alluded to, with its immense aqueducts, the conduit, its monstrous resources solely devoted to Marly, and no longer to Versailles.

Let me now speak of the amours of the King which were even more fatal to the state than his building mania.

Louis XIV in his youth more made for love than any of his subjects— being tired of gathering passing sweets, fixed himself at last upon La Vallière. The progress and the result of his love are well known.

Madame de Montespan was she whose rare beauty touched him next, even during the reign of Madame de La Vallière. She soon perceived it, and vainly pressed her husband to carry her away into Guienne. With foolish confidence he refused to listen to her. She spoke to him more in earnest. In vain. At last the King was listened to, and carried her off from her husband, with that frightful hubbub which resounded with horror among all nations, and which gave to the world the new spectacle of two mistresses at once! The King took them to the frontiers, to the camps, to the armies, both of them in the Queen's coach. The people ran from all parts to look at the three queens; and asked each other in their simplicity if they had seen them. In the end, Madame de Montespan triumphed, and disposed of the master and his Court with an éclat unconcealed.

Madame de Montespan was cross, capricious, ill-tempered, and of a haughtiness in everything which reached to the clouds, and from the effects of which nobody, not even the King was exempt. The courtiers avoided passing under her windows, above all when the King was with her. They used to say it was equivalent to being put to the sword, and this phrase became proverbial at the Court. It is true that she spared nobody, often without other design than to divert the King; and as she had infinite wit and sharp pleasantry, nothing was more dangerous than the ridicule she, better than anybody, could cast on all. With that she loved her family and her relatives, and did not fail to serve people for whom she conceived friendship. The Queen endured with difficulty her haughtiness—very different from the respect and measure with which she had been treated by the Duchesse de La Vallière, whom she always loved; whereas of Madame de Montespan she would say, 'That strumpet will cause my death.' The retirement, the austere penitence, and the pious end of Madame de Montespan have been already described.

During her reign she did not fail to have causes for jealousy. There was Mademoiselle de Fontanges, who pleased the King sufficiently to become his mistress. But she had no intellect, and without that it was impossible to maintain supremacy over the King. Her early death quickly put an end to this amour. Then there was Madame de Soubise, who, by the infamous connivance of her husband, prostituted herself to the King, and thus secured all sorts of advantages for that husband, for herself, and for her children. The love of the King for her continued until her death, although for many years before that he had ceased to see her in private. Then there was the beautiful Ludre, Canoness of Lorraine, and maid of honour to *Madame*, who was openly loved for a moment. But this amour was a flash of lightning, and Madame de Montespan remained triumphant.

Let us now pass to another kind of amour which astonished all the world as much as the other had scandalised it, and which the King carried with him to the tomb. Who does not already recognise the celebrated

Françoise d'Aubigné, Marquise de Maintenon, whose permanent reign did not last less than thirty-two years?

Born in the American islands, where her father, perhaps a gentleman, had gone to seek his bread, and where he was stifled by obscurity, she returned alone and at haphazard into France. She landed at La Rochelle, and was received in pity by Madame de Neuillant, mother of the Maréchale Duchesse de Navailles, and was reduced by that avaricious old woman to keep the keys of her granary, and to see the hay measured out to her horses, as I have already related elsewhere. She came afterwards to Paris, young, clever, witty, and beautiful, without friends and without money; and by lucky chance made acquaintance with the famous Scarron. Marriage with this joyous and learned cripple appeared to her the greatest and most unlooked-for good fortune.

The marriage being brought about, the new spouse pleased the company which went to Scarron's house. It was the fashion to go there: people of wit, people of the Court and of the city, the best and most distinguished went. Scarron was not in a state to leave his house, but the charm of his genius, of his knowledge, of his imagination, of that incomparable and ever fresh gaiety which he showed in the midst of his afflictions, that rare fecundity, and that humour, tempered by so much good taste that is still admired in his writings, drew everybody there.

Madame Scarron made at home all sorts of acquaintances, which, however, at the death of her husband, did not keep her from being reduced to the charity of the parish of St. Eustace. She took a chamber for herself and for a servant, where she lived in a very pinched manner.

Step by step, she was introduced to the Hôtel d'Albret, and thence to the Hôtel de Richelieu, and elsewhere; so she passed from one house to the other. In these houses Madame Scarron was far from being on the footing of the rest of the company. She was more like a servant than a guest.

To the intimacy between the Maréchal d'Albret and Madame de Montespan, Madame de Maintenon owed the good fortune she met with fourteen or fifteen years later. Madame de Montespan continually visited the Hôtel d'Albret, and was much impressed with Madame Scarron. She conceived a friendship for the obliging widow, and when she had her first children by the King—M. du Maine and Madame la Duchesse, whom the King wished to conceal—she proposed that they should be confided to Madame Scarron. A house in the Marais was accordingly given to her, to lodge in with them, and the means to bring them up, but in the utmost secrecy. Afterwards, these children were taken to Madame de Montespan, then shown to the King, and then by degrees drawn from secrecy and avowed.

Their governess, being established with them at the Court, more and more pleased Madame de Montespan, who several times made the King give presents to her. He, on the other hand, could not endure her; what he gave to her, always little, was by excess of complaisance and with a regret that he did not hide.

The estate of Maintenon being for sale, Madame de Montespan did not let the King rest until she had drawn from him enough to buy it for Madame Scarron, who thenceforth assumed its name. She obtained enough also for the repair of the château, and then attacked the King for means to arrange the garden, which the former owners had allowed to go to ruin.

It was at the toilette of Madame de Montespan that these demands were made. The captain of the guards alone followed the King there. M. le Maréchal de Lorges, the truest man that ever lived, held that post then, and he has often related to me the scene he witnessed. The King at first turned a deaf ear to the request of Madame de Montespan, and then refused. Annoyed that she still insisted, he said he had already done more than enough for this creature; that he could not understand the fancy of Madame de Montespan for her, and her obstinacy in keeping her after he had begged her so many times to dismiss her; that he admitted Madame Scarron was insupportable to him, and provided he never saw her more and never heard speak of her, he would open his purse again, though, to say truth, he had already given too much to a creature of this kind! Never did M. le Maréchal de Lorges forget these words; and he has always repeated them to me and others precisely as they are given here, so struck was he with them, and much more after all that he saw since, so astonishing and so contradictory. Madame de Montespan stopped short, very much troubled by having too far pressed the King.

M. du Maine was extremely lame; this was caused, it was said, by a fall he had had from his nurse's arms. Nothing done for him succeeded; the resolution was then taken to send him to various practitioners in Flanders, and elsewhere in the realm, then to the waters, among others to Barèges. The letters that the governess wrote to Madame de Montespan, giving an account of these journeys, were shown to the King. He thought them well written, relished them, and the last ones made his aversion for the writer diminish.

The ill humour of Madame de Montespan finished the work. She had a good deal of that quality, and had become accustomed to give it full swing. The King was the object of it more frequently than anybody; he was still amorous; but her ill humour pained him. Madame de Maintenon reproached Madame de Montespan for this, and thus advanced herself in the King's favour. The King, by degrees, grew accustomed to speak some-times to Madame de Maintenon; to unbosom to her what he wished her to say to Madame de Montespan; at last to relate to her the chagrins this latter caused him, and to consult her thereupon.

Admitted thus into the intimate confidence of the lover and the mistress, and this by the King's own doing, the adroit waiting woman knew how to cultivate it, and profited so well by her industry that by degrees she supplanted Madame de Montespan, who perceived, too late, that her friend had become necessary to the King. Arrived at this point, Madame de Main-tenon made, in her turn, complaints to the King of all she had to suffer, from a mistress who spared even him so little; and by dint of these mutual complaints about Madame de Montespan, Madame de Maintenon at last took her place, and knew well how to keep it.

It was while the King was in the midst of his partiality for Madame de Maintenon that the Queen died. It was at the same time, too, that the ill humour of Madame de Montespan became more and more insupportable. This imperious beauty, accustomed to domineer and to be adored, could not struggle against the despair which the prospect of her fall caused her. What carried her beyond all bounds, was that she could no longer disguise from herself, that she had an abject rival whom she had supported, who owed everything to her; whom she had so much liked that she had several times refused to dismiss her when pressed to do so by the King; a rival, too, so beneath her in beauty, and older by several years; to feel that it was this lady's-maid, not to say this servant, that the King most frequently went to see; that he sought only her; that he could not dissimulate his uneasiness if he did not find her; that he quitted all for her; in fine, that at all moments she (Madame de Montespan) needed the intervention of Madame de Maintenon, in order to attract the King to reconcile her with him, or to obtain the favours she asked for. It was then, in times so propitious to the enchantress, that the King became free by the death of the Queen.

He passed the first few days at Saint Cloud, at *Monsieur's*, whence he went to Fontainebleau, where he spent all the autumn. It was there that his liking, stimulated by absence, made him find that absence insupport-able. Upon his return it is pretended—for we must distinguish the certain from that which is not so—it is pretended, I say, that the King spoke more freely to Madame de Maintenon, and that she, venturing to put forth her strength, retrenched herself behind devotion and prudery; that the King did not cease, that she preached to him and made him afraid of the devil, and that she balanced his love against his conscience with so much art, that she succeeded in becoming what our eyes have seen her, but what posterity will never believe she was.

But what is very certain and very true, is, that some time after the return of the King from Fontainebleau, and in the midst of the winter that followed the death of the Queen (posterity will with difficulty believe it, although perfectly true and proved), Père de la Chaise, confessor of the King, said mass at the dead of night in one of the King's cabinets at Versailles. Bontems, governor of Versailles, chief valet on duty, and the most confidential of the four, was present at this mass, at which the monarch and Maintenon were married in presence of Harlay, archbishop of Paris, as diocesan, of Louvois (both of whom drew from the King a promise that he would never declare this marriage), and of Montchevreuil.

The satiety of the honeymoon, usually so fatal, and especially the honeymoon of such marriages, only consolidated the favour of Madame de Maintenon. Soon after, she astonished everybody by the apartments given to her at Versailles, at the top of the grand staircase facing those of the King and on the same floor. From that moment the King always passed some hours with her every day of his life; wherever she might be she was always lodged near him, and on the same floor if possible.

Madame de Maintenon was a woman of much wit, which the good company, in which she had at first been merely suffered, but in which she soon shone, had much polished; and ornamented with knowledge of the world, and which gallantry had rendered of the most agreeable kind. Incomparable grace, an easy manner, and yet measured and respectful, which, in consequence of her long obscurity, had become natural to her, marvellously aided her talents; with language gentle, exact, well expressed, and naturally eloquent and brief. Her best time, for she was three or four years older than the King, had been the dainty phrase period,—the superfine gallantry days,—in a word, the time of the 'Ruelles,'[1] as it was called; and it had so influenced her that she always retained evidences of it.

Her inconstancy was of the most dangerous kind. With the exception of some of her old friends, to whom she had good reasons for remaining faithful, she favoured people one moment only to cast them off the next. You were admitted to an audience with her for instance, you pleased her in some manner, and forthwith she unbosomed herself to you as though you had known her from childhood. At the second audience you found

---

[1] *Ruelle* is, properly speaking, the space left between the bed and the wall, where intimate visitors sometimes sat; but it came by degrees to signify any little *sanctum* where ladies received their gossips.

her dry, laconic, cold. You racked your brains to discover the cause of this change. Mere loss of time!—Flightiness was the sole reason of it.

Devoutness was her strong point; by that she held her place.

The profound ignorance in which the King had been kept all his life, rendered him from the first an easy prey to the Jesuits, for he was devout with the grossest ignorance.

The magnificent establishment of Saint Cyr, followed closely upon the revocation of the edict of Nantes. Madame de Montespan had founded at Paris an establishment for the instruction of young girls in all sorts of fine and ornamental work. Emulation gave Madame de Maintenon higher and vaster views which, whilst gratifying the poor nobility, would cause her to be regarded as protectress in whom all the nobility would feel interested.

It must not be imagined that in order to maintain her position Madame de Maintenon had need of no address. Her reign, on the contrary, was one of continual intrigue.

Ordinarily as soon as she rose, she went to St. Cyr, dined in her apartment there alone, or with some favourite, directed the affairs of the house, and returned to Versailles just as the King was ready to enter her rooms.

Towards nine o'clock in the evening two waiting women came to undress her. Immediately afterwards, her maître d'hôtel, or a valet de chambre brought her her supper—soup, or something light. As soon as she had finished her meal, her women put her to bed, and all this in the presence of the King and his minister, who did not cease working or speak lower. This done, ten o'clock had arrived; the curtains of Madame de Maintenon were drawn, and the King went to supper, after saying good night to her.

When with the King in her own room, they each occupied an armchair, with a table between them, at either side of the fireplace, hers towards the bed, the King's with the back to the wall, where was the door of the ante-chamber; two stools were before the table, one for the minister who came to work, the other for his papers.

During the King's working hours Madame de Maintenon read or worked at tapestry. She heard all that passed between the King and his minister, for they spoke out loud. Rarely did she say anything, or, if so, it was of no moment. The King often asked her opinion; then she replied with great discretion.

For the King was constantly on his guard, not only against Madame de Maintenon, but against his ministers also. Many a time it happened that when sufficient care had not been taken, and he perceived that a minister or a general wished to favour a relative or protégé of Madame de

Maintenon, he firmly opposed the appointment on that account alone, and the remarks he uttered thereupon made Madame de Maintenon very timid and very measured when she wished openly to ask a favour.

When the King travelled his coach was always full of women; his mistresses, afterwards his bastards, his daughters-in-law, sometimes *Madame*, and other ladies when there was room. In the coach, during his journeys, there were always all sorts of things to eat, as meat, pastry, fruit. A quarter of a league was not passed over before the King asked if somebody would not eat. He never ate anything between meals himself, not even fruit; but he amused himself by seeing others do so, aye, and to bursting. You were obliged to be hungry, merry, and to eat with appetite, otherwise he was displeased and even showed it. And yet after this, if you supped with him at table the same day, you were compelled to eat with as good a countenance as though you had tasted nothing since the previous night. He was as inconsiderate in other and more delicate matters; and ladies, in his long drives and stations, had often occasion to curse him. The Duchesse de Chevreuse once rode all the way from Versailles to Fontainebleau in such extremity, that several times she was well-nigh losing consciousness.

The King, who was fond of air, liked all the windows to be lowered; he would have been much displeased had any lady drawn a curtain for protection against sun, wind, or cold. No inconvenience or incommodity was allowed to be even perceived.

Madame de Maintenon, who feared the air and many other inconveniences, could gain no privilege over the others. All she obtained, under pretence of modesty and other reasons, was permission to journey apart; but whatever condition she might be in, she was obliged to follow the King, and be ready to receive him in her rooms by the time he was ready to enter them. She made many journeys to Marly in a state such as would have saved a servant from movement. She made one to Fontainebleau when it seemed not unlikely that she would die on the road! In whatever condition she might be, the King went to her at his ordinary hour and did what he had projected; though several times she was in bed, profusely sweating away a fever.

Nothing remains but to describe the outside life of this monarch, during my residence at the Court.

At eight o'clock the chief valet de chambre on duty, who alone had slept in the royal chamber, and who had dressed himself, awoke the King. The chief physician, the chief surgeon, and the nurse (as long as she lived), entered at the same time. The latter kissed the King; the others rubbed and often changed his shirt, because he was in the habit of sweating a great deal. At the quarter, the grand chamberlain was called (or, in his absence, the first gentleman of the chamber), and those who had, what was called the *grandes entrées*. The chamberlain (or chief gentleman) drew back the curtains which had been closed again, and presented the holy water from the vase, at the head of the bed. These gentlemen stayed but a moment, and that was the time to speak to the King, if any one had anything to ask of him; in which case the rest stood aside. When, contrary to custom, nobody had aught to say, they were there but for a few moments. He who had opened the curtains and presented the holy water, presented also a prayer-book. Then all passed into the cabinet of the council. A very short religious service being over, the King called, they re-entered. The same officer gave him his dressing-gown; immediately after, other privileged courtiers entered, and then everybody, in time to find the King putting on his shoes and stockings, for he did almost everything himself and with address and grace. Every other day we saw him shave himself; and he had a little short wig in which he always appeared, even in bed, and on medicine days. He often spoke of the chase, and sometimes said a word to somebody. No toilette table was near him; he had simply a mirror held before him.

As soon as he was dressed, he prayed to God, at the side of his bed, where all the clergy present knelt, the cardinals without cushions, all the laity remaining standing; and the captain of the guards came to the balustrade during the prayer, after which the King passed into his cabinet.

He found there, or was followed by all who had the entrée, a very numerous company, for it included everybody in any office. He gave orders to each for the day; thus within a half a quarter of an hour it was known what he meant to do; and then all this crowd left directly. The bastards, a few favourites, and the valets alone were left. It was then a good opportunity for talking with the King; for example, about plans of gardens and buildings; and conversation lasted more or less according to the person engaged in it.

All the Court meantime waited for the King in the gallery, the captain of the guard being alone in the chamber seated at the door of the cabinet. During this pause the King gave audiences when he wished to accord any, spoke with whoever he might wish to speak secretly to, and gave secret interviews to foreign ministers in presence of Torcy.

The King went to mass, where his musicians always sang an anthem. He did not go below except on grand fêtes or at ceremonies. Whilst he was going to and returning from mass, everybody spoke to him who wished, after apprising the captain of the guard, if they were not distinguished; and he came and went by the door of the cabinet into the gallery. During the mass the ministers assembled in the King's chamber where distinguished people could go and speak or chat with them. The King amused himself a little upon returning from mass and asked almost immediately for the council. Then the morning was finished.

On Sunday, and often on Monday, there was a council of state; on Tuesday a finance council; on Wednesday council of state; on Saturday finance council. Rarely were two held in one day or any on Thursday or Friday. Once or twice a month there was a council of despatches on Monday morning; but the order that the Secretaries of State took every morning between the King's rising and his mass, much abridged this kind of business. All the ministers were seated according to rank, except at the council of despatches, where all stood except the sons of France, the Chancellor, and the Duc de Beauvilliers.

Thursday morning was almost always blank. It was the day of audiences that the King wished to give—often unknown to any—back stair audiences. It was also the grand day taken advantage of by the bastards, the valets, &c., because the King had nothing to do. On Friday after the mass the King was with his confessor, and the length of their audiences was limited by nothing, and might last until dinner. At Fontainebleau on the mornings when there was no council, the King usually passed from mass to Madame de Maintenon's and so at Trianon and Marly. It was the time for their tête-à-tête without interruption. Often on the days when there was no council the dinner hour was advanced, more or less for the chase or the promenade. The ordinary hour was one o'clock; if the council still lasted, then the dinner waited and nothing was said to the King.

The dinner was always *au petit couvert*, that is, the King ate by himself in his chamber upon a square table in front of the middle window. It was more or less abundant, for he ordered in the morning whether it was to be 'a little,' or 'very little' service. But even at this last, there were always many dishes, and three courses without counting the fruit. The dinner being ready, the principal courtiers entered; then all who were known; and the first gentlemen of the chamber on duty, informed the King.

I have seen, but very rarely, *Monseigneur* and his sons standing at their dinners, the King not offering them seats. I have continually seen there the princes of the blood and the cardinals. I have often seen there also *Monsieur*, either on arriving from St. Cloud to see the King, or arriving from the council of despatches (the only one he entered), give the King his napkin and remain standing. A little while afterwards, the King, seeing that he did not go away, asked him if he would not sit down; he bowed, and the King ordered a seat to be brought for him. A stool was put behind him. Some moments after the King said, 'Nay then, sit down, my brother.' *Monsieur* bowed and seated himself until the end of the dinner, when he presented the napkin.

At other times when he came from St. Cloud, the King, on arriving at the table, asked for a plate for *Monsieur*, or asked him if he would dine. If he refused, he went away a moment after, and there was no mention of a seat; if he accepted, the King asked for a plate for him. The table was square, he placed himself at one end, his back to the cabinet. Then the Grand Chamberlain (or the first gentleman of the chamber) gave him drink and plates, taking them from him as he finished with them, exactly as he served the King; but *Monsieur* received all this attention with strongly marked politeness. When he dined thus with the King he much enlivened the conversation. The King ordinarily spoke little at table unless some familiar favourite was near. It was the same at his rising. Ladies scarcely ever were seen at these little dinners.

Upon leaving the table the King immediately entered his cabinet. That was the time for distinguished people to speak to him. He stopped at the door a moment to listen, then entered; very rarely did any one follow him, never without asking him for permission to do so; and for this few had the courage. If followed he placed himself in the embrasure of the window nearest to the door of the cabinet, which immediately closed of itself, and which you were obliged to open yourself on quitting the King. This also was the time for the bastards and the valets.

The King amused himself by feeding his dogs, and remained with them more or less time, then asked for his wardrobe, changed before the very few distinguished people it pleased the first gentleman of the chamber to admit there, and immediately went out by the backstairs into the court of marble to get into his coach. From the bottom of that staircase to the coach, any one spoke to him who wished.

The King was fond of air, and when deprived of it his health suffered; he had headaches and vapours caused by the undue use he had formerly made of perfumes, so that for many years he could not endure any, except the odour of orange flowers; therefore if you had to approach anywhere near him you did well not to carry them.

As he was but little sensitive to heat or cold, or even to rain, the weather was seldom sufficiently bad to prevent his going abroad. He went out for three objects: stag-hunting, once or more each week; shooting in his parks (and no man handled a gun with more grace or skill), once or twice each week; and walking in his gardens for exercise, and to see his workmen. Sometimes he made picnics with ladies, in the forest at Marly or at Fontainebleau, and in this last place, promenades with all the Court around the canal, which was a magnificent spectacle. Nobody followed him in his other promenades but those who held principal offices, except at Versailles or in the gardens of Trianon. Marly had a privilege unknown to the other places. On going out from the château, the King said aloud, 'Your hats, gentlemen,' and immediately courtiers, officers of the guard, everybody, in fact, covered their heads, as he would have been much displeased had they not done so; and this lasted all the promenade, that is four or five hours in summer, or in other seasons, when he dined early at Versailles to go and walk at Marly, and not sleep there.

The stag-hunting parties were on an extensive scale. The King did not like too many people at these parties. He did not care for you to go if you were not fond of the chase. He thought that ridiculous, and never bore ill-will to those who stopped away altogether.

It was the same with the play-table, which he liked to see always well frequented—with high stakes—in the saloon at Marly, for lansquenet and other games. He amused himself at Fontainebleau during bad weather by seeing good players at tennis, in which he had formerly excelled; and at Marly by seeing mall played, in which he had also been skilful. Sometimes when there was no council, he would make presents of stuff, or of silver ware, or jewels, to the ladies, by means of a lottery, for the tickets of which they paid nothing. Madame de Maintenon drew lots with the others, and almost always gave at once what she gained. The King took no ticket.

Upon returning home from walks or drives, anybody, as I have said, might speak to the King from the moment he left his coach till he reached the foot of his staircase. He changed his dress again, and rested in his cabinet an hour or more, then went to Madame de Maintenon's, and on the way any one who wished might speak to him.

At ten o'clock his supper was served. The captain of the guard announced this to him. A quarter of an hour after the King came to supper, and from the ante-chamber of Madame de Maintenon to the table again, any one spoke to him who wished. This supper was always on a grand scale, the royal household (that is, the sons and daughters of France), at table, and a large number of courtiers and ladies present, sitting or standing, and on the evening before the journey to Marly all those ladies who wished to take part in it. That was called presenting yourself for Marly. Men asked in the morning, simply saying to the King, 'Sire, Marly.' In later years the King grew tired of this, and a valet wrote up in the gallery the names of those who asked. The ladies continued to present themselves.

After supper the King stood some moments, his back to the balustrade of the foot of his bed, encircled by all his Court; then, with bows to the ladies, passed into his cabinet, where on arriving, he gave his orders. He passed a little less than an hour there, seated in an arm-chair, with his legitimate children and bastards, his grandchildren, legitimate and other-wise, and their husbands or wives. *Monsieur* in another arm-chair; the princesses upon stools, *Monseigneur* and all the other princes standing.

The King, wishing to retire, went and fed his dogs; then said good night, passed into his chamber to the *ruelle* of his bed, where he said his prayers, as in the morning, then undressed. He said good night with an inclination of the head, and whilst everybody was leaving the room stood at the corner of the mantelpiece, where he gave the order to the colonel of the guards alone. Then commenced what was called the *petit coucher*, at which only the specially privileged remained. That was short. They did not leave until he got into bed. It was a moment to speak to him.

On medicine days, which occurred about once a month, the King re-mained in bed, then heard mass. The royal household came to see him for a moment, and Madame de Maintenon seated herself in the arm-chair at the head of his bed. The King dined in bed about three o'clock, every-body being allowed to enter the room, then rose, and the privileged alone remained. He passed afterwards into his cabinet, where he held a council, and afterwards went, as usual, to Madame de Maintenon's and supped at ten o'clock, according to custom.

During all his life, the King failed only once in his attendance at mass. It was with the army, during a forced march; he missed no fast day, unless really indisposed. Some days before Lent, he publicly declared that he should be very much displeased if any one ate meat or gave it to others, under any pretext. He ordered the grand prevôt to look to this, and report all cases of disobedience. But no one dared to disobey his commands, for they would soon have found out the cost. They extended even to Paris, where the lieutenant of police kept watch and reported. For twelve or fifteen years he had himself not observed Lent, however. At church he was very respectful. During his mass everybody was obliged to kneel at the *Sanctus*, and to remain so until after the communion of the priest; and if he heard the least noise, and saw anybody talking during the mass, he was much displeased. He took the communion five times a year, in the collar of the Order, band, and cloak. On Holy Thursday, he served the poor at dinner; at the mass he said his chaplet (he knew no more), always kneeling, except at the Gospel.

He was always clad in dresses more or less brown, lightly embroidered, but never at the edges, sometimes with nothing but a gold button, sometimes black velvet. He wore always a vest of cloth, or of red, blue, or green satin, much embroidered. He wore no ring; and no jewels, except in the buckles of his shoes, garters, and hat, the latter always trimmed with Spanish point, with a white feather. He had always the *cordon bleu* outside, except on fêtes, when he wore it inside, with eight or ten millions of precious stones attached.

Rarely a fortnight passed that the King did not go to Saint Germains, even after the death of King James the Second. The Court of Saint Germains came also to Versailles, but oftener to Marly, and frequently to sup there; and no fête or ceremony took place to which they were not invited, and at which they were not received with all honours. Nothing could compare with the politeness of the King for this Court, or with the air of gallantry and of majesty with which he received it at any time.

The King was but little regretted. His valets and a few other people felt his loss, scarcely anybody else. M. le Duc d'Orléans could scarcely be expected to feel much grief for him. And those who may have been expected to did not consider it necessary to do their duty.

Paris, tired of a dependence which had enslaved everything, breathed again in the hope of liberty, and with joy at seeing at an end the authority of so many people who abused it. The provinces in despair at their ruin and their annihilation breathed again and leaped for joy; and the parliament and the robe destroyed by edicts and by revolutions, flattered themselves the first that they should figure, the other that they should find themselves free. The people ruined, overwhelmed, desperate, gave thanks to God, with a scandalous éclat, for a deliverance, their most ardent desires had not anticipated.

No foreign Court exulted: all plumed themselves upon praising and honouring his memory. As for our ministry and the intendants of the Provinces, the financiers and what may be called the *canaille*, they felt all the extent of their loss. We shall see if the realm was right or wrong in the sentiments it held, and whether it found soon after that it had gained or lost.

The death of the King surprised M. le Duc d'Orléans in the midst of his idleness as though it had not been foreseen. He had made no progress in numberless arrangements, which I had suggested he should carry out.

I learnt the death of the King upon awaking. Immediately after, I went

The Duc d'Orléans,
Regent of France

*From an engraving by
Marie Horthemels after
a portrait by J.-B.
Santerre*

Cardinal Dubois

*From an engraving by
P. Drevet, 1724, after
a portrait by H. Rigaud*

Louis XV in the courtyard of the Sainte-Chapelle as he leaves the Palace after the Lit de Justice, 1715

From a painting by P.-D. Martin

to pay my respects to the new monarch. I went thence to M. le Duc d'Orléans, and talked of the Convocation of the States-General, and reminded him of a promise he had given me, that he would allow the Dukes to keep their hats on when their votes were asked for.[1]

The next morning a number of us met, and, in accordance with a resolution previously agreed upon, it was arranged that I should make a protest to the Parliament before the opening of the King's will there, against certain other usurpations, and state that it was solely because M. le Duc d'Orléans had given us his word that our complaints should be attended to as soon as the public affairs of the government were settled, that we postponed further measures upon this subject. It was past seven before our debate ended, and then we went straight to the Parliament.

We found it already assembled, and a few Ducs who had not attended our meeting, but had promised to be guided by us, were also present; and then a quarter of an hour after we were seated the bastards arrived. M. du Maine was bursting with joy; the term is strange, but his bearing cannot otherwise be described. The smiling and satisfied air prevailed over that of audacity and of confidence, which shone, nevertheless, and over politeness which seemed to struggle with them. He saluted right and left, and pierced everybody with his looks. His salutation to the Presidents had an air of rejoicing. To the peers he was serious, nay, respectful; the slowness, the lowness of his inclination, was eloquent. I rigidly followed him everywhere with my eyes, and I remarked that his salute was returned by the peers in a very dry and cold manner.

Scarcely were we re-seated than M. le Duc arrived, and the instant after M. le Duc d'Orléans. I allowed the stir that accompanied his appearance to subside a little, and then, seeing that the Chief President was about to speak, I forestalled him, uncovered my head, and then covered it, and made my speech in the terms agreed upon. I concluded by appealing to M. le Duc d'Orléans to verify the truth of what I had said, in so far as it affected him.

The profound silence with which I was listened to showed the surprise of all present. M. le Duc d'Orléans uncovered himself, and in a low tone, and with an embarrassed manner, confirmed what I had said, then covered himself again.

---

[1] This revelation gives the measure of Saint-Simon's political calibre. The first thing that comes into his head, and about which he begins to busy himself at so important a crisis, is a dispute about the right of his Order to wear, or not to wear, hats on a particular occasion.

Immediately afterwards I looked at M. du Maine, who appeared to be well content at being let off so easily, and who, my neighbours said to me, appeared much troubled at my commencement.

A very short silence followed my protest, after which I saw the Chief President say something in a low tone to M. le Duc d'Orléans, then arrange a deputation of the Parliament to go in search of the King's will, and its codicil.

The deputation was not long in returning. It placed the will and the codicil in the hands of the Chief President who presented them, without parting with them, to M. le Duc d'Orléans, then passed them from hand to hand to Dreux, conseiller of the Parliament, and father of the grand master of the ceremonies, saying that he read well, and in a loud voice that would be well heard by everybody. It may be imagined with what silence he was listened to, and how all eyes and ears were turned towards him. Through all his joy the Duc de Maine showed that his soul was troubled, as though about to undergo an operation. M. le Duc d'Orléans showed only a tranquil attention.

I will not dwell upon these two documents, in which nothing is provided but the grandeur and the power of the bastards, Madame de Maintenon and Saint Cyr, the choice of the King's education and of the council of the regency, by which M. le Duc d'Orléans was to be shorn of all authority to the advantage of M. le Duc du Maine.

I remarked a sadness and a kind of indignation which were painted upon all cheeks, as the reading advanced, and which turned into a sort of tranquil fermentation at the reading of the codicil. The Duc du Maine felt it and grew pale, for he was solely occupied in looking at every face, and I in following his looks, and in glancing occasionally at M. le Duc d'Orléans.

The reading being finished, that prince spoke, commencing by a word of praise and of regret for the late King; afterwards raising his voice, he declared that he had only to approve everything just read respecting the education of the King, and everything respecting an establishment so fine and so useful as that of Saint Cyr; that with respect to the dispositions concerning the government of the state, he would speak separately of those in the will and those in the codicil; that he could with difficulty harmonise them with the assurances the King, during the last days of his life, had given him. Since the council of the regency was chosen, and M. du Maine's authority so established by the will, that the Regent remained almost without power.

The Duc du Maine wished to speak. As he was about to do so, M. le Duc d'Orléans put his head in front of M. le Duc and said, in a dry tone,

'Monsieur, you will speak in your turn.' In one moment the affair turned according to the desires of M. le Duc d'Orléans. The power of the council of the regency and its composition fell. The choice of the council was awarded to M. le Duc d'Orléans, with all the authority of the regency, and to the plurality of the votes of the council, the decision of affairs, the vote of the Regent to be counted as two in the event of an equal division. Thus all favours and all punishments remained in the hands of M. le Duc d'Orléans alone. The acclamation was such that the Duc du Maine did not dare to say a word. He reserved himself for the codicil, which, if adopted, would have annulled all that M. le Duc d'Orléans had just obtained.

After some few moments of silence, M. le Duc d'Orléans spoke again. He testified fresh surprise that the dispositions of the will had not been sufficient for those who had suggested them, and that, not content with having established themselves as masters of the State, they themselves should have thought those dispositions so strange that in order to re-assure them, it had been thought necessary to make them masters of the person of the King, of the Regent, of the Court, and of Paris. He added, that if his honour and all law and rule had been wounded by the dis-positions of the will, still more violated were they by those of the codicil, which left neither his life nor his liberty in safety, and placed the person of the King in the absolute dependence of those who had dared to profit by the feeble state of a dying monarch, to draw from him conditions he did not understand. He concluded by declaring that the regency was impossible under such conditions, and that he doubted not the wisdom of the assembly would annul a codicil which could not be sustained, and the regulations of which would plunge France into the greater and most troublesome mis-fortune.

The Duc du Maine became of all colours, and began to speak. He said that the education of the King, and consequently his person, being confided to him, as a natural result, entire authority over his civil and military household followed, without which he could not properly serve him or answer for his person. Then he vaunted his well-known attachment to the deceased King, who had put all confidence in him.

M. le Duc d'Orléans interrupted him at this word, and commented upon it. M. du Maine wished to calm him by praising the Maréchal de Villeroy, who was to assist him in his charge. M. le Duc d'Orléans replied that it would be strange if the chief and most complete confidence were not placed in the Regent, and stranger still if he were obliged to live under the pro-tection and authority of those who had rendered themselves the absolute masters within and without, and of Paris even, by the regiment of guards.

The dispute grew warm when, troubled about the end of an altercation which became indecent, I made a sign with my hand to M. le Duc d'Orléans to go out and finish this discussion in another room leading out of the grand-chamber and where there was nobody. What led me to this action was that I perceived M. du Maine grew stronger, that confused murmurs for a division were heard, and that M. le Duc d'Orléans did not show to the best advantage since he descended to plead his cause, so to speak, against that of the Duc du Maine.

M. le Duc d'Orléans was short-sighted. He was entirely absorbed in attacking and repelling; so that he did not see the sign I made. Some moments after I rose, advanced some steps, and said to him, though rather distant, 'Monsieur, if you passed into the fourth chamber with M. du Maine you could speak there more easily,' and advancing nearer at the same time I pressed him by a sign of the head and the eyes that he could distinguish. He replied to me with another sign, and scarcely was I reseated than I saw him advance in front of M. le Duc to the Duc du Maine, and immediately after both rose and went into the chamber I had indicated. I could not see who of the scattered group around followed them, for all present rose at their departure, and seated themselves again directly in complete silence. Some time after, M. le Comte de Toulouse left his place and went into the chamber. M. le Duc followed him in a little while: soon again the Duc de la Force did the same.

He did not stay long. Returning to the assembly, he passed the Duc de la Rochefoucauld and me, put his head between that of the Duc de Sully and mine, because he did not wish to be heard by La Rochefoucauld, and said to me, 'In the name of God go there; things are getting on badly. M. le Duc d'Orléans gives way; stop the dispute; make M. le Duc d'Orléans come back; and, as soon as he is in his place, let him say that it is too late to finish, that the company had better go to dinner, and return to finish afterwards, and during this interval,' added La Force, 'send the King's people to the Palais Royal, and let doubtful peers be spoken to, and the chiefs among other magistrates.'

The advice appeared to be good and important. I left the assembly and went to the chamber. I found a large circle of spectators. M. le Duc d'Orléans and the Duc du Maine stood before the fireplace, looking both very excited. I looked at this spectacle some moments; then approached the mantelpiece like a man who wishes to speak. 'What is this, Monsieur?' said M. le Duc d'Orléans to me, with an impatient manner. 'A pressing word, Monsieur, that I have to say to you,' said I. He continued speaking to the Duc du Maine, I being close by. I redoubled my instances; he lent me his ear. 'No, no,' said I, 'not like that, come here,' and I took him into a corner by the chimney.

I said to M. le Duc d'Orléans, in his ear, that he could not hope to gain anything from M. du Maine, who would not sacrifice the codicil to his reasonings; that the only thing to be done was to return to the assembly, and, when there, dissolve it. 'You are right,' said he, 'I will do it.' He quitted me without another word, went to M. du Maine, told him in two words that it was too late, and that the matter must be finished after dinner.

I had remained where he left me. I saw the Duc du Maine bow to him immediately, and the two separated, and retired at the same moment into the assembly.

The noise which always accompanies these entrances being appeased, M. le Duc d'Orléans said it was too late to abuse the patience of the company any longer; that dinner must be eaten, and the work finished afterwards. He immediately added, he believed it fitting that *M. le Duc* should enter the council of the regency as its chief; and that since the company had rendered the justice due to his birth and his position as Regent, he would explain what he thought upon the form to be given to the government, and that meanwhile he profited by the power he had to avail himself of the knowledge and the wisdom of the company, and restored to them from that time their former liberty of remonstrance. These words were followed by striking and general applause, and the assembly was immediately adjourned.

We returned to the Parliament a little before four o'clock. M. le Duc d'Orléans arrived, and said that matters must be recommenced from the point where they had been broken off in the morning; that it was his duty to say to the Court that in nothing had he agreed with M. du Maine and to bring again before all eyes the monstrous clauses of a codicil, drawn from a dying prince; clauses much more strange than the dispositions of the testament that the Court had not deemed fit to be put in execution, and that the Court could not allow M. du Maine to be master of the person of the King, of the camp, of Paris, consequently of the State, of the person, life, and liberty of the Regent, whom he would be in a position to arrest at any moment as soon as he became master of the civil and military household of the King; that the Court saw what must inevitably result from an unheard-of novelty, which placed everything in the hands of M. du Maine; and that he left it to the enlightenment, to the prudence, to the wisdom, to the equity of the company, and its love for the State, to declare what they thought on this subject.

M. du Maine appeared then as contemptible in the broad open daylight as he had appeared redoubtable in the obscurity of the cabinets. He replied in a very low and scarcely intelligible voice, and with an air as respectful and as humble as it had been audacious in the morning.

People opined without listening to him; and tumultuously, but with one voice, the entire abrogation of the codicil was passed.

After they had spoken, the Duc du Maine tried a last resource. He represented, with more force than could have been expected from his demeanour at this second sitting, but yet with measure, that since he had been stripped of the authority confided to him by the codicil, he asked to be discharged from the responsibility of answering for the person of the King, and to be allowed simply to preserve the superintendence of his education. M. le Duc d'Orléans replied, 'With all my heart, Monsieur; nothing more is wanted.' Thereupon the Chief President formally put the question to the vote.

A decree was passed by which all power was taken from the hands of M. du Maine and placed in those of the Regent, with the right of placing whom he pleased in the council; of dismissing anybody as it should seem good to him; and of doing all he might think fit respecting the form to be given to the government; authority over public affairs, nevertheless, to remain with the council, and decision to be taken by the plurality of votes, the vote of the Regent to count double in case of division; M. le Duc to be chief of the council under him, with the right to enter it at once and opine there.

The Regent thanked the company in brief, polished, and majestic terms; declared with what care he would employ for the good of the state, the authority with which he was invested; then said it was time he should inform them what he judged ought to be established in order to aid him in the administration of affairs. He added that he did so with the more confidence, because what he proposed was exactly what M. le Duc de Bourgogne ('twas thus he named him) had resolved, as shown by papers found in his bureau. He passed a short and graceful eulogy upon the enlightenment and intentions of that prince; then declared that, besides the council of the regency, which would be the supreme centre from which all the affairs of the government would spring, he proposed to establish a council for foreign affairs, one for war, one for the navy, one for finance, one for ecclesiastical matters, and one for home affairs, and to choose some of the magistrates of the company to enter these last two councils, and aid them by their knowledge upon the police of the realm, the jurisprudence, and what related to the liberties of the Gallican church.

The applause of the magistrates burst out at this, and all the crowd replied to it. The Chief President concluded the sitting by a very short compliment to the Regent, who rose, and at the same time all the assembly, which then broke up.

On the 9th of September, the Regent worked all the morning, with all the secretaries of State separately, whom he had charged to bring him the list of all the *lettres de cachet* issued from their bureaux, and a statement of the reasons for which they were delivered, as such oftentimes were slight. The majority of the *lettres de cachet* of exile and of imprisonment had been drawn up against Jansenists, and people who had opposed the *Constitution*; numbers the reasons of which were known only to the deceased King, and to those who had induced him to grant them; others were of the time of previous ministers, and among them were many which had been long forgotten and unknown. The Regent restored everybody to liberty, exiles and prisoners, except those whom he knew to have been arrested for grave crimes, or affairs of State; and brought down infinite benedictions upon himself by this act of justice and humanity.

A few days after, the finances being in such a bad state, the Regent made Crosat treasurer of the Order, in return for which he obtained from him a loan of a million, in bars of silver, and the promise of another two million. It was found that there were sixteen hundred thousand francs owing to our ambassadors, and to our agents in foreign countries, the majority of whom literally had not enough to pay the postage of their letters, having spent all they possessed.

I have already alluded to the presence of Lord Stair at this time in our Court, as ambassador from England. By means of intrigues he had succeeded in ingratiating himself into the favour of the Regent and in convincing him that the interests of France and England were identical. One of the reasons—the main one—which he brought forward to show this, was that King George was an usurper; and that if anything happened to our King, M. le Duc d'Orléans would become, in mounting the throne of France, an usurper also, the King of Spain being the real heir to the French monarchy; that, in consequence of this, France and England ought to march together, protect each other; France assisting England against the Pretender, and England assisting France, if need be, against the King of Spain.

Stair wished, above all, to hinder the Regent from giving any assistance to the Pretender, and to prevent him passing through the realm in order to reach a seaport. Now the Regent was between two stools, for he had promised the Pretender to wink at his doings, and to favour his passage through France, if it were made secretly, and, at the same time, he had assented to the demand of Stair. Things had arrived at this pass when the troubles increased in England, and the Earl of Mar obtained some success in Scotland. Soon after news came that the Pretender had departed from Bar, and was making his way to the coast. Thereupon Stair ran in hot haste to M. le Duc d'Orléans to ask him to keep his promise, and hinder the Pretender's journey. The Regent immediately sent off Contades, major in the guards, very intelligent, and in whom he could trust, with his brother, a lieutenant in the same regiment, and two sergeants of their choice, to go to Château-Thierry, and wait for the Pretender, Stair having sure information that he would pass there. Contades set out at night on the 9th of November, well resolved and instructed to miss the person he was to seek.

It is time now to speak of the public and private occupations of the Regent, of his conduct, his pleasure parties, and the employment of his days.

Up to five o'clock in the evening he devoted himself exclusively to public business, reception of ministers, councils, &c., never dining during the day, but taking chocolate between two and three o'clock, when everybody was allowed to enter his room. After the council of the day, that is to say, at about five o'clock, there was no more talk of business. It was now the time of the Opera or the Luxembourg (if he had not been to the latter place before his chocolate), or he went to Madame la Duchesse d'Orléans' apartments, or supped or went out privately, or received company privately; or, in the fine season, he went to Saint-Cloud, or elsewhere out of town, now supping there, or at the Luxembourg, or at home. When *Madame* was at Paris, he spoke to her for a moment before his mass; and when she was at Saint-Cloud he went to see her there, and always paid her much attention and respect.

His suppers were always composed of very strange company. His mistresses, sometimes an opera girl, often Madame la Duchesse de Berry, and a dozen men whom he called his *Roués*, formed the party. The requisite cheer was prepared in places made expressly, on the same floor; all the utensils were of silver; the company often lent a hand to the cooks. It was at these parties that the character of every one was passed in review, ministers and favourites like the rest, with a liberty which was unbridled licence. The gallantries past and present of the Court and of the town; all old stories, disputes, jokes, absurdities were raked up; nobody was spared; M. le Duc d'Orléans had his say like the rest, but very rarely did these discourses make the slightest impression upon him. The company drank as much as they could, inflamed themselves, said the filthiest things without stint, uttered impieties with emulation, and when they had made a good deal of noise and were very drunk, they went to bed to recommence the same game the next day. From the moment when supper was ready, business, no matter of what importance, no matter whether private or national, was entirely banished from view. Until the next morning everybody and everything were compelled to wait.

The Regent lost then an infinite amount of time in private, in amusements, and debauchery. He lost much also in audiences too long, too extended, too easily granted, and drowned himself in those same details which during the lifetime of the late King we had both so often reproached him with. Questions he might have decided in half an hour he prolonged, sometimes from weakness, sometimes from that miserable desire to set people at loggerheads, and that poisonous maxim which occasionally escaped him or his favourite, *divide et impera*; often from his general mistrust of everybody and everything; nothings become hydras with which he himself afterwards was much embarrassed. His familiarity and his readiness of access extremely pleased people, but were much abused. Folks sometimes were even wanting in respect to him, which at last was an inconvenience all the more dangerous because he could not, when he wished, reprimand those who embarrassed him; inasmuch as they themselves did not feel embarrassed.

What is extraordinary is, neither his mistress nor Madame la Duchesse de Berry, nor his *Roués*, could ever draw anything from him, even when drunk, concerning the affairs of the government, however important. He publicly lived with Madame de Parabère; he lived at the same time with others; he amused himself with the jealousy and vexation of these women; he was not the less on good terms with them all; and the scandal of this public seraglio, and that of the daily filthiness and impiety at his suppers, were extreme and spread everywhere.

A Scotchman, I do not know of what family, had come to Paris during the last days of the deceased King. His name was Law. He was spoken of to M. le Duc d'Orléans as a man deep in banking and commercial matters; the Regent, from this description, was desirous to see him. He conversed with Law some time, and was so pleased with him, that he spoke of him to Desmarets as a man from whom information was to be drawn. I recollect that the Prince spoke of him to me at the same time. Desmarets sent for Law, and was a long while with him several times; I know nothing of what passed between them or its result, except that Desmarets was pleased with Law, and formed some esteem for him.

M. le Duc d'Orléans, after that, only saw him from time to time; but after the first rush of affairs, which followed the death of the King, Law, who had formed some subaltern acquaintances at the Palais Royal, and an intimacy with the Abbé Dubois, presented himself anew before M. le Duc d'Orléans, soon after conversed with him in private, and proposed some finance plans to him. The bank project pleased that Prince so much that he wished to carry it out. He spoke in private to the heads of finance, in whom he found great opposition. When he had entirely formed his resolution, he summoned a financial and commercial assembly, in which Law explained the whole plan of the bank he wished to establish (this was on the 24th of October, 1715). He was listened to as long as he liked to talk. Some, who saw that the Regent was almost decided, acquiesced; but the majority opposed.

M. le Duc d'Orléans took the trouble to speak in private to each member of the council, and gently to make them understand that he wished the bank to meet with no opposition. He spoke his mind to me thoroughly: therefore a reply was necessary. I said to him that I did not hide my ignorance or my disgust for all finance matters; that, nevertheless, what he had just explained to me appeared good in itself, that without any new tax, without expense, and without wronging or embarrassing anybody, money should double itself at once by means of the notes of this bank, and become transferable with the greatest facility. But along with this advantage I found two inconveniences, the first, how to govern the bank with sufficient foresight and wisdom, so as not to issue more notes than could be paid whenever presented: the second, that what is excellent in a republic, or in a monarchy where the finance is entirely popular, as in England, is of pernicious use in an absolute monarchy, such as France, where the necessities of a war badly undertaken and ill sustained, the avidity of a first minister, favourite or mistress, the luxury, the wild expenses, the prodigality of a King, might soon exhaust a bank, and ruin all the holders of notes, that is to say, overthrow the realm. M. le Duc d'Orléans agreed to this; but at the same time maintained that a King would have so much interest in never meddling or allowing minister, mistress, or favourite to meddle with the bank, that this capital inconvenience was never to be feared. Upon that we for a long time disputed without convincing each other, so that when, some few days afterwards, he proposed the bank to the regency council, I gave my opinion as I have just explained it, but with more force and at length: and my conclusion was to reject the bank, as a bait the most fatal, in an absolute country, while in a free country it would be a very good and very wise establishment.

Few dared to be of this opinion: the bank passed.

Some time after, to relate all at once, M. le Duc d'Orléans wished me to see Law in order that he might explain to me his plans, and asked me to do so as a favour. I represented to him my unskilfulness in all finance matters; that Law would in vain speak a language to me of which I understood nothing, that we should both lose our time very uselessly. I tried to back out thus, as well as I could. The Regent several times reverted to the charge, and at last demanded my submission. Law came then to my house. Though there was much of the foreigner in his bearing, in his expressions, and in his accent, he expressed himself in very good terms, with much clearness and precision. He conversed with me a long while upon his bank, which, indeed, was an excellent thing in itself, but for another country rather than for France, and with a prince less easy than the Regent. Law had no other solutions to give me, of my two objections, than those the Regent himself had given, which did not satisfy me. But as the affair had passed, and there was nothing now to do but direct it well, our conversation turned principally upon that. I made him feel as much as I could the importance of not showing such facility, that it might be abused, with a Regent so good, so easy, so open, so surrounded. I masked as well as I could what I wished to make him understand thereupon; and I dwelt especially upon the necessity of being prepared to satisfy instantly all bearers of notes, who should demand payment: for upon this depended the credit or the overthrow of the bank.

Arouet, son of a notary, who was employed by my father and me until his death, was exiled and sent to Tulle at this time (the early part of 1716), for some verses very satirical and very impudent. I should not amuse myself by writing down such a trifle, if this same Arouet, having become a great poet and academician under the name of Voltaire, had not also become— after many tragical adventures—a manner of personage in the republic of letters, and even achieved a sort of importance among certain people.[1]

1716

Ever since the Regent's accession to power, an intimacy had gradually been growing up between the two governments of France and England.

---

[1] This delicious reference to the most famous Frenchman of his own age is the most striking example I know of Saint-Simon's complete detachment from the eighteenth century.

This was mainly owing to the intrigues of the Abbé Dubois, who had sold himself to the English Court, from which he secretly received an enormous pension. He was, therefore, devoted heart and soul—if such a despicable personage can be said to have the one or the other—to the interests of King George, and tried to serve them in every way. He had but little difficulty—comparatively speaking—in inducing M. le Duc d'Orléans to fall into his nets, and to declare himself in favour of an English alliance. Negotiations with this end in view were, in fact, set on foot, had been for some time; and about the month of September of this year (1716), assumed a more smiling face than they had yet displayed.

Both France and England, from different motives, wished to draw Spain into this alliance. The Regent, therefore, in order to further this desire, obtained from England a promise that she would give up Gibraltar to its former owners, the Spaniards. The King of England consented to do so, but on one condition: it was, that in order not to expose himself to the cries of the party opposed to him, this arrangement should be kept profoundly secret until executed. In order that this secrecy might be secured, he stipulated that the negotiation should not in any way pass through the hands of Alberoni, or any Spanish minister, but be treated directly between the Regent and the King of Spain, through a confidential agent chosen by the former.

This confidential agent was to take a letter respecting the treaty to the King of Spain, a letter full of insignificant trifles, and at the same time a positive order from the King of England, written and signed by his hand, to the Governor of Gibraltar, commanding him to surrender the place to the King of Spain the very moment he received this order, and to retire with his garrison, &c., to Tangiers. In order to execute this, a Spanish general was suddenly to march to Gibraltar, under pretence of repressing the incursions of its garrison—summon the Governor to appear, deliver to him the King of England's order, and enter into possession of the place.

Louville was the secret agent whom the Regent determined to send. He had already been in Spain, had gained the confidence of the King, and knew him better than any other person who could have been chosen. Precisely because of all these reasons, I thought him the most unfit person to be charged with this commission. The more intimate he had been with the King of Spain, the more firm in his confidence, the more would he be feared by the Queen and Alberoni; and the more would they do to cover his embassy with failure, so as to guard their credit and their authority. Louville in due time departed to Madrid, on his strange and secret embassy.

Upon arriving he went straight to the house of the Duc de Saint-Aignan, our ambassador, and took up his quarters there. Saint-Aignan who had received not the slightest information of his arriving, was surprised beyond measure at it. Alberoni was something more than surprised.

He instantly despatched a courier to meet Louville with an order prohibiting him to approach any nearer to Madrid. The courier missed Louville, but a quarter of an hour after this latter had alighted at Saint-Aignan's, he received a note from Grimaldo inclosing an order from the King of Spain, commanding him to leave the city that instant! Louville replied that he was charged with a confidential letter from the King of France, and with another from M. le Duc d'Orléans, for the King of Spain; and with a commission for his Catholic Majesty which would not permit him to leave until he had executed it. In consequence of this reply, a courier was at once despatched to the Prince de Cellamare, Spanish ambassador at Paris, ordering him to ask for the recall of Louville, and to declare that the King of Spain so disliked his person that he would neither see him, nor allow him to treat with any of the ministers!

Alberoni, not satisfied with what he had already done, came himself to the Duc de Saint-Aignan's, in order to persuade Louville to depart at once. Grimaldo came afterwards to intimate to Louville an absolute order to depart, and to inform the Duc de Saint-Aignan that the King of Spain was so angry with the obstinacy of this delay, that he would not say what might happen if the stay of Louville was protracted; but that he feared the respect due to an ambassador of France would be disregarded.

Both Louville and Saint-Aignan clearly saw that all audience was impossible, and that in consequence a longer stay could only lead to disturbances which might embroil the two crowns; so that, at the end of seven or eight days, Louville departed, returning as he came. Alberoni began then to breathe again after the extreme fear he had had. He was consoled by this proof of his power, which showed he need no longer fear that any one could approach the King without his aid, or that any business could be conducted without him. Thus Spain lost Gibraltar, and she has never been able to recover it since.

Louville having returned, it was necessary to send word to the King of England of all he had done in Spain; and this business came to nothing, except that it set Alberoni against the Regent for trying to execute a secret commission without his knowledge; and that it set the Regent against Alberoni for frustrating a project so openly, and for showing the full force of his power. Neither of the two ever forgot this matter; and the dislike of Alberoni to the Regent led, as will be seen, to some strange results.

I will add here, that the treaty of alliance between France and England was signed a short time after this event. I did my utmost to prevent it, representing to the Regent that his best policy was to favour the cause of the Pretender, and thus by keeping the attention of Great Britain continually fixed upon her domestic concerns, he would effectually prevent her from influencing the affairs of the continent. Many and long were the conversations I had with him, insisting upon this point. But although, while he was with me, my arguments might appear to have some weight with him, they were forgotten, clean swept from his mind, directly the Abbé Dubois, who had begun to obtain a most complete and pernicious influence over him, brought his persuasiveness to bear. Dubois' palm had been so well greased by the English that he was afraid of nothing. He succeeded then in inducing the Regent to sign a treaty with England, in every way, it may safely be said, advantageous to that power, and in no way advantageous to France. Amongst other conditions, the Regent agreed to send the so-called Pretender out of the realm, and to force him to seek an asylum in Italy. This was, in fact, executed to the letter. King James, who for some time had retired to Avignon, crossed the Alps and settled in Rome, where he lived ever afterwards. I could not but deplore the adoption of a policy so contrary to the true interests of France; but the business being done I held my peace, and let matters take their course. It was the only course of conduct open to me.

It is known that Peter I, Czar of Muscovy, wished to come into France during the time of the late King, who civilly refused to receive him. There being no longer this obstacle, he wished to satisfy his curiosity, and he informed the Regent through Prince Kourakin, his ambassador at Paris, that he was going to quit the Low Countries, and come and see the King.

There was nothing for it but to appear very pleased, although the Regent would gladly have dispensed with this visit. The expenses to be defrayed were great; the trouble would be not less great with a prince so powerful and so clear-sighted, but full of whims, with a remnant of barbarous manners, and a grand suite of people, of behaviour very different from that common in these countries, full of caprices and of strange fashions, and both they and their master very touchy and very positive upon what they claimed to be due or permitted to them.

Moreover the Czar was at daggers drawn with the King of England, the enmity between them passing all decent limits, and being the more bitter because personal. This troubled the Regent not a little, whose intimacy with the King of England was public.

1717

The Czar arrived at Beaumont on Friday, the 7th of May, 1717, about mid-day. Tessé made his reverences to him as he descended from his coach, had the honour of dining with him, and of escorting him that very day to Paris.

The Czar alighted at nine o'clock in the evening at the Louvre, and walked all through the apartments of the Queen-Mother. He considered them to be too magnificently hung and lighted, jumped into his coach again, and went to the Hôtel de Lesdiguières, where he wished to lodge. He thought the apartment destined for him too fine also, and had his camp-bed immediately spread out in a dressing-room. The Maréchal de Tessé, who was to do the honours of his house and of his table, to accompany him everywhere, and not quit the place where he might be, lodged in an apartment of the Hôtel de Lesdiguières, and had enough to do in following and sometimes running after him. Verton, one of the King's maîtres d'hôtel, was charged with serving him and all the tables of the Czar and his suite. The suite consisted of forty persons of all sorts, twelve or fifteen of whom were considerable people in themselves, or by their appointments; they all ate with the Czar.

The Czar excited admiration by his extreme curiosity, always bearing upon his views of government, trade, instruction, police, and this curiosity embraced everything, disdained nothing in the smallest degree useful; it was marked and enlightened, esteeming only what merited to be esteemed, and exhibited in a clear light the intelligence, justness, ready appreciation of his mind. Everything showed in the Czar the vast extent of his knowledge, and a sort of logical harmony of ideas. He allied in the most surprising manner the highest, the proudest, the most delicate, the most sustained, and at the same time the least embarrassing majesty, when he had established it in all its safety with a marked politeness. Yet he was always and with everybody the master everywhere, but with gradations, according to the persons he was with. He had a kind of familiarity which sprang from liberty, but he was not without a strong dash of that ancient barbarism of his country, which rendered all his actions rapid, nay, precipitous, his will uncertain, and not to be constrained or contradicted in anything. His desire for liberty, his dislike to be made a show of, his free and easy habits, often made him prefer hired coaches, common cabs even; nay, the first which he could lay his hands on, though belonging to people below him, of whom he knew nothing. He jumped in, and had himself driven all over the city, and outside it.

The Czar was a very tall man, his look majestic and gracious when he liked. All his bearing showed his intellect, his reflectiveness, and his greatness, and was not devoid of a certain grace. What he ate and drank at his two regular meals is inconceivable, without reckoning the beer, lemonade, and other drinks he swallowed between these repasts, his suite following his example; a bottle or two of beer, as many more of wine, and, occasionally, liqueurs afterwards; at the end of the meal strong drinks, such as brandy, as much sometimes as a quart. This was about the usual quantity at each meal. His suite at his table drank more and ate in proportion, at eleven o'clock in the morning and at eight at night. There was a chaplain who ate at the table of the Czar, who consumed half as much again as the rest, and with whom the monarch, who was fond of him, much amused himself.

The Czar understood French well, and I think could have spoken it, if he had wished, but for greatness' sake he always had an interpreter. Latin and many other languages he spoke very well.

On Monday, the 10th of May, the King went to see the Czar, who received him at the door, saw him alight from his coach, walked with him at his left into his chamber, where they found two arm-chairs equally placed. The King sat down in the right-hand one, the Czar in the other, Prince Kourakin served as interpreter. It was astonishing to see the Czar take the King under both arms, hoist him up to his level, embrace him thus in the air; and the King, young as he was, show no fear, although he could not possibly have been prepared for such a reception. It was striking, too, to see the grace which the Czar displayed before the King, the air of tenderness he assumed towards him, the politeness which flowed as it were naturally, and which nevertheless was mixed with greatness, with equality of rank, and slightly with superiority of age: for all these things made themselves felt. He praised the King, appeared charmed with him, and persuaded everybody he was. He embraced him again and again. The King paid his brief compliment very prettily; and M. du Maine, the Maréchal de Villeroy, and the distinguished people present, filled up the conversation. The meeting lasted a short quarter of an hour. The Czar accompanied the King as he had received him, and saw him to his coach.

On Tuesday, the 11th of May, between four and five o'clock, the Czar went to see the King. He was received by the King at his carriage door, took up a position on his right, and was conducted within. All these ceremonies had been agreed on before the King went to see him. The Czar showed the same affection and the same attentions to the King as before; and his visit was not longer than the one he had received, but the crowd much surprised him.

M. le Duc d'Orléans came afterwards and took him to the Opera, into his grand box, where they sat upon the front seat upon a splendid carpet. Some time after, the Czar asked if there was no beer to be had? Immediately a large goblet of it was brought to him, on a salver. The Regent rose, took it, and presented it to the Czar, who with a smile and an inclination of politeness, received the goblet without any ceremony, drank, and put it back on the salver which the Regent still held. In handing it back, the Regent took a plate, in which was a napkin, presented it to the Czar, who without rising made use of it, at which the house appeared rather astonished. At the fourth act the Czar went away to supper, but did not wish the Regent to leave the box. The next morning he jumped into a hired coach, and went to see a number of curiosities among the workmen.

On the 16th of May, Whit Sunday, he went to the Invalides, where he wished to see and examine everything. At the refectory he tasted the soldier's soup and their wine, drank to their healths, struck them on the shoulders, and called them comrades. He much admired the church, the dispensary, and the infirmary, and appeared much pleased with the order of the establishment.

On Friday, the 11th of June, he went from Versailles to Saint Cyr, where he saw all the household, and the girls in their classes. He was received there like the King. He wished to see Madame de Maintenon, who, expecting his curiosity, had buried herself in her bed, all the curtains closed, except one, which was half-open. The Czar entered her chamber, pulled back the window-curtains upon arriving, then the bed-curtains, took a good long stare at her, said not a word to her,—nor did she open her lips,—and, without making her any kind of reverence, went his way.

On Sunday, the 20th of June, the Czar departed, and slept at Ivry, bound straight for Spa, where he was expected by the Czarina.

The Czar had an extreme desire to unite himself to France. Nothing would have been more advantageous to our commerce; to our importance in the north, in Germany, in all Europe. The Czar kept England in restraint as to her commerce, and King George in fear for his German states. He kept Holland respectful, and the Emperor measured. It cannot be denied that he made a grand figure in Europe and in Asia, or that France would not have infinitely profited by close union with him. He did not like the Emperor; he wished to sever us from England, and it was England which rendered us deaf to his invitations, unbecomingly so, though they lasted after his departure. Often I vainly pressed the Regent upon this subject, and gave him reasons of which he felt all the force, and to which he could not reply. He was bewitched by Dubois, who panted to become Cardinal, and who built all his hopes of success upon England. The English saw his ambition, and took advantage of it for their own interests. Dubois' aim was to make use of the intimacy between the King of England and the Emperor, in order that the latter might be induced by the former to obtain a Cardinalship from the Pope, over whom he had great power. It will be seen, in due time, what success has attended the intrigues of the scheming and unscrupulous Abbé.

The Abbé Alberoni, having risen by the means I have described, and acquired power by following in the track of the Princesse des Ursins, governed Spain like a master. He had the most ambitious projects. One of his ideas was to drive all strangers, especially the French, out of the West Indies; and he hoped to make use of the Dutch to attain this end. But Holland was too much in the dependence of England.

At home Alberoni proposed many useful reforms, and endeavoured to diminish the expenses of the royal household. He thought, with reason, that a strong navy was the necessary basis of the power of Spain; and to create one he endeavoured to economise the public money. Alberoni had persuaded the Queen of Spain to keep her husband shut up, as had the Princesse des Ursins. This was a certain means of governing a prince, whose temperament and whose conscience equally attached him to his spouse. He was soon completely governed once more—under lock and key, as it were, night and day. By this means the Queen was jailoress and prisoner at the same time. As she was constantly with the King nobody could come to her. Thus Alberoni kept them both shut up, with the key of their prison in his pocket.

Alberoni was made Cardinal on the 12th of July, 1717. Not a soul approved this promotion when it was announced at the consistory.

1718

By chance I learnt one day what M. le Duc d'Orléans really thought of me. I know not what had occurred at the Council to occasion it. All that I can say is that he insisted upon his happiness in having a friend so faithful, so unchanging at all times, so useful to him as I was, and always had been; so sure, so true, so disinterested, so firm, such as he could meet with in no one else, and upon whom he could always count. This eulogy lasted from the Tuileries to the Palais Royal, the Regent saying to his son that he wished to teach him how to make my acquaintance, as a support and a source of happiness (all that I relate here is in his own words); such as he had always found in my friendship and counsel. The Bailli de Conflans, astonished at this abundant eloquence, repeated it to me two days after, and I admit that I never have forgotten it.

It is time now that I should speak of matters of very great importance, which led to changes that filled my heart with excessive joy, such as it had never known before.

For a long time past the Parliament had made many encroachments upon the privileges belonging to the Dukes. Even under the late King it had begun these impudent enterprises, and no word was said against it; for nothing gave the King greater pleasure than to mix all ranks together in a cauldron of confusion. He hated and feared the nobility, was jealous of their power, which in former reigns had often so successfully balanced that of the crown; he was glad therefore of any opportunity which presented itself that enabled him to see our order weakened and robbed of its dignity.

The Parliament grew bolder as its encroachments one by one succeeded. It began to fancy itself armed with powers of the highest kind. It began to imagine that it possessed all the authority of the English Parliament, forgetting that that assembly is charged with the legislative administration of the country, that it has the right to make laws and repeal laws, and that the monarch can do but little, comparatively speaking, without the support and sanction of this representative chamber; whereas, our own Parliament is but a tribunal of justice, with no control or influence over the royal authority or state affairs.

But, as I have said, success gave it new impudence. Now that the King was dead, at whose name alone it trembled, this assembly thought that a fine opportunity had come to give its power the rein. It had to do with a Regent, notorious for his easy-going disposition, his indifference to form and rule, his dislike to all vigorous measures. It fancied that victory over such an opponent would be easy; that it could successfully overcome all the opposition he could put in action, and in due time make his authority secondary to its own. The Chief-President of the Parliament, I should observe, was the principal promoter of these sentiments. He was the bosom friend of M. and Madame du Maine, and by them was encouraged in his views. Incited by his encouragement, he seized an opportunity which presented itself now, to throw down the glove to M. le Duc d'Orléans, in the name of the Parliament, and to prepare for something like a struggle. The Parliament of Brittany had recently manifested a very turbulent spirit, and this was an additional encouragement to that of Paris.

At first the Parliament men scarcely knew what to lay hold of and bring forward, as an excuse for the battle. They wished of course to gain the applause of the people as protectors of their interests—likewise those who for their private ends try to trouble and embroil the state—but could not at first see their way clear. They sent for Trudaine, Prévôt des Marchands, Councillor of State, to give an account to them of the state of the Hôtel de Ville funds. He declared that they had never been so well paid, and that there was no cause of complaint against the government. Baffled upon this point, they fastened upon an edict, recently rendered, respecting the money of the realm. They deliberated thereon, deputed a commission to examine the matter, made a great fuss, and came to the conclusion that the edict would, if acted upon, be very prejudicial to the country.

Thus much done, the Parliament assembled anew on Friday morning, the 17th of June, 1718, and again in the afternoon. At the end they decided upon sending a deputation to the Regent, asking him to suspend the operation of the edict, introduce into it the changes suggested by their body, and then send it to them to be registered. The deputation was sent, and said all it had to say.

On the morrow the Parliament again assembled, morning and afternoon, and sent a message to the Regent, saying, it would not separate until it had received his reply. That reply was very short and simple. The Regent sent word that he was tired of the meddling interference of the Parliament (this was not the first time, let me add, that he experienced it), that he had ordered all the troops in Paris, and round about, to hold themselves ready to march, and that the King must be obeyed. Such was in fact true. He had really ordered the soldiers to keep under arms and to be supplied with powder and shot.

The message did not intimidate the Parliament. The next day, Sunday, the Chief-President, accompanied by all the other presidents, and by several councillors, came to the Palais Royal. Although, as I have said, the leader of his company, and the right-hand man of M. and Madame du Maine, he wished for his own sake to keep on good terms with the Regent, and at the same time to preserve all authority over his brethren, so as to have them under his thumb. His discourse then to the Regent commenced with many praises and much flattery, in order to smooth the way for the three fine requests he wound up with. The first of these was that the edict should be sent to the Parliament to be examined, and to suffer such changes as the members should think fit to introduce, and then be registered; the second, that the King should pay attention to their remonstrances in an affair of this importance, which they believed prejudicial to the State; the third, that the works recently undertaken at the Mint for recasting the specie should be suspended.

To these modest requests the Regent replied that the edict had been registered at the Cour des Monnaies, which is a superior court, and consequently sufficient for such registration; that there was only a single instance of an edict respecting the money of the realm having been sent before the Parliament, and then out of pure civility; that the matter had been well sifted, and all its inconveniences weighed; that it was to the advantage of the State to put in force this edict; that the works of the Mint could not be interfered with in any way; finally, that the King must be obeyed.

Notwithstanding the decisive answer they had received, the Parliament met the very next day, and passed a decree against the edict. The council of the regency, at its sitting on the afternoon of the same day, abrogated this decree. Thus, since war was in a measure declared between the Regent's authority and that of the Parliament, the orders emanating from the one were disputed by the other, and *vice versâ*.

The Regent was determined to be obeyed. He prohibited, therefore, the printing and posting up of the decree of the Parliament. Soldiers of the guards, too, were placed in the markets to enforce the acceptance of the new money which had been issued. The fact is, by the edict which had been passed, the louis worth thirty livres was taken at thirty-six livres, and the crown piece, worth a hundred sous, at six livres instead of five. By this edict also government notes were made legal tender until the new money should be ready. The finances were thus relieved, and the King gained largely from the recasting of the coin. But private people lost by this increase, which much exceeded the intrinsic value of the metal used, and which caused everything to rise in price. Thus the Parliament had a fine opportunity of trumpeting forth its solicitude for the public interest, and did not fail to avail itself of it.

During the night a councillor of the Parliament was surprised on horseback in the streets tearing down and disfiguring the decree of the regency council, which abrogated that of the Parliament. He was taken to prison.

On Monday, the 27th of June, the Chief-President, at the head of all the other presidents, and of forty councillors, went to the Tuileries, and in the presence of the Regent read the wire-drawn remonstrance of the Parliament upon this famous edict. The keeper of the seals said that in a few days the King would reply. Accordingly on Saturday, the 2nd of July, the same deputation came again to the Tuileries to hear the reply. The Regent and all the princes of the blood were there, the bastards also. Argenson, who from lieutenant of police had been made keeper of the seals, and who in his former capacity had often been ill-used—nay, even attacked by the Parliament—took good care to show his superiority over that assembly. He answered that deputation in the name of the King, and concluded by saying that the edict would in no way be altered, but would receive complete application. The parliamentary gentlemen did not expect so firm a reply, and withdrew much mortified.

They were not, however, vanquished. They reassembled on the 11th and 12th of August, and spat forth all their venom in another decree specially aimed at the authority of the Regent. By this decree the administration of the finance was henceforth to be entirely at the mercy of the Parliament. Law, the Scotchman, who, under the favour of M. le Duc d'Orléans, had been allowed some influence over the State money matters, was to possess that influence no longer; in fact, all power on the part of the Regent over the finances was to be taken from him.

After this the Parliament had to take but one step in order to become the guardian of the King and the master of the realm (as in fact it madly claimed to be), the Regent more at its mercy than the King, and perhaps as exposed as King Charles I of England. Our parliamentary gentlemen began as humbly as those of England, and though, as I have said, their assembly was but a simple court of justice, limited in its jurisdiction like the other courts of the realm, to judge disputes between private people, yet by dint of hammering upon the word parliament, they believed themselves not less important than their English brethren, who form the legislative assembly, and represent all the nation.

M. and Madame du Maine had done not a little to bring about these fancies, and they continued in secret to do more. Madame du Maine, it may be recollected, had said that she would throw the whole country into combustion, in order not to lose her husband's prerogative. She was as good as her word. Encouraged doubtless by the support they received from this precious pair, the Parliament continued on its mad career of impudent presumption, pride, and arrogance. It assembled on the 22nd of August, and ordered inquiry to be made of the Regent as to what had become of all the State notes that had been passed at the Chamber of Justice; those which had been given for the lotteries that were held every month; those which had been given for the Mississippi or Western Company; finally, those which had been taken to the Mint since the change in the specie.

These questions were communicated to the Regent by the King's officers. In reply he turned his back upon them, and went away into his cabinet, leaving these people slightly bewildered. Immediately after this occurrence it was rumoured that a Bed of Justice would soon be held.

At the first movements of the Parliament, of the bastards, and of those who had usurped the name of nobility, I had warned M. le Duc d'Orléans. I had done so again as soon as I saw the cadence and the harmony of the designs in progress. I had pointed out to him their inevitable sequel; how easy it was to hinder them at the commencement; how difficult after, especially for a person of his character and disposition. But I was not the man for such work as this. He was on his guard against what he called my warmth, and against the love I had for my dignity, so attacked by the usurpations of the bastards; the designs of the Parliament, and the modern fancies of a sham nobility. As soon as I perceived his suspicions I told him so, and I added that, content with having done my duty as citizen and as his servitor, I would say no more on the subject. I kept my word. For more than a year I had not of myself opened my mouth thereon.

Judge of my surprise, therefore, when as I was working as usual one afternoon with the Regent, he interrupted me to speak with bitterness of the Parliament. As the subject was now reopened I reminded him of a prophecy I had uttered long before, that he had missed the opportunity of governing the Parliament when he might have done so with a frown, and that step by step he would allow himself to be conducted by his easy-going disposition, until he found himself on the very verge of the abyss; that if he wished to recover his position he must begin at once to retrace his steps, or lose his footing for ever.

It was indeed high time to do something, as I have before remarked. The Parliament, we found, after passing its last decree, had named a commission to inquire into the financial edict; this commission was working in the utmost secrecy; a number of witnesses had already been examined, and preparations were quietly making to arrest Law some fine morning, and hang him three hours after within the enclosure of the Palais de Justice.

Immediately this fact became known, the Duc de la Force and Fagon went to the Regent—it was on the 19th of August, 1718—and spoke to him with such effect, that he ordered them to assemble with Law that very day at my house in order to see what was to be done. They came, in fact, and this was the first intimation I had that the Regent had begun to feel the gravity of his position, and that he was ready to do something. In this conference at my house the firmness of Law, hitherto so great, was shaken so that tears escaped him. Arguments did not satisfy us at first, because the question could only be decided by force, and we could not rely upon that of the Regent. The safe-conduct with which Law was supplied would not have stopped the Parliament an instant. On every side we were embarrassed. Law, more dead than alive, knew not what to say; much less what to do. His safety appeared to us the most pressing matter to ensure. If he had been taken it would have been all over with him before the ordinary machinery of negotiation (delayed as it was likely to be by the weakness of the Regent) could have been set in motion; certainly, before there would have been leisure to think of better, or to send a regiment of guards to force open the Palais de Justice; a critical remedy at all times, and grievous to the last degree, even when it succeeds; frightful, if instead of Law, only his corpse had been found!

I advised Law, therefore, to retire to the Palais Royal, and occupy the chamber of Nancré, his friend, then away in Spain. Law breathed again at this suggestion and put it in execution the moment he left my house. He might have been kept in safety at the Bank, but I thought the Palais Royal would be better: that his retirement there would create more effect, and induce the Regent to hold firm to his purpose, besides allowing His Royal Highness to see the financier whenever he pleased.

This done I proposed, and the others approved my proposition, that a Bed of Justice should be held as the only means left by which the abrogation of the parliamentary decrees could be registered. But while our arguments were moving, I stopped them all short by a reflection which came into my mind. I represented to my guests that the Duc du Maine was in secret the principal leader of the parliament, and was closely allied with Maréchal de Villeroy; and that both would oppose might and main the assembling of a Bed of Justice.

I said, 'Let the Bed of Justice be held at the Tuileries; let it be kept a profound secret until the very morning it is to take place; and let those who are to attend it be told so only a few hours before they are to assemble. By these means no time will be allowed for anybody to object to the proceeding, to plead the health of the King, the heat of the weather, or to interfere with the arrangements of the troops which it will be necessary to make.'

We stopped at this: Law went away, and I dictated to Fagon the full details of my scheme, by which secrecy was to be ensured and all obstacles provided against. We finished about nine o'clock in the evening, and I counselled Fagon to carry what he had written to the Abbé Dubois, who had just returned from England with new credit over the mind of his master.

The next day I repaired to the Palais Royal about four o'clock. When M. le Duc d'Orléans was free he led me into the cabinet behind the grand salon, by the Rue de Richelieu, and on entering said he was at the crisis of his Regency, and that everything was needed in order to sustain him on this occasion. He added that he was resolved to strike a heavy blow at the Parliament; that he much approved my proposition respecting the Bed of Justice at the Tuileries, and that it would be held exactly as I had suggested.

I was delighted at his animation, and at the firmness he appeared to possess.

Our preparations for the Bed of Justice continued to be actively but silently made during the next few days. In the course of the numberless discussions which arose upon the subject, it was agreed, after much opposition on my part, to strike a blow, not only at the Parliament, but at M. du Maine, who had fomented its discontent. M. le Duc, who had been admitted to our councils, and who was heart and soul against the bastards, proposed that at the Bed of Justice the education of the young King should be taken out of the control of M. du Maine and placed in his hands. He proposed also that the title of Prince of the Blood should be taken from him, with all the privileges it conferred, and that he should be reduced to the rank of a simple Duke and Peer, taking his place among the rest according to the date of his erection; thus, at a bound, going down to the bottom of the peerage!

Should these memoirs ever see the light, every one who reads them will be able to judge how such a proposition as this harmonised with my personal wishes. No man could be more against M. du Maine than I, and yet I opposed this proposition of M. le Duc because I thought one blow was enough at a time, and that it might be dangerous to attempt the two at once. M. du Maine had supporters, nay, he was at the head of a sort of party; strip him of the important post he held, and what might not his rage, his disappointment, and his wounded ambition lead him to attempt? Civil war, perhaps, would be the result of his disgrace.

Again and again I urged these views, not only upon M. le Duc d'Orléans, but upon M. le Duc. But M. le Duc was not to be shaken, and as I could do no more than I had done to move him, I was obliged at last to give in. It was resolved, however, that disgrace should fall upon M. du Maine alone; that his brother, the Comte de Toulouse, on account of the devotion to the State he had ever exhibited, and his excellent conduct since the death of the late King, should, when stripped of his title like the other, receive it back again the moment after, in acknowledgment of the services he had rendered to the Regent as Councillor of State, and as an expression of personal good feeling towards him, which his excellent qualities so justly merited.

I returned home from my last interview with M. le Duc, and went to mass at the Jacobins, to which I entered from my garden. It was not without a distracted mind. But I prayed to God sincerely and earnestly to guide my steps, so that I might labour for His glory and the good of the State without private ends. My prayer was heard, and in the sequel I had nothing to reproach myself with. I followed the straight road without turning to the right or to the left.

Fontanieu was waiting for me in my house as I returned home from mass, and I was obliged to listen to his questions and to reply to them, as though I had nothing on my mind. I arranged my chamber like a Bed of Justice, I made him understand several things connected with the ceremonial that he had not understood before, and that it was essential he should in no way omit. Thus everything went on satisfactorily, and I began to count the hours, by day as well as by night, until the great day was to arrive on which the arrogant pride of the Parliament was to receive a check, and the false plumage which adorned the bastards was to be plucked from them.

In the midst of the sweet joy that I felt, no bitterness entered. I was satisfied with the part I had played in this affair, satisfied that I had acted sincerely, honestly, that I had not allowed my own private motives to sway me; that in the interests of the State, as opposed to my own interests, I had done all in my power to save the Duc du Maine. And yet I did not dare to give myself up to the rosy thoughts suggested by the great event, now so rapidly approaching. I toyed with them instead of allowing myself to embrace them. I shrunk from them as it were like a cold lover who fears the too ardent caresses of his mistress. I could not believe that the supreme happiness I had so long pined for was at last so near. Might not M. le Duc d'Orléans falter at the last moment? Might not all our preparations so carefully conducted, so cleverly planned, weigh upon his feebleness until they fell to the ground? It was not improbable. He was often firm in promises. How often was he firm in carrying them out? All these questions, all these restless doubts—natural as it appears to me under the circumstances—winged their way through my mind, and kept me excited and feverish as though life and death were hanging on one thread.

In the midst of my reflections, a messenger from M. le Duc d'Orléans, Millain by name, arrived at my house. It was on the afternoon of Thursday, the 25th of August, 1718. His message was simple. M. le Duc d'Orléans was in the same mood as ever, and I was to join him at the Palais Royal, according to previous agreement, at eight o'clock in the evening. The Bed of Justice was to be held on the morrow.

Never was kiss given to a beautiful mistress sweeter than that which I imprinted upon the fat old face of this charming messenger. A close embrace, eagerly repeated, was my first reply, followed afterwards by an overflow of feeling for M. le Duc, and for Millain even, who had worthily served in this great undertaking.

The arrangements respecting the troops and for summoning the Parliament, &c., were all carried out to the letter during the night and early morning. Towards five o'clock in the morning drums began to be heard throughout the town, and soon soldiers were seen in movement. At six o'clock a message was sent to the Parliament requesting it to attend at the Tuileries. The reply was that the request should be obeyed. At the same time, horsemen went to all the Peers and officers of the Crown, and to all the chevaliers of the order, the governors and lieutenant-governors of the provinces (who were to accompany the King), informing them of the Bed of Justice. The French and Swiss guards were under arms in various quarters; the watch, the light horse, and the two companies of musketeers all ready in their barracks; the usual guard at the Tuileries.

Towards eight o'clock in the morning a messenger from M. le Duc d'Orléans came to remind me of the Regency Council at eight o'clock, and to attend it in my mantle. I dressed myself in black, because I had only that suit with a mantle, and another, a magnificent one in cloth of gold, which I did not wish to wear lest it should cause the remark to be made, though much out of season, that I wished to insult the Parliament and M. du Maine. I took two gentlemen with me in my coach, and I went in order to witness all that was to take place. I was at the same time full of fear, hope, joy, reflection, and mistrust of M. le Duc d'Orléans' weakness, and all that might result from it. I was also firmly resolved to do my best, whatever might happen, but without appearing to know anything, and without eagerness, and I resolved to show presence of mind, attention, circumspection, modesty, and much moderation.

I arrived at the grand court of the Tuileries about eight o'clock, asked where I was to await the assembling of the Council, and was admitted to a room upstairs, where I found a good number of people already congregated.

The Council was held in a room which ever since the very hot weather the King had slept in. The hangings of his bed, and of the Maréchal de Villeroy's were drawn back. The Council table was placed at the foot of one of the beds. After a passing glance upon this crowd I entered the Council chamber. I found scattered there the majority of those who composed the Council with serious and troubled looks, which increased my seriousness. Scarcely anybody spoke; and each, standing or seated here and there, kept himself in his place. The better to examine all I joined nobody. A moment after M. le Duc d'Orléans entered with a gay, easy, untroubled air, and looked smilingly upon the company. I considered this of good augury. Immediately afterwards I asked him his news. He replied aloud that he was tolerably well; then approaching my ear, added that except when aroused to give his orders, he had slept very well, and that he was determined to hold firm. This infinitely pleased me, for it seemed to me by his manner that he was in earnest, and I briefly exhorted him to remain so.

In due time M. du Maine appeared in his mantle, entering by the King's little door. Never before had he made so many or such profound reverences as he did now—though he was not usually very stingy of them—then standing alone, resting upon his stick near the Council table, he looked around at everybody. Then and there, being in front of him, with the table between us, I making him the most smiling bow I had ever given him, and did it with extreme pleasure. He repaid me in the same coin, and continued to fix his eyes upon everybody in turn, his face agitated, and nearly always speaking to himself.

The Comte de Toulouse arrived as the Regent had just quitted the two persons with whom he had been talking. The Comte de Toulouse was in his mantle, and saluted the company with a grave and meditative manner, neither accosting nor accosted.

A short time afterwards the Comte de Toulouse had a conversation with his brother, both speaking with agitation and without appearing to agree very well. Then the Comte approached M. le Duc d'Orléans, who was talking again to M. le Duc, and they spoke at some length to each other. As their faces were towards the wall, nothing but their backs could be seen, no emotion and scarcely a gesture was visible.

The Duc du Maine had remained where he had spoken to his brother. He seemed half dead, looked askance upon the company with wandering eyes, and the troubled agitated manner of a criminal, or a man condemned to death. Shortly afterwards he became pale as a corpse, and appeared to me to have been taken ill. He crawled to the end of the table, during which the Comte de Toulouse came and said a word to the Regent, and began to walk out of the room.

All these movements took place in a trice. The Regent, who was near the King's arm-chair, said aloud, 'Now, gentlemen, let us take our places.' Each approached to do so, and as I looked behind mine I saw the two brothers at the door as though about to leave the room. I leaped, so to speak, between the King's arm-chair and M. le Duc d'Orléans, and whispered in the Regent's ear so as not to be heard by the Prince de Conti:

'Monsieur, look at them. They are going.'

'I know it,' he replied tranquilly.

'Yes,' I exclaimed with animation, 'but do you know what they will do when they are outside?'

'Nothing at all,' said he: 'the Comte de Toulouse has asked me for permission to go out with his brother; he has assured me that they will be discreet.'

'And if they are not?' I asked.

'They will be. But if they are not, they will be well looked after.'

'But if they commit some absurdity, or leave Paris?'

'They will be arrested. Orders have been given, and I will answer for their execution.'

Therefore, more tranquil, I sat down in my place. Scarcely had I got there than the Regent called me back, and said that since they had left the room, he should like to tell the council what was going to be done with respect to them. I replied that the only objection to this, their presence, being now removed—I thought it would be wrong not to do so. He asked M. le Duc in a whisper, across the table,—afterwards called to the Keeper of the Seals; both agreed, and then we really seated ourselves.

These movements had augmented the anxiety and curiosity of every one. The eyes of all, occupied with the Regent, had been removed from the door, so that the absence of the bastards was by no means generally remarked. As soon as it was perceived, everybody looked inquiringly

around, and remained standing in expectation. I sat down in the seat of
the Comte de Toulouse. The Duc de Guiche, who sat on the other side
of me, left a seat between us, and still waited for the bastards. He told me
to approach nearer to him, saying I had mistaken my place. I replied not
a word, looking on at the company, which was a sight to see. At the second
or third summons, I replied that he, on the contrary, must approach me.

'And M. le Comte de Toulouse?' replied he.

'Approach,' said I, and seeing him motionless with astonishment, looking
towards the Duc du Maine's seat, which had been taken by the Keeper of
the Seals, I pulled him by his coat (I was seated), saying to him, 'Come
here and sit down.'

I pulled him so hard that he seated himself near me without understanding aught.

'But what is the meaning of all this?' he demanded; 'where are these
gentlemen?'

'I don't know,' replied I, impatiently; 'but they are not here.'

At the same time, the Duc de Noailles, who sat next to the Duc de
Guiche, and who, enraged at counting for nothing in preparations for such
a great day, had apparently divined that I was in the plot, vanquished by
his curiosity, stretched over the table in front of the Duc de Guise, and
said to me:

'In the name of Heaven, M. le Duc, do me the favour to say what all
this means?'

I was at daggers-drawn with him, as I have explained, and had no
mercy for him. I turned, therefore, towards him with a cold and disdainful
air, and, after having heard him out, and looked at him, I turned away
again. That was all my reply. The Duc de Guiche pressed me to say something, even if it was only that I knew all. I denied it, and yet each seated
himself slowly, because intent only upon looking around, and divining
what all this could mean, and because it was a long time before any one
could comprehend that we must proceed to business without the bastards,
although nobody opened his mouth.

When everybody was in his place, M. le Duc d'Orléans after having for
a moment looked all around, every eye fixed upon him, said that he had
assembled this regency council to hear read the resolutions adopted at the
last; that he had come to the conclusion there was no other means of
obtaining the registration of the finance edict recently passed than that
of holding a Bed of Justice; that the heat rendering it unadvisable to
jeopardise the King's health in the midst of the crowd of the Palais de
Justice, he had thought it best to follow the example of the late King, who

had sometimes sent for the Parliament to the Tuileries; that, as it had become necessary to hold this Bed of Justice, he had thought it right to profit by the occasion, and register the *lettres de provision* of the Keeper of the Seals at the commencement of the sitting; and he ordered the Keeper of the Seals to read them.

During this reading, which had no other importance than to seize an occasion of forcing the Parliament to recognise the Keeper of the Seals, whose person and whose commission they hated, I occupied myself in examining the faces.

I saw M. le Duc d'Orléans with an air of authority and of attention, so new that I was struck with it. M. le Duc, gay and brilliant, appeared quite at his ease, and confident. The Prince de Conti, astonished, absent, meditative, seemed to see nothing and to take part in nothing. The Keeper of the Seals, grave and pensive, appeared to have too many things in his head; nevertheless, with bag, wax, and seals near him, he looked very decided and very firm. The Duc de la Force hung his head, but examined on the sly the faces of us all. Maréchal Villeroy and Maréchal de Villars spoke to each other now and then; both had irritated eyes and long faces. Nobody was more composed than the Maréchal de Tallard; but he could not hide an internal agitation which often peeped out. The Maréchal d'Estrées had a stupefied air, as though he saw nothing but a mist before him. The Maréchal de Besons enveloped more than ordinarily in his big wig, appeared deeply meditative, his look cast down and angry. Pelletier, very buoyant, simple, curious, looking at everything. Torcy, three times more starched than usual, seemed to look at everything by stealth. D'Effiat, meddlesome, piqued, outraged, ready to boil over, fuming at everybody, his look haggard, as it passed rapidly, and by fits and starts, from side to side. Those on my side I could not well examine; I saw them only by moments as they changed their postures or I mine; and then not well or for long. I have already spoken of the astonishment of the Duc de Guiche, and of the vexation and curiosity of the Duc de Noailles. D'Antin, usually of such easy carriage, appeared to me as though in fetters, and quite scared. The Maréchal d'Huxelles tried to put a good face on the matter, but could not hide the despair which pierced him. Old Troyes, all abroad, showed nothing but surprise and embarrassment, and did not appear to know where he was.

From the first moment of this reading and the departure of the bastards, everybody saw that something was in preparation against them. What that something was to be, kept every mind in suspense.

After a short but marked pause, the Regent developed, in few words, the reasons which had induced the Council at its last sitting, to abrogate the decree of the Parliament. He added that the Keeper of the Seals would now read to the Council the act of abrogation, and the rules that were to be observed in future. Then, looking at the Keeper of the Seals, 'Monsieur,' said he, 'you will explain this better than I. Have the goodness to do so before reading the decree.'

The Keeper of the Seals then spoke, and paraphrased what his Royal Highness had said more briefly; he explained in what manner the Parliament had the right to remonstrate, showed the distinction between its power and that of the Crown; the incompetence of the tribunals in all matters of state and finance; and the necessity of repressing the remonstrances of Parliament by passing a code (that was the term used), which was to serve as their inviolable guide.

The reading finished, the Regent, contrary to his custom, showed his opinion by the praises he gave to this document: and then, assuming the Regent's tone and air he had never before put on, and which completed the astonishment of the company, he added, 'To-day, gentlemen, I shall deviate from the usual rule in taking your votes, and I think it will be well to do so during all this Council.'

Then after a slight glance upon both sides of the table, during which you might have heard a worm crawl, he turned to M. le Duc and asked him his opinion. M. le Duc declared for the decree, alleging several short but strong reasons. The Prince de Conti spoke in the same sense. I spoke after, for the Keeper of the Seals had done so directly his reading was finished. The Duc de la Force was longer. All spoke, but the majority said but little, and some allowed their vexation to be seen, but did not dare to oppose, feeling that it would be of no use. Dejection was painted upon their faces; it was evident this affair of the Parliament was not what they expected or wished. Tallard was the only one whose face did not betray him; but the suffocated monosyllable of the Maréchal d'Huxelles tore off the rest of the mask. The Duc de Noailles could scarcely contain himself. M. le Duc d'Orléans spoke last, and with unusual force; then made a pause, piercing all the company with his eyes.

These little movements over, M. le Duc d'Orléans, rising a little in his seat, said to the company, in a tone more firm, and more like that of a master than before, that there was another matter now to attend to, much more important than the one just heard. This prelude increased the general astonishment, and rendered everybody motionless. After a moment of silence the Regent said, that the peers had had for some time good grounds of complaints against certain persons, who by unaccustomed favour, had been allowed to assume rank and dignity to which their birth did not entitle them; that it was time this irregularity should be corrected, and that with this view, an instrument had been drawn up, which the Keeper of the Seals would read to them.

A profound silence followed this discourse, so unexpected, and which began to explain the absence of the bastards. Upon many visages a sombre hue was painted. As for me I had enough to do to compose my own visage, upon which all eyes successively passed; I had put upon it an extra coat of gravity and of modesty; I steered my eyes with care, and only looked horizontally at most, not an inch higher. As soon as the Regent opened his mouth on this business, M. le Duc cast upon me a triumphant look which almost routed my seriousness, and which warned me to increase it, and no longer expose myself to meet his glance. Contained in this manner, attentive in devouring the aspect of all, alive to everything and to myself, motionless, glued to my chair, all my body fixed, penetrated with the most acute and most sensible pleasure that joy could impart, with the most charming anxiety, with an enjoyment, so perseveringly and so immoderately hoped for, I sweated with the agony of self control, and this agony was of a voluptuousness such as I had never felt before,—such as I have never felt since. How inferior are the pleasures of the senses to those of the mind!

A moment after the Regent had ceased speaking, he told the Keeper of the Seals to read the declaration.

When it was finished, M. le Duc d'Orléans said he was very sorry for this necessity, but that justice must be done to the peers as well as to the princes of the blood: then turning to the Keeper of the Seals asked him for his opinion.

This latter spake briefly and well; but was like a dog running over hot ashes. He declared for the Declaration. His Royal Highness then called upon M. le Duc for his opinion. It was short, but nervous, and polite to the peers. M. le Prince de Conti the same. Then the Regent asked me my opinion. I made, contrary to my custom, a profound inclination, but without rising, and said, that having the honour to find myself the eldest of the peers of the Council, I offered to his Royal Highness my very humble thanks and those of all the peers of France, for the justice so ardently desired,—and touching so closely our dignity and our persons,—that he had resolved to render us; that I begged him to be persuaded of our gratitude, and to count upon our utmost attachment to his person for an act of equity so longed for, and so complete; that in this sincere expression of our sentiments consisted all our opinion, because, being pleaders, we could not be judges also. I terminated these few words with a profound inclination, without rising, imitated by the Duc de la Force at the same moment; all the rest of the Council briefly gave their opinions, approving what the majority of them evidently did not approve at all.

The opinions taken almost as soon as demanded, M. le Duc d'Orléans said, 'Gentlemen, it is finished, then: justice is done, and the rights of Messieurs the Peers are in safety. I have now an act of grace to propose to you. What I am going to explain to you, regards the Comte de Toulouse alone.

'Nobody is ignorant how he has disapproved all that has been done in favour of him and his brother, and that he has sustained it since the regency only out of respect for the wishes of the late King. Everybody knows also his virtue, his merit, his application, his probity, his disinterestedness. Nevertheless, I could not avoid including him in the declaration you have just heard. Justice furnishes no exception in his favour, and the rights of the Peers must be assured. Now that they are no longer attacked, I have thought fitly to render to merit, what from equity, I have taken from birth; and to make an exception of M. le Comte de Toulouse, which (while confirming the rule), will leave him in full possession of all the honours he enjoys to the exclusion of every other. Those honours are not to pass to his children, should he marry and have any, or their restitution be considered as a precedent to be made use of at any future time.

'I have the pleasure to announce that the Princes of the Blood consent to this, and that such of the Peers to whom I have been able to explain myself, share my sentiments. I doubt not that the esteem he has acquired here will render this proposition agreeable to you.' And then turning to the Keeper of the Seals, 'Monsieur, will you read the declaration?'

It was read at once.

I had, during the discourse of his Royal Highness, thrown all my attention into an examination of the impression it made upon the assembly. Villeroy confounded, Villars raging, Effiat rolling his eyes, Estrées beside himself with surprise, were the most marked. Tallard, with his head stretched forward, sucked in, so to speak, all the Regent's words as they were proffered, and those of the declaration, as the Keeper of the Seals read them. Noailles, inwardly distracted, could not hide his distraction; Huxelles, entirely occupied in smoothing himself, forgot to frown. I divided my attention between the declaration and these persons.

The document read, M. le Duc d'Orléans praised it in two words, and called upon the Keeper of the Seals to give his opinion.

All opinions having been expressed, M. le Duc cast a brilliant leer at me, and prepared to speak. Raising himself majestically from his seat, the

Regent then said: 'Gentlemen, M. le Duc has a proposition to make to you. I have found it just and reasonable; I doubt not, you will find it so too.' Then turning towards M. le Duc, he added, 'Monsieur, will you explain it?'

The movement these few words made among the company is inexpressible. 'Twas as though I saw before me people deprived of all power, and surprised by a new assembly rising up from the midst of them in an asylum they had breathlessly reached.

'Monsieur,' said M. le Duc, addressing himself to the Regent, as usual; 'since you have rendered justice to the Dukes, I think I am justified in asking for it myself. The deceased King gave the education of His Majesty to M. le Duc du Maine. I was a minor then, and according to the idea of the deceased King, M. du Maine was prince of the blood, capable of succeeding to the crown. Now I am of age, and not only M. du Maine is no longer prince of the blood, but he is reduced to the rank of his peerage. M. le Maréchal de Villeroy is now his senior, and precedes him everywhere; M. le Maréchal can therefore no longer remain governor of the King, under the superintendence of M. du Maine. I ask you, then, for M. du Maine's post, that I think my age, my rank, my attachment to the King and the State, qualify me for. I hope,' he added, turning towards his left, 'that I shall profit by the lessons of M. le Maréchal de Villeroy, acquit myself of my duties with distinction, and merit his friendship.'

As soon as M. le Duc had finished, M. le Duc d'Orléans reviewed all the company with his eyes, and then said, that the request of M. le Duc was just; that he did not think it could be refused; that M. le Maréchal de Villeroy could not be allowed to remain under a person whom he preceded in rank; that the superintendence of the King's education could not be more worthily filled than by M. le Duc; and that he was persuaded all would be of one voice in this matter. Immediately afterwards, he asked M. le Prince de Conti to give his opinion, who did so in two words; then he asked the Keeper of the Seals, whose reply was equally brief; then he asked me.

I simply said, looking at M. le Duc, that I was for the change with all my heart. The rest, M. de la Force excepted (who said a single word), voted without speaking, simply bowing; the Marshals and D'Effiat scarcely moved their eyes, and those of Villars glistened with fury.

Maréchal de Villeroy, pale and agitated, muttered to himself. At last, like a man who has made up his mind, he turned with bended head, expiring eyes, and feeble voice, towards the Regent, and said, 'I will simply say these two words; here are all the dispositions of the late king overturned, I cannot see it without grief. M. du Maine is very unfortunate.'

'Monsieur,' replied the Regent, in a loud and animated tone, 'M. du Maine is my brother-in-law, but I prefer an open enemy to a hidden one.'

The Keeper of the Seals, to make a diversion, proposed to read the speech he had prepared to serve as preface to the decree to be read at the Bed of Justice, abrogating the Parliament decrees.

A short time afterwards it was announced to M. le Duc d'Orléans that the Parliament had set out on foot, and had begun to defile through the Palace. This news much cooled the blood of the company, M. le Duc d'Orléans more than that of any one else.

I walked about, slowly and incessantly without fixing myself on any one, in order that nothing should escape me principally attending to the doors. I took advantage of the opportunity to say a word here and a word there, to pass continually near those who were suspected, to skim and interrupt all conversations. I went to break in upon the colloquy of D'Effiat and his friends, and taking them by surprise, caused D'Effiat to say that he had just heard strange resolutions, that he did not know who had advised them, that he prayed that M. d'Orléans would find them advantageous. I replied, agreeing with him. The Maréchal de Villeroy sighed, muttered, and shook his wig, Villars spoke more at length, and blamed sharply what had been done. I assented to everything, being there not to persuade but to watch.

At last the Parliament arrived, and behold us! like children, all at the windows. The members came in red robes, two by two, by the grand door of the court, which they passed in order to reach the Hall of the Ambassadors, where the Chief President, who had come in his carriage with the president Haligre, awaited them.

The Parliament being in its place, a messenger came to inform us that all was ready. As soon as it was announced to the Regent that we could set out, his Royal Highness sent word to the Parliament, to prepare the deputation to receive the King, and then said aloud to the company, that it was time to go in search of His Majesty.

At these words I felt a storm of joy sweep over me, at the thought of the grand spectacle that was going to pass in my presence, which warned me to be doubly on my guard. I tried to furnish myself with the strongest dose of seriousness, gravity, and modesty. I followed M. le Duc d'Orléans, who entered the King's room by the little door, and who found the King in his cabinet. When the Duc d'Orléans had been a few moments with him, he asked him if he would be pleased to go: and the way was instantly cleared, a procession formed, and the King moved towards the Hall of the Swiss Guard.

I now hastened to the chamber, where the Bed of Justice was to be held. I stopped a moment in the passage at the entrance to the room, seized with joy upon seeing this grand spectacle, and at the thought of the grand movement that was drawing nigh I needed a pause in order to recover myself sufficiently to see distinctly what I looked at, and to put on a new coat of seriousness and of modesty.

As soon as I appeared, all eyes were fixed upon me. I slowly advanced towards the chief *greffier*, and introducing myself between the two seats, I traversed the length of the room, in front of the King's people, who saluted me with a smiling air, and I ascended over three rows of high seats, where all the peers were in their places, and who rose as I approached the steps. I respectfully saluted them from the third row.

Seated in my elevated place, and with nothing before me, I was able to glance over the whole assembly. I did so at once piercing everybody with my eyes. One thing alone restrained me; it was that I did not dare to fix my eyes upon certain objects. I feared the fire and brilliant significance of my looks at that moment so appreciated by everybody: and the more I saw I attracted attention, the more anxious was I to kill curiosity by my discreetness. I cast, nevertheless, a glittering glance upon the Chief President and his friends, for the examination of whom I was admirably placed. I carried my looks over all the Parliament, and saw there an astonishment, a silence, a consternation, such as I had not expected, and which was of good augury to me. The Chief President, insolently crest-fallen, the other presidents disconcerted, and attentive to all, furnished me the most agreeable spectacle.

I had but little leisure for this examination, for the King immediately arrived.

When all was ready, Argenson, the Keeper of the Seals, remained some minutes at his desk motionless, looking down, and the fire which sprang from his eyes seemed to burn every breast. An extreme silence eloquently announced the fear, the attention, the trouble, and the curiosity of all the expectants. The Parliament, which under the deceased King had often summoned this same Argenson, and as lieutenant of police had often given him its orders, he standing uncovered at the bar of the house;—the Parliament, which since the Regency had displayed its ill-will towards him so far as to excite public remark, and which still detained prisoners and papers to vex him; this Chief President so superior to him, so haughty, so proud of his Duc du Maine; this Lamoignon, who had boasted he would have him hanged at his chamber of Justice; where he had so completely dishonoured himself;—this Parliament and all saw him clad in the ornaments of the chief office of the robe, presiding over them, effacing them, and entering upon his functions to teach them their duty, to read them a public lesson the first time he found himself at their head.

After the Keeper of the Seals (according to the manner of the preachers) had accustomed himself to this august audience, he uncovered himself, rose, mounted to the King, knelt before the steps of the throne, by the side of the middle of the steps, where the grand chamberlain was lying upon cushions, and took the King's orders, descended, placed himself in his chair and covered himself. Having returned back into his place, he opened, after some moments of silence, this great scene by a discourse. This first discourse, served only as the preface to all the rest.

This first act finished, the second was announced by the discourse of the Keeper of the Seals, the force of which penetrated all the Parliament. General consternation spread itself over their faces. Scarcely one of the members dared to speak to his neighbour. Bitter grief, obviously full of vexation, obscured the visage of the Chief President. Shame and confusion were painted there.

After the vote, and when the Keeper of the Seals had pronounced, I saw the principal members of the Parliament in commotion. The Chief President was about to speak. He did so by uttering the remonstrance of the Parliament, full of the most subtle and impudent malice against the Regent, and of insolence against the King. The villain trembled, nevertheless, in pronouncing it. His voice broken, his eyes constrained, his flurry and confusion, contradicted the venomous words he uttered; libations he could not abstain from offering to himself and his company. This was the moment when I relished, with delight utterly impossible to express, the sight of these haughty lawyers (who had dared to refuse us the salutation), prostrated upon their knees, and rendering, at our feet, homage to the throne, whilst we sat covered upon elevated seats, at the side of that same throne. These situations and these postures, so widely disproportioned, plead of themselves with all the force of evidence, the cause of those who are really and truly *laterales regis* against this *vas electum* of the third estate. My eyes fixed, glued, upon these haughty bourgeois, with their uncovered heads humiliated to the level of our feet, traversed the chief members kneeling or standing, and the ample folds of those fur robes of rabbit-skin that would imitate ermine, which waved at each long and re-doubled genuflexion; genuflexions which only finished by command of the King.

The remonstrance being finished, the Keeper of the Seals mentioned to the King their wishes, asking further opinions; took his place again; cast his eyes on the Chief President, and said: *The King wishes to be obeyed, and obeyed immediately.*

This grand speech was a thunder-bolt which overturned councillors and presidents in the most marked manner. All of them lowered their heads, and the majority kept them lowered for a long time. The rest of the spectators, except the Marshals of France, appeared little affected by this desolation.

But this—an ordinary triumph—was nothing to that which was to follow. After an interval of some few minutes, the Keeper of the Seals went up again to the King, returned to his place, and remained there in silence some little time. Then everybody clearly saw that the Parliamentary affair being finished, something else must be in the wind. Some thought that a dispute which the Dukes had had with the Parliament, concerning one of its usurpations, was now to be settled in our favour. Others who had noticed the absence of the bastards, guessed it was something that affected them; but nobody divined what, much less its extent.

At last the Keeper of the Seals opened his mouth, and in his first sentence announced the fall of one brother and the preservation of the other. The effect of this upon every one was inexpressible. Astonishment prevailed over every other sentiment. Many appeared glad, either from hatred to the Duc du Maine, or from affection for the Comte de Toulouse; several were in consternation. The Chief President lost all countenance; his visage, so self-sufficient and so audacious, was seized with a convulsive movement; the excess alone of his rage kept him from swooning. It was even worse at the reading of the declaration. Each word was legislative and decreed a fresh fall. The attention was general; every one was motionless, so as not to lose a word; all eyes were fixed upon the *greffier* who was reading. A third of this reading over, the Chief President, gnashing the few teeth left in his head, rested his forehead upon his stick that he held in both hands, and in this singular and marked position finished listening to the declaration, so overwhelming for him, so resurrectionary for us.

As for me, I was dying with joy. I was so oppressed that I feared I should swoon; my heart dilated to excess, and no longer found room to beat. The violence I did myself, in order to let nothing escape me, was infinite; and, nevertheless, this torment was delicious. I compared the years and the time of servitude; the grievous days, when dragged at the tail of the Parliamentary car as a victim, I had served as a triumph for the bastards; the various steps by which they had mounted to the summit above our heads; I compared them, I say, to this court of justice and of rule, to this frightful fall which, at the same time, raised us by the force of the shock. I thanked myself that it was through me this had been brought about. I had triumphed, I was revenged; I swam in my vengeance; I enjoyed the full accomplishment of desires the most vehement and the most continuous of all my life. I was tempted to fling away all thought and care. Nevertheless, I did not fail to listen to this vivifying reading (every note of which sounded upon my heart as the bow upon an instrument), or to examine, at the same time, the impressions it made upon every one.

During the registration I gently passed my eyes over the whole assembly, and though I constantly constrained them, I could not resist the temptation to indemnify myself upon the Chief President; I perseveringly overwhelmed him, therefore, a hundred different times during the sitting, with my hard-hitting regards. Insult, contempt, disdain, triumph, were darted at him from my eyes, and pierced him to the very marrow: often he lowered his eyes when he caught my gaze: once or twice he raised his upon me, and I took pleasure in annoying him by sly but malicious smiles which completed his vexation. I bathed myself in his rage, and amused myself by making him feel it. I sometimes played with him by pointing him out to my two neighbours when he could perceive this movement; in a word, I pressed upon him without mercy, as heavily as I could.

Saint-Simon's hatred of the Duc du Maine causes him to give an account of the Cellamare conspiracy which is contradicted by reliable contemporary evidence. So far was the Duc du Maine from being the chief plotter that his wife later on confessed that one of the difficulties was to keep her husband in ignorance of what was going on. The unfortunate Duc du Maine's sin, such as it was, consisted in his failure to control his uncontrollable Duchess.

It was scarcely to be expected, perhaps, that M. du Maine would remain altogether quiet under the disgrace which had been heaped upon him by the proceedings at the Bed of Justice. Soon indeed we found that he had been secretly working out the most perfidious and horrible schemes for a long time before that assembly; and that after his fall, he gave himself up with redoubled energy to his devilish devices.

Towards the end of this memorable year, 1718, it was discovered that Alberoni, by means of Cellamare, Spanish ambassador at our Court, was preparing a plot against the Regent. The scheme was nothing less than to throw all the realm into revolt against the government of M. le Duc d'Orléans; to put the King of Spain at the head of the affairs of France, with a council and ministers named by him, and a lieutenant, who would in fact have been Regent; this self-same lieutenant to be no other than the Duc du Maine!

This precious plot was, fortunately, discovered before it had come to maturity. Had such not happened, the consequences might have been very serious, although they could scarcely have been fatal. The conspirators counted upon the Parliaments of Paris and of Brittany, upon all the old Court accustomed to the yoke of the bastards, and to that of Madame de Maintenon; and they flung about promises with an unsparing hand to all who supported them.

Cellamare was Spanish ambassador at our Court. He had been one of the chief movers in the plot. He had excited, as much as lay in his power, discontent against the Regent's government; he had done his best to embroil France with Spain; he had worked heart and soul with M. du Maine, to carry out the common end they had in view. So much preparation had been made; so much of the treason train laid, that at last it became necessary to send to Alberoni a full and clear account of all that had been done, so as to paint exactly the position of affairs, and determine the measures that remained to be taken. But how to send such an account as this? To trust it to the ordinary channels of communication would have been to run a great risk of exposure and detection. To send it by private hand would have been suspicious, if the hand were known, and dangerous if it were not: Cellamare had long since provided for this difficulty.

He had caused a young ecclesiastic to be sent from Spain, who came to Paris as though for his pleasure. There he was introduced to young Monteléon, son of a former ambassador at our Court, who had been much liked. The young ecclesiastic was called the Abbé Portocarrero, a name regarded with favour in France. Monteléon came from the Hague, and was going to Madrid. Portocarrero came from Madrid, and was going back there. What more natural than that the two young men should travel in company? What less natural than that the two young men, meeting each other by pure accident in Paris, should be charged by the ambassador with any packet of consequence, he having his own couriers, and the use, for the return journey, of those sent to him from Spain?

They set out, then, at the commencement of December, furnished with passports from the King—with a Spanish banker, who had been established in England, where he had become bankrupt for a large amount, so that the English government had obtained permission from the Regent to arrest him, if they could, anywhere in France.

Whether the arrival of Portocarrero in Paris, and his short stay there, seemed suspicious to Dubois and his emissaries, or whether he had corrupted some of the principal people of the Spanish ambassador and this Court, and learned that these young men were charged with a packet of importance; whether there was no other mystery than the bad company of the bankrupt banker, and that the anxiety of Dubois to oblige his friends the English, induced him to arrest the three travellers and seize their papers, lest the banker should have confided his to the young men, I know not: but however it may have been, it is certain that he arrested the three travellers at Poitiers, and carried off their papers, a courier bringing these papers to him immediately afterwards.

The day after the arrival of the courier from Poitiers, Cellamare, informed of what had occurred, but who flattered himself that the presence of the banker had caused the arrest of the young men, and the seizure of their papers, hid his fears under a very tranquil bearing, and went, at one o'clock in the day, to M. le Blanc, to ask for a packet of letters he had entrusted to Portocarrero and Monteléon on their return to Spain. Le Blanc (who had had his lesson prepared beforehand by the Abbé Dubois) replied that the packet had been seen; that it contained important things, and that, far from being restored to him, he himself must go back to his hotel under escort, to meet Dubois.

During the three hours, passed in his house, in the examination of all his bureaux and his boxes, and his papers, Cellamare treated M. le Blanc very civilly; as for the Abbé Dubois, with whom he felt he had no measure to keep (all the plot being discovered), he affected to treat him with the utmost disdain.

When all was examined, the King's seal, and that of the ambassador, were put upon all the bureaux and the caskets which contained papers. The Abbé Dubois and Le Blanc went off together to give an account of their proceedings to the Regent, leaving a company of musketeers to guard the ambassador and his household.

I heard of the capture effected at Poitiers, at home, the morning after it occurred, without knowing anything of those arrested. As I was at table, a servant came to me from M. le Duc d'Orléans, summoning me to a council of the regency, at four o'clock that day. He opened the council with a discourse upon the people and the papers seized at Poitiers, the latter proving that a very dangerous conspiracy against the State was on the eve of breaking, and of which the ambassador of Spain was the principal promoter. He explained the orders he had given so as to inform all the foreign ministers in Paris of what had occurred, and had ordered Dubois to render an account to the council of what he had done at the ambassador's, and offered to read the letters from Cellamare to Cardinal Alberoni, found among the papers brought from Poitiers.

The Abbé Dubois stammered out a short and ill-arranged recital of what he had done at the ambassador's house, and dwelt upon the importance of the discovery and upon that of the conspiracy as far as already known. We were much scandalised with the expressions in these letters against M. le Duc d'Orléans, who was in no way spared.

This prince spoke again, to say he did not suspect the King or Queen of Spain to be mixed up in this affair, but that he attributed it all to the passion of Alberoni, and that of his ambassador to please him, and that he would ask for justice from their Catholic Majesties.

On Tuesday, the 13th of December, in the afternoon, Cellamare was placed in a coach with two officers, chosen to conduct him to Blois, until Saint Aignan, our ambassador in Spain, should arrive in France.

On Sunday, the 25th of December, Christmas Day, M. le Duc d'Orléans sent for me to come and see him at the Palais Royal, about four o'clock in the afternoon. I went accordingly, and after despatching some business with him, other people being present, I followed him into his little winter cabinet at the end of the little gallery, M. le Duc being present.

M. le Duc d'Orléans said that we should not be surprised to learn that M. and Madame du Maine had been mixed up all along with this affair of the Spanish ambassador Cellamare; that he had written proofs of this, and that the project was exactly that which I have already described, and he finished by saying that he wished, above all things, to consult M. le Duc and me upon the course he ought to adopt.

M. le Duc said M. and Madame du Maine must at once be arrested and put where they could cause no apprehension. I supported this opinion, and showed the perilous annoyances that might arise if this step were not instantly taken. Our advice was accepted by M. le Duc d'Orléans, after some little debate. But now the question arose, where are the prisoners to be put? The Bastille and Vincennes both seemed to me too near to Paris. Several places were named without one appearing to suit. At last, M. le Duc d'Orléans mentioned Dourlens. I stopped him short at the name, and recommended it warmly. Upon this it was agreed to send M. du Maine to Dourlens.

Then we had to fix upon a place for his wife, and this was more difficult; there were her sex, her fiery temper, her courage, her daring,—all to be considered; whereas, her husband, we knew, so dangerous as a hidden enemy, was contemptible without his mask, and would fall into the lowest state of dejection in prison, trembling all over with the fear of the scaffold, and attempting nothing; his wife, on the contrary, being capable of attempting anything.

Various places discussed, M. le Duc d'Orléans smiled, and proposed the château of Dijon! Now, the joke of this suggestion was, that Dijon belonged to M. le Duc, and that he was nephew of Madame du Maine, whom the Regent proposed to lock up there! M. le Duc smiled also, and said it was a little too bad to make him the gaoler of his aunt! But all things considered, it was found that a better choice than Dijon could not be made, so M. le Duc gave way.

On Wednesday we assembled again. Our conference was long, and the result of it was, that M. and Madame du Maine were to be arrested on the morrow.

The morrow, about ten o'clock in the morning, having noiselessly and without show placed the body-guard around Sceaux, La Billardière, lieutenant of the regiment, entered there, and arrested the Duc du Maine as he was leaving his chapel after hearing mass, and very respectfully begged him not to re-enter the house, but to mount immediately into a coach which he had brought. M. du Maine, who had expected this arrest, and who had had time to put his papers in order, made not the slightest resistance. He replied that he had anticipated this compliment for some days, and at once moved into the coach. La Billardière placed himself by his side, and in front was a warrant officer of the body-guards, and Favancourt, brigadier in the first company of musketeers, destined to guard him in his prison.

As these two latter persons did not appear before the Duc du Maine until the moment he entered the coach, he appeared surprised and moved to see Favancourt. He would not have been at the warrant officer, but the sight of the other depressed him. He asked La Billardière what this meant. Billardière could not dissimulate that Favancourt had orders to accompany him, and to remain with him in the place to which they were going. Favancourt himself took this moment to pay his compliments as best he might to the Duc du Maine, to which the Duc replied but little, and that in a civil and apprehensive manner. These proceedings conducted them to the end of the avenue of Sceaux, where the body-guards appeared. The sight of them made the Duc du Maine change colour.

Silence was but little interrupted in the coach. Now and then M. du Maine would say that he was very innocent of the accusation which had been formed against him. He took his meals in the coach, ate very little, was alone at night, but with good precautions taken. He did not know until the morrow that he was going to Dourlens. He showed no emotion thereupon.

At the moment of the arrest of M. du Maine, Ancenis, captain of the body-guard, arrested the Duchesse du Maine in her house in the Rue St. Honoré. A lieutenant, and warrant officer of the foot body-guards, with other troops, took possession of the house at the same time, and guarded the doors. The compliment of the Duc d'Ancenis was sharply received. Madame du Maine wished to take away some caskets. Ancenis objected. She demanded, at the least, her jewels; altercations very strong on one side, very modest on the other: but she was obliged to yield. She delayed her departure as long as she could, despite the instances of Ancenis, who at last presented his hand to her, and politely, but firmly, said she must go. She found at her door two six-horse coaches, the sight of which much shocked her. She was obliged, however, to mount. Ancenis placed himself by her side, the lieutenant and the warrant officer of the guard in front, two chambermaids whom she had chosen were in the other coach, with her apparel, which had been examined. The ramparts were followed, the principal streets avoided; there was no stir, and at this she could not restrain her surprise and vexation, or check a tear, declaiming by fits and starts against the violence done her. She complained of the rough coach, the indignity it cast upon her, and from time to time asked where she was being led to. She was simply told that she would sleep at Essonne, nothing more. Her three guardians maintained profound silence. At night all possible precautions were taken. When she set out the next day, the Duc d'Ancenis took leave of her, and left her to the lieutenant, and to the warrant officer of the body-guards, with troops to conduct her. She asked where they were leading her to: he simply replied, 'To Fontainebleau'. The disquietude of Madame du Maine augmented as she left Paris farther behind, but when she found herself in Burgundy, and knew at last she was to go to Dijon, she stormed at a fine rate.

1719

It was worse when she was forced to enter the castle, and found herself the prisoner of M. le Duc. Fury suffocated her. She raged against her nephew, and the horrible place chosen for her. Nevertheless, after her first transports, she returned to herself, and began to comprehend that she was in no place and no condition to play the fury. Her extreme rage she kept to herself, affected nothing but indifference for all, and disdainful of the precaution for her security. The King's lieutenant of the castle, absolutely devoted to M. le Duc, kept her fast, and closely watched her and her chambermaids. The Prince de Dombes and the Comte d'Eu (her sons) were at the same time exiled to Eu, where a gentleman in ordinary always was near them; Mademoiselle du Maine was sent to Maubuisson.

The commotion caused by the arrest and imprisonment of M. and Madame du Maine was great; many faces, already elongated by the Bed of Justice, were still further pulled out by these events.

As for the Comte de Toulouse he remained as upright and loyal as ever. The very day of the double arrest he came to M. le Duc d'Orléans and said that he regarded the King, the Regent, and the State as one and the same thing; that he should never be wanting in his duty or in his fidelity towards them; that he was very sorry for what had happened to his brother, but that he was in no way answerable for him. The Regent stated this to me the same day, and appeared, with reason, to be charmed with such straightforward honesty.

Let me finish at once with all I shall have to say respecting M. and Madame du Maine.

They remained in their prison during the whole of the year 1719, supplied with all the comforts and attentions befitting their state, and much less rigorously watched than at first, thanks to the easy disposition of M. le Duc d'Orléans, whose firmness yielded even more rapidly than beauty to the effects of time. The consequence of his indulgence towards the two conspirators was, that at about the commencement of the following year, 1720, they began to play a very ridiculous comedy, of which not a soul was the dupe, not even the public, nor the principal actors, nor the Regent.

Madame du Maine, supported by her sex and birth, muffled herself up in her dignity, protected as much as possible her friends, her husband above all, by charging herself with all; by declaring that what she had done M. du Maine had no knowledge of; and that its object went no farther than to obtain from the Regent such reforms in his administration as were wanted.

The Duc du Maine, shorn of his rank and of his title of prince of the blood, trembled for his life. His crimes against the state,—against the blood royal,—against the person of the Regent, so long, so artfully, and so cruelly offended, troubled him all the more because he felt they deserved severe punishment. He soon, therefore, conceived the idea of screening himself beneath his wife's petticoats. His replies, and all his observations were to the same tune; perfect ignorance of everything. Therefore when the Duchesse had made her confessions, and they were communicated to him, he cried out against his misfortune in having a wife capable of conspiring, and daring enough to implicate him in everything without having spoken to him; making him thus a criminal without being so the least in the world; and keeping him so ignorant of her doings, that it was out of his power to stop them, to chide her, or inform M. le Duc d'Orléans if things had been pushed so far that he ought to have done so!

From that time the Duc du Maine would no longer hear talk of a woman who, without his knowledge, had cast him and his children into this abyss; and when at their release from prison, they were permitted to write and send messages to each other, he would receive nothing from her, or give any signs of life. They were at this point when they were allowed to come near Paris. M. du Maine went to live at Clagny, a château near Versailles, built for Madame de Montespan. Madame du Maine went to Sceaux. They came separately to see M. le Duc d'Orléans at Paris, without sleeping there; both played their parts, and as the Abbé Dubois judged the time had come to take credit to himself in their eyes for finishing their disgrace, he easily persuaded M. le Duc d'Orléans to appear convinced of the innocence of M. du Maine.

During their stay in the two country-houses above-named, where they saw but little company, Madame du Maine made many attempts at reconciliation with her husband, which he repelled. This farce lasted from the month of January (when they arrived at Sceaux and at Clagny) to the end of July. Then they thought the game had lasted long enough to be put an end to.

At last the resolution being taken to put an end to the comedy, this is how it was terminated by another.

Madame la Princesse made an appointment with the Duc du Maine at Vaugirard on the last of July, and in the house of Landais, treasurer of difficult to undersand; the piece had been well studied. The Duchesse du Maine, whom she left in her carriage. She said to M. du Maine she had brought a lady with her who much desired to see him. The thing was not difficult to understand; the piece had been well studied. The Duchesse du Maine was sent for. The apparent reconcilement took place. The three were a long time together. To play out the comedy, M. and Madame du Maine still kept apart, but saw and approached each other by degrees, until at last the former returned to Sceaux, and lived with his wife as before.

About this time appeared some verses under the title of *Philippiques*, which were distributed with extraordinary promptitude and abundance. La Grange, formerly page of Madame la Princesse de Conti, was the author, and did not deny it. All that Hell could vomit forth, true and false, was expressed in the most beautiful verses, most poetic in style, and with all the art and talent imaginable. M. le Duc d'Orléans knew it, and wished to see the poem, but he could not succeed in getting it, for no one dared to show it to him.

He spoke of it several times to me, and at last demanded with such earnestness that I should bring it to him, that I could not refuse. I brought it to him accordingly, but read it to him I declared I never would. He took it, therefore, and read it in a low tone, standing in the window of his little winter cabinet, where we were.

'Ah,' said he, 'this is too much, this horrible poem beats me completely——'

He was at the part where the scoundrel shows M. le Duc d'Orléans having the design to poison the King, and quite ready to execute his crime.

I never saw a man so penetrated, so deeply touched, so overwhelmed with injustice so enormous and sustained. As for me, I could not contain myself. To see him, the most prejudiced, if of good faith, would have been convinced he was innocent of the crime imputed to him, by the horror he displayed at it. I have said all, when I state that I recovered myself with difficulty, and that I had all the pains in the world to compose him a little.

This La Grange was arrested shortly afterwards, and sent to the Isles of Sainte Marguerite, which he obtained permission to leave before the end of the Regency. He had the audacity to show himself everywhere in Paris, and while he was appearing at the theatres and in all public places, people had the impudence to spread the report that M. le Duc d'Orléans had had him killed! M. le Duc d'Orléans and his enemies have been equally indefatigable; the latter in the blackest villainies, the Prince in the most unfruitful clemency, to call it by no more expressive name.

On Saturday evening, the 15th of April, 1719, Madame de Maintenon died at St. Cyr. What a stir this event would have made in Europe, had it happened a few years earlier!

I have already said so much respecting this woman, so unfortunately famous, that I will say but little more now. Her life at St. Cyr was divided between her spiritual duties, the letters she received from her religious correspondents, and the answers she gave to them. She took the communion twice a-week, ordinarily between seven and eight o'clock in the morning; not, as Dangeau says in his *Mémoires*, at midnight or every day. She was very rich, having four thousand livres pension per month from the Regent, besides other emoluments. She had, too, her estate at

Maintenon, and some other property. With all this wealth, too, she had not a farthing of expense at St. Cyr. Everything was provided for herself and servants and their horses, even wood, coals, and candles. She had nothing to buy, except dress for herself and for her people. She kept a steward, a valet, people for the horses and the kitchen, a coach, seven or eight horses, one or two others for the saddle, besides having the young ladies of Saint Cyr, chambermaids, and Mademoiselle d'Aumale to wait upon her.

The fall of the Duc du Maine at the Bed of Justice struck the first blow at her. It is not too much to presume that she was well informed of the measures and the designs of this darling, and that this hope had sustained her; but when she saw him arrested she succumbed; continuous fever seized her, and she died at eighty-three years of age, in the full possession of all her intellect.

Madame la Duchesse de Berry was living as usual, when lo! she fell ill at the Luxembourg.

She was in the family-way by Rion, but hid it as much as she could. Madame de Mouchy was their go-between, although her conduct was as clear as day. Rion and Mouchy, in fact, were in love with each other, and had innumerable facilities for indulging their passion. They laughed at the Princesse, who was their dupe, and from whom they drew in council all they could.

The illness of Madame la Duchesse de Berry came on, and this illness, ill prepared for by suppers washed down by wine and strong liquors, became stormy and dangerous. The danger increasing, Languet, a celebrated curé of Saint-Sulpice, who had always rendered himself assiduous, spoke of the sacraments to M. le Duc d'Orléans. The difficulty was how to propose them to Madame la Duchesse de Berry. But another and greater difficulty soon appeared. The curé, like a man knowing his duty, refused to administer the sacrament, or to suffer it to be administered, while Rion or Madame de Mouchy remained in the chamber, or even in the Luxembourg.

He declared this aloud before everybody, expressly in presence of M. le Duc d'Orléans, who was less shocked than embarrassed. He took the curé aside, and for a long time tried to make him give way. Seeing him inflexible, he proposed reference to the Cardinal de Noailles. The curé immediately agreed, and promised to defer to his orders, Noailles being his bishop, provided he was allowed to explain his reasons.

The Cardinal de Noailles arrived; M. le Duc d'Orléans took him aside with the curé, and their conversation lasted more than half an hour. As the declaration of the curé had been public, the Cardinal Archbishop of Paris judged it fitting that his should be so also. As all three approached the door of the chamber, filled with company, the Cardinal de Noailles said aloud to the curé, that he had very worthily done his duty, and that if he wanted further authorisation he prohibited him from administering the sacraments, or allowing them to be administered, to Madame la Duchesse de Berry while Rion and Mouchy were in the chamber, or even in the Luxembourg.

Now came the question between the Regent, the Cardinal, and curé, which should announce this determination to Madame la Duchesse de Berry, who in no way expected it, and who, having confessed, expected every moment to see the Holy Sacrament enter, and to take it. After a short colloquy urged on by the state of the patient, the Cardinal and the curé withdrew a little, while M. le Duc d'Orléans slightly opened the door and called Madame de Mouchy.

The conclusion was that Mouchy undertook to announce to Madame la Duchesse de Berry the resolution that had been taken respecting the sacraments: what she added of her own may be imagined. A negative response did not fail to be quickly delivered to M. le Duc d'Orléans through the half-opened door. Coming through such a messenger, it was just the reply he might have expected. Immediately after, he repeated it to the Cardinal, and to the curé; the curé being supported by his archbishop, contented himself with shrugging his shoulders. But the Cardinal said to M. le Duc d'Orléans that Madame de Mouchy, one of the two who ought to be sent away, was not a fit person to bring Madame la Duchesse to reason; that it was his duty to carry this message to her, and to exhort her to do her duty as a Christian shortly about to appear before God; and the Archbishop pressed the Regent to go and say so to her. It will be believed, without difficulty, that his eloquence gained nothing. This Prince feared his daughter too much, and would have been but a feeble apostle with her.

Reiterated refusals determined the Cardinal to go and speak to Madame la Duchesse de Berry, accompanied by the curé, and as he wished to set about it at once, M. le Duc d'Orléans, who did not dare to hinder him, but who feared some sudden and dangerous revulsion in his daughter at the sight and at the discourses of the two pastors, conjured him to wait until preparations could be made to receive him. He went, therefore, and held another colloquy through the door with Madame de Mouchy, the success of which was equal to the other. Madame la Duchesse de Berry flew into fury, railed in unruly terms against these hypocritical humbugs, who took advantage of her state and their calling to dishonour her by an unheard-of scandal, not in the least sparing her father for his stupidity and feebleness in allowing it. To have heard her, you would have thought that the curé and the Cardinal ought to be kicked downstairs.

M. le Duc d'Orléans returned to the ecclesiastics, looking very small, and not knowing what to do between his daughter and them. However, he said to them that she was so weak and suffering that they must put off their visit, persuading them as well as he could.

The Cardinal, seeing that he could not enter the chamber without a sort of violence, much opposed to persuasion, thought it indecent and useless to wait any longer. In going away, he reiterated his orders to the curé, and begged him to watch so as not to be deceived respecting the sacraments. M. le Duc d'Orléans hastened to announce to his daughter the departure of the Cardinal, at which he himself was much relieved. But on leaving the chamber he was astonished to find the curé glued against the door, and still more so to hear that he had taken up his post there, and meant to remain, happen what might, because he did not wish to be deceived respecting the sacraments. And, indeed, he remained there four days and four nights, except during short intervals for food and repose that he took at home, quite close to the Luxembourg, and during which his place was filled by two priests whom he left there. At last, the danger being passed, he raised the siege.

Her illness had begun on the 26th of March, 1719, and Easter day fell on the 9th of April.

In order to steer clear of Easter, the Duchesse resolved to go away to Meudon on Easter Monday. It was in vain that the danger was represented to her, of the air, of the movement of the coach, and of the change of place at the end of a fortnight.

The premature journey to Meudon was not calculated to re-establish a person just returned from the gates of death. The extreme desire she had to hide her state from the public, and to conceal the terms on which she was with her father (for the rarity of his visits to her began to be remarked), induced her to give a supper to him on the terrace of Meudon about eight o'clock one evening.

This supper in the open air did not succeed. The same night she was taken ill. She grew disgusted with Meudon, like people ill in body and mind, who in their grief attribute everything to the air and the place. She was annoyed at the few visits she received from M. le Duc and Madame la Duchesse d'Orléans,—her pride, however, suffering more than her tenderness.

In despite of all reason, nothing could hinder her from changing her abode. She was transferred from Meudon to the Muette, wrapped up in sheets, and in a large coach, on Sunday, the 14th of May, 1719. Arrived so near Paris, she hoped M. le Duc and Madame la Duchesse d'Orléans would come and see her more frequently, if only for form's sake.

This journey was painful by the sufferings it caused her, added to those she already had, which no remedies could appease, except for short intervals, and which became very violent. Her illness augmented; but hopes and fears sustained her until the commencement of July. The month of July brought augmentation of pain and fever. These ills increased so much, in fact, that, by the 14th of July, fears for her life began to be felt.

The night of the 14th was so stormy, that M. le Duc d'Orléans was sent to at the Palais Royal, and awakened. At the same time Madame de Pons wrote to Madame de Saint-Simon, pressing her to come and establish herself at the Muette. Madame de Saint-Simon, although she made a point of scarcely ever sleeping under the same roof as Madame la Duchesse de Berry, complied at once with this request.

Upon arriving, she found the danger great. Madame la Duchesse de Berry had been bled in the arm and in the foot on the 10th, and her confessor had been sent for. But the malady still went on increasing. As the pain which had so long afflicted her could not induce her to follow a regimen necessary for her condition, or to think of a future state, relations and doctors were at last obliged to speak a language to her, not used towards princesses, except at the most urgent extremity. This, at last, had its effect. She submitted to the medical treatment prescribed for her, and received the sacrament with open doors, speaking to those present upon her life and upon her state, but like a queen in both instances. After this sight was over, alone with her familiars, she applauded herself for the firmness she had displayed, asked them if she had not spoken well, and if she was not dying with greatness and courage.

A day or two after, she wished to receive Our Lord once more. She received, accordingly, and as it appeared, with much piety, quite differently from the first time.

While the end was yet approaching, Madame de Saint-Simon, seeing that there was no one to bear M. le Duc d'Orléans company, sent for me. I was not altogether useless to him in relieving his grief. The rest of the day was passed in entering for a moment at a time into the sick chamber. In the evening I was nearly always alone with him.

The night was well advanced, and Madame la Duchesse de Berry grew worse and worse. M. le Duc d'Orléans returned into the chamber, approached the head of the bed—all the curtains being pulled back; I allowed him to remain there but a few moments, and hurried him into the cabinet, which was deserted just then. The windows were open, he leaned upon the iron balustrade, and his tears increased so much that I feared lest they should suffocate him. When this attack had a little subsided, he began to talk of the misfortunes of this world, and of the short duration of its most agreeable pleasures. I urged the occasion to say to him everything God gave me the power to say, with all the gentleness, emotion, and tenderness, I could command. Not only did he receive well what I said to him, but he replied to it and prolonged the conversation.

At last, about midnight, on the 21st of July, 1719, Madame la Duchesse de Berry died. M. le Duc d'Orléans was the only person touched. Some people grieved; but not one of them who had enough to live upon appeared ever to regret her loss. I have little need to say anything more of Madame la Duchesse de Berry. These pages have already painted her. She was a strange mixture of pride and shamelessness. Drunkenness, filthy conversation, debauchery of the vilest kind, and impiety, were her diversions, varied, as has been seen, by occasional religious fits. Her indecency in everything, language, acts, behaviour, passed all bounds; and yet her pride was so sublime that she could not endure that people should dare to speak of her amid her depravity, so universal and so public; she had the hardihood to declare that nobody had the right to speak of persons of her rank, or blame their most notorious actions!

Yet she had by nature a superior intellect, and, when she wished, could be agreeable and amiable. Her face was commanding, though somewhat spoiled at last by fat. She had much eloquence, speaking with an ease and precision that charmed and overpowered. What might she not have become, with the talents she possessed! But her pride, her violent temper, her irreligion, and her falsehood, spoiled all, and made her what we have seen her.

Law had established his Mississippi Company, and now began to do marvels with it. A sort of language had been invented, to talk of this scheme, language which, however, I shall no more undertake to explain than the other finance operations. Everybody was mad upon Mississippi Stock.

Law often pressed me to receive some shares for nothing, but I never would lend myself to it. The Regent attacked me more than once, but I always eluded him.

At last, one day when we were together by appointment, at Saint Cloud, seated upon the balustrade of the orangery, which covers the descent into the wood of the goulottes, the Regent spoke again to me of the Mississippi, and pressed me to receive some shares from Law.

The more I resisted, the more he pressed me, and argued; at last he grew angry, and said that I was too conceited, thus to refuse what the king wished to give me (for everything was done in the King's name), while so many of my equals in rank and dignity were running after these shares. I replied that such conduct would be that of a fool, the conduct of impertinence, rather than of conceit; that it was not mine, and that since he pressed me so much I would tell him my reasons. They were, that since the fable of Midas, I had nowhere read, still less seen, that anybody had the faculty of converting into gold all he touched; that I did not believe this virtue was given to Law, but thought that all his knowledge was a learned trick, a new and skilful juggle, which put the wealth of Peter into the pockets of Paul, and which enriched one at the expense of the other; that sooner or later the game would be played out, that an infinity of people would be ruined; finally, that I abhorred to gain at the expense of others, and would in no way mix myself up with the Mississippi scheme.

M. le Duc d'Orléans distributed a large number of the Company's shares to all the general officers and others employed in the war against Spain. A month after, the value of the specie was diminished; then the whole of the coin was re-cast. Day by day Law's bank and his Mississippi increased in favour. The confidence in them was complete. People could not change their lands and their houses into paper fast enough, and the result of this paper was, that everything became dear beyond all previous experience.

1720

About the commencement of the new year, 1720, the system of Law approached its end. If he had been content with his bank—his bank within wise and proper limits—the money of the realm might have been doubled, and an extreme facility afforded to commerce and to private enterprise, because, the establishment always being prepared to meet its liabilities, the notes it issued would have been as good as ready money, and sometimes even preferable, on account of the facility of transport. It must be admitted, however, as I declared to M. le Duc d'Orléans in his cabinet, and as I openly said in the Council of the Regency when the bank passed there, that good as this establishment might be in itself, it could only be so in a republic, or in a monarchy, like that of England, where the finances are absolutely governed by those who furnish them, and who simply furnish as much or as little as they please; but in a trivial, changing, and more than absolute state like France, solidity necessarily is wanting, consequently confidence (at least of a discreet and proper kind): since a king, and under his name, a mistress, a minister, favourites; still more, extreme necessities, such as the deceased King experienced in the years 1707–8–9 and 10,—a hundred things, in fact, could overthrow the bank, the allurements of which were, at once, too great and too easy. But to add to the reality of this bank, the chimera of the Mississippi, with its shares, its special jargon, its science (a continual juggle for drawing money from one person to give it to another), was almost to guarantee that these shares should at last end in smoke (since we had neither mines, nor quarries of the philosopher's stone), and that the few would be enriched at the expense of the many, as in fact happened.

What hastened the fall of the bank, and of the system, was the inconceivable prodigality of M. le Duc d'Orléans, who, without bounds, and worse still, if it can be, without choice, could not resist the importunities even of those whom he knew, beyond all doubt, to have been the most opposed to him, and who were completely despicable, but gave with open hands; and more frequently allowed money to be drawn from him by people who laughed at him, and who were grateful only to their effrontery. People with difficulty believe what they have seen; and posterity will consider as a fable what we ourselves look upon as a dream. At last, so much was given to a greedy and prodigal nation, always covetous and in want on account of its luxury, its disorder, and its confusion of ranks, that paper became scarce, and the mills could not furnish enough.

It may be imagined by this, what abuse had been made of a bank, established as a resource always ready, but which could not exist as such without being always delicately adjusted; and above all, kept in a state to meet the obligations it had contracted. The notes began to lose favour; then to fall into discredit, and the discredit to become public. Then came the necessity to sustain them by force, since they could no longer be sustained by industry; and the moment force showed itself every one felt that all was over. Coercive authority was resorted to; the use of gold, silver, and jewels was suppressed, so that everybody was obliged to take all the ready money he possessed to the bank, for fear of its being discovered by a valet. But nobody, as may be imagined, was persuaded of the justice of the power accorded to the Company, and accordingly authority was more and more exerted; all private houses were searched, informations were laid against people in order that no money might be kept back, or if it were, that the guilty parties might be severely punished.

Never before had sovereign power been so violently exercised; never had it attacked in such a manner the temporal interests of the community.

This violence was, however, too excessive, and in every respect too indefensible to last long; new paper and new juggling tricks were of necessity resorted to; the latter were known to be such—people felt them to be such—but they submitted to them rather than not have twenty crowns in safety in their houses; and a greater violence made people suffer the smaller. Hence so many projects, so many different faces in finance, and all tending to establish one issue of paper upon another; that is to say, always causing loss to the holders of the different paper (everybody being obliged to hold it), and the universal multitude. This is what occupied all the rest of the government, and of the life of M. le Duc d'Orléans; which drove Law out of the realm; which increased six-fold the price of all merchandise, all food even the commonest; which ruinously augmented every kind of wages, and ruined public and private commerce; which gave, at the expense of the public, sudden riches to a few noblemen who dissipated it, and were all the poorer in a short time; which enabled many financiers' clerks, and the lowest dregs of the people, profiting by the general confusion, to take advantage of the Mississippi, and make enormous fortunes; which occupied the government several years after the death of M. le Duc d'Orléans; and which, to conclude, France never will recover from, although it may be true that the value of land is considerably augmented.

The 22nd of this year, 1720, became celebrated by the publication of a decree of the Council of State, concerning the shares of the Company of the Indies (the same as that known under the name of Mississippi) and the notes of Law's bank. This decree diminished by degrees, and from month to month, the value of the shares and the note; so that, by the end of the year, that value would have been reduced one-half.

This, in the language of finance and of bankruptcy, was to turn tail with a vengeance; and its effect, while remedying nothing, was to make people believe that things were in a worse state than was actually the case. The little confidence in Law remaining was now radically extinguished; not an atom of it could ever be set afloat again.

On the 5th July, a decree of the Council was issued, prohibiting people from possessing jewels, from keeping them locked up, or from selling them to foreigners. It may be imagined what a commotion ensued. This decree was grafted upon a number of others, the object of all, too visibly, being to seize upon all coin, in favour of the discredited paper, in which nobody could any longer have the slightest confidence.

Immediately after the issue of this decree an edict was drawn up for the establishment of an Indian commercial company, which was to undertake to reimburse in a year six hundred millions of bank notes, by paying fifty thousand dollars per month. Such was the last resource of Law and his system. For the juggling tricks of the Mississippi, it was found necessary to substitute something real; especially since the edict of the 22nd of May, so celebrated and so disastrous for the paper. Chimeras were replaced by realities—by a true India Company; and it was this name and this thing which succeeded, which took the place of the undertaking previously known as the Mississippi. It was in vain that the tobacco monopoly and a number of other immense monopolies were given to the new company; they could not enable it to meet the proper claims spread among the public, no matter what trouble might be taken to diminish them at all hazard and at all loss.

It was necessary to seek other expedients. None could be found except that of rendering this company a commercial one; this was, under a gentler name, a name vague and unpretending, to hand over to it the entire and exclusive commerce of the country. It may be imagined how such a resolution was received by the public, exasperated by the severe decree, prohibiting people, under heavy penalties, from having more than five hundred livres, in coin, in their possession, subjecting them to visits of inspection, and leaving them nothing but bank notes to pay for the commonest necessaries of daily life. Two things resulted; first, fury, which day by day was so embittered by the difficulty of obtaining money for daily subsistence, that it was a marvel all Paris did not revolt at once, and that the émeute was appeased: second, the Parliament, taking its stand upon this public emotion, held firm to the end in refusing to register the edict instituting the new company.

On the 15th of July, the chancellor showed in his own house the draught of the edict to deputies from the Parliament, who remained with him until nine o'clock at night, without being persuaded. On the morrow, the 16th, the edict was brought forward in the regency council. M. le Duc d'Orléans, sustained by M. le Duc, spoke well upon it, because he could not speak ill, however bad his theme. Nobody said a word, and all bowed their necks. It was resolved, in this manner, to send the edict to the Parliament on the morrow, the 17th of July.

That same 17th of July, there was such a crowd in the morning, at the bank and in the neighbouring streets, for the purpose of obtaining enough money to go to market with, that ten or twelve people were stifled. Three of the bodies were tumultuously carried to the Palais Royal, where the mob was shouting for admittance. A detachment of the King's guards at the Tuileries was promptly sent there. La Vrillière and Le Blanc separately harangued the people. The lieutenant of police came; brigades of the watch were sent for. The dead bodies were afterwards carried away, and by gentleness and cajoleries the people were at length dispersed. The detachment of the King's guards returned to the Tuileries. By about ten o'clock in the morning, all being over, Law took it into his head to go to the Palais Royal. He received many imprecations as he passed through the streets. M. le Duc d'Orléans thought it would be well not to let him leave the Palais Royal, and gave him a lodging there.

This same morning the edict was carried to the Parliament, which refused to register it, and sent a deputation to M. le Duc d'Orléans with its reasons for this, at which the Regent was much vexed. The next morning an ordonnance of the King was pasted all over the town, prohibiting the people, under heavy penalties, to assemble, and announcing that in consequence of the disturbances which had taken place the previous day at the bank, that establishment would remain closed until further notice, and no more money would be paid by it. Money was sent to Gonesse to induce the bakers to come as usual, and for fear they should refuse bank notes, like the Paris workmen and shopkeepers, nearly all of whom would no longer receive any paper, the regiment of guards had orders to hold itself ready, and the musketeers to keep within their quarters, their horses saddled and bridled.

As for the Parliament, M. le Duc d'Orléans determined to punish its disobedience by sending it to Blois. This resolution was carried in full council. The Regent hoped that the Parliamentary men, accustomed to the comfort of their Paris homes, and to the society there of their wives, children, and friends, would soon grow tired of being separated from them, and of the extra expense they would be put to, and would give in. I agreed to the project, although I saw, alas! that by this exile the Parliament would be punished, but would be neither conciliated nor tamed into submission. To make matters worse, Blois was given up, and Pontoise was substituted for it! This latter town being close to Paris, the chastisement became ridiculous, showed the vacillating weakness of the Regent, and encouraged the Parliament to laugh at him.

All this time the public stock-jobbing still continued on the Place Vendôme. The Mississippi had tempted everybody. It was who should fill his pockets first with millions, through M. le Duc d'Orléans and Law. At last it was found that this stock-jobbing too much embarrassed the Place Vendôme and the public way; it was transferred, therefore, to the vast garden of the Hôtel de Soissons. This was, in fact, its proper place. Law, who had remained at the Palais Royal some time, had returned to his own house, where he received many visits.

I have a few more words to say of Law and of his Mississippi. The bubble finally burst at the end of the year (1720). Law, who had no more resources, being obliged secretly to depart from the realm, was sacrificed to the public. His flight was known only through the eldest son of Argenson, intendant at Maubeuge, who had the stupidity to arrest him. The courier he despatched with the news was immediately sent back, with a strong reprimand for not having deferred to the passport with which Law had been furnished by the Regent. The financier was with his son, and they both went to Brussels where the Marquis de Prié, governor of the Imperial Low Countries, received them very well, and entertained them. Law did not stop long, gained Liège and Germany, where he offered his talents to several princes, who all thanked him; nothing more. After having thus roamed, he passed through the Tyrol, visited several Italian courts, not one of which would have him, and at last retired to Venice. This republic, however, did not employ him. His wife and daughter followed him some time after. I don't know what became of them or of the son.

On the 24th of January, 1721, a council was held principally for the purpose of examining the state of the finances and of Law's Bank and India Company. The administration of the finances had passed into the hands of La Houssaye, and his first act was to call the attention of the regency council to the position of the bank and the company. We were prepared to hear that things were in a very bad state, but we were scarcely prepared to find that they so clearly resembled utter ruin and bankruptcy.

I need not relate all that passed at this council; the substance of it is enough. From the statement there of M. le Duc d'Orléans, it appeared that Law had issued 1,200,000,000 livres of bank notes more than he ought to have issued. The first 600,000,000 livres had not done much harm, because they had been kept locked up in the bank; but after the 22nd of May, another issue of 600,000,000 had taken place, and been circulated among the public, without the knowledge of the Regent, without the authorisation of any decree.

The 22nd of May was the day on which commenced the final decay of the Company, and of the bank, and the extinction of all confidence by the sad discovery that there was no longer any money wherewith to pay the bank notes, they being so prodigiously in excess of the coin. After this, each step had been but a stumble: each operation a very feeble palliation.

Alberoni had made himself detested by all Europe,—for all Europe, in one way or another, was the victim of his crimes. He braved successively all the powers of Europe, and aspired to nothing less than to deceive them all, then to govern them, making them serve all his ends; and seeing at last his cunning exhausted, tried to execute alone, and without allies, the plan he had formed.

This plan was nothing less than to take away from the Emperor all that the peace of Utrecht had left him in Italy; all that the Spanish house of Austria had possessed there; to dominate the Pope and the King of Sicily; to deprive the Emperor of the help of France and England, by exciting the first against the Regent through the schemes of the ambassador Cellamare and the Duc du Maine; and by sending King James to England, via Scotland, so as to keep King George occupied with a civil war.

The Regent and Dubois, who, for a long time had only too many reasons to regard Alberoni as their personal enemy, were unceasingly occupied in silently plotting his fall; they believed the present moment favourable, and did not fail to profit by it.

Alberoni, at the moment he least expected it, received a note from the King of Spain ordering him to withdraw at once, without attempting to see him or the Queen, or to write to them; and to leave Spain in 48 hours. So few precautions had been taken, that he carried off an immense number of papers, money, and jewels; and it was not until a few days had elapsed, that the King of Spain was informed that the original will of Charles the Second could not be found. It was at once supposed that Alberoni had carried away this precious document (by which Charles the Second named Philippe V King of Spain), in order to offer it, perhaps, to the Emperor, so as to gain his favour and good graces. Alberoni was stopped. It was not without trouble, the most terrible menaces, and loud protests from him, that he surrendered the testament, and some other important papers which it was perceived were missing.

M. le Duc d'Orléans did not restrain his joy, still less did Abbé Dubois; it was their work which had overthrown their personal enemy; with him fell the wall of separation, so firmly erected by Alberoni between the Regent and the King of Spain; and (at the same time) the sole obstacle against peace. This last reason caused joy in Italy, in Vienna, in London; and peace between France and Spain soon resulted. The allied princes felicitated themselves on what had happened; even the Dutch were ravished to be delivered of a minister so double-dealing, so impetuous, so powerful.

But what ought not to be forgotten is the last mark of rage, despair, and madness that he gave in traversing France. He wrote to M. le Duc d'Orléans, offering to supply him with the means of making a most dangerous war against Spain; and at Marseilles, ready to embark, he again wrote to reiterate the same offers, and press them on the Regent.

The King attended the Royal Council for the first time on Sunday, the 18th of February, 1720. He said nothing while there, or on going away, excepting that when M. le Duc d'Orléans, who feared he might grow weary of the proceedings, proposed to him to leave, he said he would stop to the end. After this he did not come always, but often, invariably remaining to the last, without moving or speaking. His presence changed nothing in the order of our arrangements, because his arm-chair was always there, alone, at the end of the table, and M. le Duc d'Orléans, whether his Majesty came or not, had but a 'stool' similar to those we all sat upon. Step by step this council had been so much increased, that now, by the entry of the Duc de Berwick, it numbered sixteen members! To say truth, we were far too many, and we had several among us who would have been much better away. I had tried, but in vain, to make the Regent see this.

Dubois still maintained his pernicious influence over the Regent, and still looked forward to a cardinalship. In the meantime, the Archbishopric of Cambrai became vacant. That is to say, the richest archbishopric, and one of the best posts in the Church, and M. le Duc d'Orléans had not the strength to refuse to confer it upon him.

The Comte de Horn had been in Paris for the last two months, leading an obscure life of gaming and debauchery. He was a man of two-and-twenty, tall and well made, of that ancient and grand family of Horn, known in the eleventh century among the little dynasties of the Low Countries, and afterwards by a long series of illustrious generations.

On Friday, the 22nd of March, 1720, he went to the Rue Quincampoix, wishing, he said, to buy 100,000 écus worth of shares, and for that purpose made an appointment with a stockbroker in a cabaret. The stockbroker came there with his pocket-book and his shares; the Comte de Horn came also, accompanied, as he said, by two of his friends; a moment after, they all three threw themselves upon this unfortunate stockbroker; the Comte de Horn stabbed him several times with a poniard, and seized his pocket-book; one of his pretended friends (a Piedmontese named Mille), seeing that the stockbroker was not dead, finished the work. At the noise they made the people of the house came, not sufficiently quickly to prevent the murder, but in time to render themselves masters of the assassins, and to arrest them. In the midst of the scuffle, the other cut-throat escaped, but the Comte de Horn and Mille were not so fortunate. The cabaret people sent for the officers of justice, who conducted the criminals to the Conciergerie. This horrible crime, committed in broad daylight, immediately made an immense stir, and several kinsmen of this illustrious family at once went to M. le Duc d'Orléans to beg for mercy; but the Regent avoided speaking to them as much as possible, and very rightly ordered full and prompt justice to be done.

At last, the relatives of Horn penetrated to the Regent: they tried to make the Comte pass for mad, saying even that he had an uncle confined in an asylum, and begging that he might be confined also. But the reply was, that madmen who carried their madness to fury, could not be got rid of too quickly. Repulsed in this manner, they represented what an infamy it would be to their illustrious family, related to nearly all the sovereigns of Europe, to have one of its members tried and condemned. M. le Duc d'Orléans replied that the infamy was in the crime, and not in the punishment. They pressed him upon the honour the family had in being related to him. 'Very well, gentlemen,' said he, 'I will divide the shame with you.'

The trial was neither long nor difficult.

I learnt at La Ferté that the Comte de Horn had been broken alive on the wheel at the Grêve, on Holy Friday, the 26th of March, 1720, about 4 o'clock in the afternoon, and the scoundrel Mille with him on the same scaffold, after having both suffered torture.

On the last day of this year, 1720, a Prince of Wales was born at Rome.

The Prince was immediately baptised by the Bishop of Montefiascone, and named Charles. The event caused a great stir in the Holy City. The Pope sent his compliments to their Britannic Majesties, and forwarded to the King of England (the Pretender) 10,000 Roman crowns; gave him, for his life, a country house at Albano, which, until then, he had only lent him, and 2000 crowns to furnish it. A *Te Deum* was sung in the chapel of the Pope, in his presence, and there were rejoicings at Rome.

In France we were afraid to show any public feeling upon the event. We were too much in the hands of England; the Regent and Dubois too much the humble servants of the house of Hanover; Dubois especially, waiting, as he was, so anxiously for his cardinal's hat. He did not, as will be seen, have to wait much longer.

1721

The new Pope had given, in writing, a promise to Dubois, that if elected to the chair of St. Peter he would make him cardinal. Time had flown, and the promise was not yet fulfilled. The impatience of Dubois increased with his hopes, and gave him no repose. He was much bewildered when he learnt that, on the 16th of June, 1721, the Pope had elevated to the cardinalship his brother, who for ten years had been Bishop of Terracine and Benedictine monk of Mount Cassini. Dubois had expected that no promotion would be made in which he was not included. But here was a promotion of a single person only. He was furious; this fury did not last long, however; a month after, that is to say, on the 16th of July, the Pope made him cardinal with Dion Alexander Albani, nephew of the deceased pope, and brother of the Cardinal Camarlingue.

Dubois received the news and the compliment that followed with extreme joy, but managed to contain himself with some little decency, and to give all the honour of his nomination to M. le Duc d'Orléans, who, sooth to say, had had scarcely anything to do with it.

On the last day of July, the King, who had until then been in perfect health, woke with headache and pain in the throat; shivering followed, and towards afternoon, the pains in the head and throat being augmented, he went to bed.

During this illness, which lasted only five days (but of which the first three were violent) I was much troubled, but at the same time I was exceedingly glad that I had refused to be the King's governor, though the Regent had over and over again pressed me to accept the office. There were too many evil reports in circulation against M. le Duc d'Orléans for me to dream of filling this position. For was I not his bosom friend—known to have been on the most intimate terms with him ever since his childhood —and if anything had happened to excite new suspicions against him, what would not have been said? The thought of this so troubled me during the King's illness, that I used to wake in the night with a start, and, oh, what joy was mine when I remembered that I had not this duty on my head!

Before this illness of the King, that is to say, at the commencement of June, I went one day to work with M. le Duc d'Orléans, and found him alone, walking up and down the grand apartment.

'Holloa! there,' said he, as soon as he saw me; then, taking me by the hand, 'I cannot leave you in ignorance of a thing which I desire above all others, which is of the utmost importance to me, and which will cause you as much joy as me; but you must keep it profoundly secret.' Then bursting out laughing 'If M. de Cambrai knew that I had told it to you, he would never pardon me.' And he proceeded to state that perfect reconciliation had been established between himself and the King and Queen of Spain; that arrangements had been made by which our young King was to marry the Infanta of Spain, as soon as she should be old enough; and the Prince of the Asturias (the heir to the Spanish throne) was to marry Mademoiselle de Chartres, the Regent's daughter.

After we had well talked over the matter and rejoiced thereon, I said to the Regent that the proposed marriage of his daughter must be kept profoundly secret until the moment of her departure for Spain; and that of the King also, until the time for the execution arrived; so as to prevent the jealousy of all Europe. At this union, so grand and so intimate, of the two branches of the Royal Family, such a union having always been the terror of Europe and disunion the object of all its policy—this policy having only too well succeeded—I urged that the sovereigns must be left as long as possible in the confidence they had acquired, the Infanta above all, being but three years old, by which means the fears of Europe upon the marriage of Mademoiselle de Chartres with the Prince of the Asturias would be coloured—the prince could wait, he being only fourteen years of age. 'You are quite right,' replied M. le Duc d'Orléans, 'but this can't be, because in Spain they wish to make public the declaration of marriage at once, indeed, as soon as the demand is made and the declaration can be signed.'

'What madness!' cried I; 'what end can this tocsin have except to arouse all Europe and put it in movement! They must be made to understand this, and we must stick to it; nothing is so important.'

'All this is true,' said M. le Duc d'Orléans. 'I think exactly like you, but they are obstinate in Spain; they have wished matters to be arranged thus, and their wishes have been agreed to. Everything is arranged, fixed, finished. I am so much interested in the matter that you surely would not have advised me to break off for this condition.'

During the discussion which followed, I did not forget to think of myself, the occasion being so opportune for making the fortunes of my second son. I remembered then, that as matters were advanced to this point, a special ambassador must be sent to Spain, to ask the hand of the Infanta for the King, and to sign the contract of marriage; that the ambassador must be a nobleman of mark and title, and thus I begged the Duke to give me this commission, with a recommendation to the King of Spain, so as to make my second son the Marquis of Ruffec, grandee of Spain.

M. le Duc d'Orléans scarcely allowed me to finish, immediately accorded me what I had asked, promised me the recommendation with many expressions of friendship, and asked me to keep the whole matter secret, and make no preparation that would disclose it.

Dubois, as I expected, was vexed beyond measure at my embassy, and resolved to ruin me and throw me into disgrace. As soon as the marriages were declared, I asked to be declared as ambassador, so that I might openly make my preparations, which, it will be remembered, I had been forbidden to do, but the prohibition remained. The Cardinal hoped, too, I should not be able to provide myself with everything in time; and that he might represent this to M. le Duc d'Orléans, and in Spain, as a fault, and excite envious clamour against me.

The Cardinal next examined the list of persons I intended to have with me, and approved it. To my extreme surprise he said, however, that I must add forty officers of cavalry and infantry, from the regiments of my sons. I cried out against the madness and the expense of such a numerous military accompaniment. Nothing could be more evident, true, and reasonable than my representations, nothing more useless or worse received. The Cardinal had resolved to ruin me, and to leave me in Spain with all the embarrassments, business, and annoyances he could. He rightly thought that nothing was more likely to make him succeed than to charge me with forty officers. Not finding them, I took only twenty-nine.

The Cardinal now began ardently to press my departure; and, in fact, there was no more time to lose.

At last, on the 23rd of October, 1721, I set out, having with me the Comte de Lorge, my children, the Abbé de Saint-Simon, and his brother, and many others. The rest of the company joined me at Blaye. From Ruffec I went in two days to La Cassine, a small house at four leagues from Blaye, which my father had built on the borders of his marshes of Blaye, and which I felt much pleasure in visiting; I stopped there during All Saints' Day and the evening before, and the next day I early betook myself to Blaye again, where I sojourned two days. I found several persons of quality there, many of the nobility of the country and of the adjoining provinces, and Boucher, intendant of Bordeaux, who was waiting for me, and whom I entertained with good cheer morning and evening during this short stay.

We crossed to Bordeaux in the midst of such bad weather that everybody pressed me to delay the trip; but I had so few days at my command that I did not accede to their representations. Boucher had brought his brigantine magnificently equipped, and boats enough to carry over all my company, most of whom went with us.

After thanking M. and Madame Boucher for their attention, we set out again, traversed the great Landes, and reached Bayonne in due time.

Passing the Pyrenees, I quitted with France, rain and bad weather, and found a clear sky, a charming temperature, with views and perspectives which changed at each moment, and which were not less charming. We were all mounted upon mules, the pace of which is good but easy. I turned a little out of my way to visit Loyola, famous by the birth of Saint Ignatius, and situated all alone in a narrow valley.

On the 15th, we arrived at Vittoria, where I found a deputation of the province, whom I invited to supper, and the next day to breakfast. They spoke French, and I was surprised to see Spaniards so gay and such good company at table. Joy on account of my journey burst out in every place through which I passed in France and Spain, and obtained for me a good reception. At Salinas, among others which I passed through without stopping, ladies, who, to judge by their houses and by themselves, appeared to me to be quality folks, asked me with such good grace to let them see the man who was bringing happiness to Spain, that I thought it would only be proper gallantry to enter their dwellings. They appeared ravished, and I had all the trouble in the world to get rid of them, and to continue my road.

I arrived on the 18th at Burgos, where I meant to stay at least one day, to see what turn would take a rather strong fever which had seized my eldest son; but I was so pressed to hasten on that I was obliged to leave my son behind with nearly all his attendants.

I left Burgos therefore on the 19th. We found but few relays, and those ill-established. We travelled night and day without going to bed, until we reached Madrid, using such vehicles as we could obtain. I performed the last twelve leagues on a post-horse, which cost twice as much as in France. In this manner we arrived in Madrid on Friday, the 21st, at eleven o'clock at night.

We found at the entrance of the town (which has neither gates nor walls, neither barriers nor faubourgs,) people on guard, who asked us who we were, and whence we came. They had been placed there expressly so as to know the moment of my arrival. As I was much fatigued by travelling incessantly from Burgos without stopping, I replied that we were the people of the Ambassador of France, who would arrive the next day.

Early the next morning, I received a visit from Grimaldo, Minister of Foreign Affairs, who, overjoyed at my arrival, had announced it to their Catholic Majesties before coming to me. Grimaldo at once conducted me to the palace, and introduced me to the King. I made a profound reverence to him; he testified to me his joy at my arrival, and asked me for news of the King, of M. le Duc d'Orléans, of my journey, and of my eldest son, whom, as he knew, I had left behind at Burgos. He then entered alone into the Cabinet of the Mirrors.

A half quarter of an hour after the King had entered his cabinet, he sent for me. I entered alone into the Hall of Mirrors which is very vast, but much less wide than long. The King, with the Queen on his left, was nearly at the bottom of the salon,—both their Majesties standing and touching each other. The audience lasted half an hour, and was principally occupied on the part of the King and Queen, with compliments and expressions of joy at the marriages that were to take place. At its close, the Queen asked me if I would like to see the children, and conducted me to them.

I never saw prettier boys than Don Carlos and Don Ferdinand, nor a prettier babe than Don Philip. The King and Queen took pleasure in making me look at them, and in making them turn and walk before me with very good grace. Their Majesties entered afterwards into the Infanta's chamber, where I tried to exhibit as much gallantry as possible. In fact, the Infanta was charming—like a little woman—and not at all embarrassed. The Queen said to me that she had already begun to learn French, and the King that she would soon forget Spain. A few moments after the King recalled me, in order to see the Prince of the Asturias. I found him tall, with fine light-brown hair, fresh-coloured complexion, long face, but agreeable; good eyes, but too near the nose. I found in him also much grace and politeness.

On Tuesday, the 25th of November, I had my solemn audience. I went to the palace in a magnificent coach, belonging to the King, drawn by eight grey horses, admirably dappled. There were no postilions, and the coachman drove me, his hat under his arm.

The audience passed off admirably. I asked the hand of the Infanta in marriage on the part of the King; my request was graciously complied with, compliments passed on both sides, and I returned to my house, well pleased with the reception I had met with from both their Catholic Majesties.

On Thursday, the 27th of November, the King and Queen were to depart from Madrid to Lerma, a pretty hamlet six leagues from Burgos, where they had a palace. On the same day, very early in the morning, our ambassador, Maulevrier, came to me with despatches from Cardinal Dubois, announcing that the Regent's daughter, Mademoiselle de Montpensier, had departed on the 18th of November for Spain, and giving information as to the places she would stop at, the people she would be accompanied by, the day she would arrive at the frontier, and the persons charged with the exchange of the Princesses.

Maulevrier and I thought this news so important that we felt there was no time to lose, and at once hastened away to the palace to communicate it to their Majesties, who we knew were waiting for it most impatiently. We arrived at such an early hour that all was deserted in the palace, and when we reached the door of the Hall of Mirrors, we were obliged to knock loudly in order to be heard. A French valet opened the door, and told us that their Catholic Majesties were still in bed. We did not doubt it, and begged him to apprise them that we wished to have the honour of speaking to them. Such an honour was unheard of, except under extraordinary circumstances; nevertheless the valet quickly returned, saying that their Majesties would receive us, though it was against all rule and usage to do so while they were in bed.

We traversed therefore the long and grand Hall of Mirrors, turned to the left at the end into a large and fine room, then short off to the left again into a very little chamber, portioned off from the other, and lighted by the door and by two little windows at the top of the partition wall. There was a bed of four feet and a half at most, of crimson damask, with gold fringe, four posts, the curtains open at the foot and at the side the King occupied. The King was almost stretched out upon pillows with a little bed-gown of white satin; the Queen sitting upright, a piece of tapestry in her hand, at the left of the King, some skeins of thread near her, papers scattered upon the rest of the bed and upon an arm-chair at the side of it. She was quite close to the King, who was in his night-cap, she also, and in her bed-gown, both between the sheets, which were only very imperfectly hidden by the papers.

They made us abridge our reverences, and the King, raising himself a little impatiently, asked us our business.

'Good news, Sire,' replied I. 'Mademoiselle de Montpensier set out on the 18th; the courier has this instant brought us the news, and we have at once come to present ourselves to you and apprise your Majesties of it.'

Joy instantly painted itself on their faces, and immediately they began to question us at great length upon the details the courier had brought us. After an animated conversation, in which Maulevrier took but little part, their Catholic Majesties dismissed us, testifying to us the great pleasure we had caused them by not losing a minute in acquainting them with the departure of Mademoiselle de Montpensier, above all in not having been stopped by the hour, and by the fact that they were in bed.

Both the King and Queen, but especially the latter, several times insisted that I must not lose any time in following them to Lerma; upon which I assured them they would find me there as they alighted from their coach.

I set out on the 2nd of December, from Madrid, to join the court, and was to sleep at the Escurial.

We arrived on the 9th, at our village of Villahalmanzo where I found most comfortable quarters for myself and all who were with me. I found there, also, my eldest son, still merely convalescent, with the Abbé de Monthon, who came from Burgos. We supped very gaily, and I reckoned upon taking a good excursion the next day, and upon amusing myself in reconnoitring the village and the environs; but fever seized me during the night, augmented during the day, became violent the following night, so that there was no more talk of going on the 11th to meet the King and Queen at Lerma, as they alighted from their coach, according to arrangement.

The malady increased with such rapidity that I was found to be in great danger, and immediately after, on the point of death. I was bled shortly after. The small-pox, with which the whole country was filled, appeared. The small-pox came out very abundantly all over me; it was of a good kind, and I had no dangerous accident. Every one who waited upon me, master or man, was cut off from all intercourse with the rest of the world; even those who cooked for us, from those who did not.

The chief physician nearly every day provided new remedies in case of need, and yet administered none to me, except in giving me, as my sole beverage, water, in which, according to its quantity, oranges were thrown, cut in two with their skins on, and which gently simmered before my fire; occasionally some spoonful of a gentle and agreeable cordial during the height of the suppuration, and afterwards a little Rota wine, and some broth, made of beef and partridge.

The King and Queen, not content with having sent me their chief physician, M. Hyghens, to be with me night and day, wished to hear how I was twice a day, and when I was better, unceasingly showed to me a thousand favours, in which they were imitated by all the Court.

But I was six weeks ill in all.

1722

Here I think will be the fitting place to introduce an account of the daily life of the King and Queen of Spain.

About nine o'clock in the morning the curtains were drawn by the Asafeta, followed by a single valet carrying a basin full of caudle. While the King partook of this brief breakfast, the Asafeta brought the Queen some tapestry to work at, passed bedgowns to their Majesties, and put upon the bed some of the papers she found upon the adjoining seats, then withdrew with the valet and what he had brought. Their Majesties then said their morning prayers. Grimaldo afterwards entered, displayed his papers, drew from his pocket an inkstand, and worked with the King; the Queen not being hindered by her tapestry from giving her opinion.

Grimaldo, upon leaving with his papers, found the adjoining room empty, and a valet in that beyond, who, seeing him pass, entered into the empty room, crossed it, and summoned the Asafeta, who immediately came and presented to the King his slippers and his dressing-gown; he at once passed across the empty room and entered into a cabinet, where he dressed himself, followed by three valets (never changed) and by the Duc del Arco, or the Marquis de Santa Cruz, and after by both, nobody else ever being present at the ceremony.

The Queen, as soon as the King had passed into his cabinet, put on her stockings and shoes alone with the Asafeta, who gave her her dressing-gown. It was the only moment in which this person could speak to the Queen, or the Queen to her; but this moment did not stretch at the most to more than a half a quarter of an hour. Had they been longer together the King would have known it, and would have wanted to hear what kept them. The Queen passed through the empty chamber and entered into a fine large cabinet, where her toilette awaited her. When the King had dressed in his cabinet—where he often spoke to his confessor—he went to the Queen's toilette, followed by the two seigneurs just named. A few of the specially-privileged were also admitted there. This toilette lasted about three-quarters of an hour, the King and all the rest of the company standing.

When it was over, the King half opened the door of the Hall of Mirrors, which leads into the saloon where the Court assembled, and gave his orders; then rejoined the Queen in that room which I have so often called the empty room. There and then took place the private audiences of the foreign ministers, and of the seigneurs, or other subjects who obtained them. Once a week, on Monday, there was a public audience, a practice which cannot be too much praised where it is not abused. The King, instead of half opening the door, threw it wide open, and admitted whoever liked to enter. People spoke to the King as much as they liked, how they liked, and gave him in writing what they liked. But the Spaniards resemble in nothing the French; they are measured, discreet, respectful, brief.

After the audiences, or after amusing himself with the Queen if there were none, the King went to dress. The Queen accompanied him, and they took the communion together (never separately) about once a week, and then they heard a second mass. The confession of the King was said after he rose, and before he went to the Queen's toilette.

Upon returning from mass, or very shortly after, the dinner was served. It was always in the Queen's apartment, as well as the supper, but the King and Queen had each their dishes; the former, few, the latter, many, for she liked eating, and ate of everything; the King always kept to the same things—soup, capon, pigeons, boiled and roast, and always a roast loin of veal—no fruit, or salad, or cheese; pastry, rarely, never *maigre*; eggs, often cooked in various fashions; and he drank nothing but champagne; the Queen the same. When the dinner was finished, they prayed to God together. If anything pressing happened, Grimaldo came and gave them a brief account of it.

About an hour after dinner, they left the apartment by a short passage accessible to the Court, and descended by a little staircase to their coach, returning by the same way. The Queen always said something pleasant to whoever was there.

Upon returning, the King gave his orders. If they had not partaken of a collation in the coach, they partook of one upon arriving. It was for the King, a morsel of bread, a big biscuit, some water and wine; and for the Queen, pastry and fruit in season; sometimes cheese. The Prince and the Princess of the Asturias, and the children, followed and waited for them in the inner apartment. This company withdrew in less than half a quarter of an hour. Grimaldo came and worked ordinarily for a long time; it was the time for the real work of the day. When the Queen went to confession this also was the time she selected. Except what related to the confession, she and her confessor had no time to say anything to each other. The cabinet in which she confessed to him was contiguous to the room occupied by the King, and when the latter thought the confession too long, he opened the door and called her. Grimaldo being gone, they prayed together, or sometimes occupied themselves with spiritual reading until supper. It was served like the dinner. At both meals there were more dishes in the French style, than in the Spanish, or even the Italian.

After supper, conversation or prayers conducted them to the hour for bed, when nearly the same observances took place as in the morning. Finally, their Catholic Majesties everywhere had but one dressing room between them, and were never in private one from another.

They passed their lives in one long *tête-à-tête*. When they travelled it was at the merest snail's pace, and they slept on the road, night after night, in houses prepared for them. In their coach they were always alone; when in the palace it was the same.

The King had been accustomed to this monotonous life by his first queen, and he did not care for any other. The new queen, upon arriving, soon found this out, and found also that if she wished to rule him, she must keep him in the same room, confined as he had been kept by her predecessor.

Philip V was not gifted with superior understanding or with any stock of what is called imagination. He was cold, silent, sad, sober, fond of no pleasure except the chase, fearing society, fearing himself, unexpansive, a recluse by taste and habits, rarely touched by others, of good sense nevertheless, and upright, with a tolerably good knowledge of things, obstinate when he liked, and often then not to be moved; nevertheless, easy at other times to govern and influence.

He was cold. In his campaigns he allowed himself to be led into any position, even under a brisk fire, without budging in the slightest; nay, amusing himself by seeing whether anybody was afraid.

He was extremely vain; could bear no opposition in any of his enterprises; and what made me judge he liked praise, was that the Queen invariably praised him—even his face; and asked me one day, at the end of an audience which had led us into conversation, if I did not think him very handsome, and more so than any one I knew? His piety was only custom,—scruples, fears, little observances, without knowing anything of religion: the Pope a divinity when not opposed by him; in fact he had the outside religion of the Jesuits, of whom he was passionately fond.

He believed himself an usurper! and in this idea nourished his desire to return to France, and abandon Spain and his scruples at one and the same time. It cannot be disguised that all this was very ill-arranged in his head, but there it was, and he would have abandoned Spain had it been possible, because he felt compelled by duty to do so.

Let me now more particularly describe the Queen.

This princess had much intellect and natural graces, which she knew how to put to account. Her sense, her reflection, and her conduct, were guided by that intellect, from which she drew all the charms and all the advantages possible. Whoever knew her was astonished to find how her intelligence and natural capacity supplied the place of her want of knowledge of the world, of persons, of affairs, upon all of which subjects, her garret life in Parma, and afterwards her secluded life with the King of Spain, hindered her from obtaining any real instruction. The perspicuity she possessed, which enabled her to see the right sight of everything that came under her inspection, was undeniable, and this singular gift would have become developed in her to perfection if its growth had not been interrupted by the ill-humour she possessed; which it must be admitted the life she led was more than enough to give her. She felt her talent and her strength, but did not feel the fatuity and pride which weakened them and rendered them ridiculous. The current of her life was simple, smooth, with a natural gaiety even, which sparkled through the eternal restraint of her existence; and despite the ill-temper and the sharpness which this restraint without rest gave her, she was a woman ordinarily without pretension, and really charming.

I have shown in its place the motive which made me desire my embassy; it was to obtain the *grandesse* for my second son, and thus to 'branch' my house. I also desired to obtain the Toison d'Or for my eldest son, that he might derive from this journey an ornament which, at his age, was a decoration.

I regarded the moment at which the marriage would be celebrated as that at which I stood most chance of obtaining what I desired, and I considered that if it passed over without result to me, all would grow cold, and become uncertain, and very disagreeable. I had forgotten nothing during this first stay in Madrid, in order to please everybody, and I make bold to say that I had all the better succeeded because I had tried to give weight and merit to my politeness, measuring it according to the persons I addressed, without prostitution and without avarice, and that's what made me hasten to learn all I could of the birth, of the dignities, of the posts, of the alliances, of the reputation of each, so as to play my cards well, and secure the game.

But still I needed the letters of M. le Duc d'Orléans, and of Cardinal Dubois. I did not doubt the willingness of the Regent, but I did doubt, and very much too, that of his minister. It has been seen what reason I had for this.

A few days before going to Lerma I received letters from Cardinal Dubois upon my affair. Nobody could be more eager or more earnest than the Cardinal, for he gave me advice how to arrive at my aim, and pressed me to look out for everything which could aid me; assuring me that his letters, and those of M. le Duc d'Orléans, would arrive in time. In the midst of the perfume of so many flowers, the odour of falsehood could nevertheless be smelt.

Upon arriving at Lerma I fell ill as I have described, and the small-pox kept me confined forty days. The letters so long promised and so long expected did not arrive until the end of my quarantine. They were just what I expected. Cardinal Dubois explained himself to Grimaldo in turns and circumlocution, and if one phrase displayed eagerness and desire, the next destroyed it by an air of respect and of discretion.

This written stammering savoured of the bombast of a man who had no desire to serve me, but who, not daring to break his word, used all his wits to twist and overrate the little he could not hinder himself from saying. This letter was simply for Grimaldo as the letter of M. le Duc d'Orléans was simply for the King of Spain. The last was even weaker than the first. It scarcely touched upon the real point, but lost itself in respects, in reservations, in deference, and would propose nothing that was not according to the taste of the King.

Grimaldo came to the conclusion that these letters would assuredly do me more harm than good; that they must be suppressed, never spoken of to the King, who must be confirmed without them in the belief that in according me these favours he would confer upon M. le Duc d'Orléans a pleasure, all the greater, because he saw to what point extended all his reserve in not speaking to him about this matter, and mine in not asking for these favours through His Royal Highness, as there was every reason to believe I should do.

The Regent's daughter arrived in Spain at the commencement of the year 1722, and it was arranged that her marriage with the Prince of the Asturias should be celebrated on the 30th of January at Lerma, where their Catholic Majesties were then staying. It was some little distance from my house. I was obliged therefore to start early in the morning in order to arrive in time.

The chapel was void of courtiers. I placed myself to the right of the King's cushion just beyond the edge of the carpet, and amused myself there better than I had expected. Cardinal Borgia, pontifically clad, was in the corner, his face turned towards me, learning his lesson between two chaplains in surplices, who held a large book open in front of him. The good prelate did not know how to read; he tried, however, and read aloud, but inaccurately. The chaplains took him up, he grew angry, scolded them, recommenced, was again corrected, again grew angry, and to such an extent, that he turned round upon them and shook them by their surplices.

Amidst the amusement supplied to us by the poor cardinal, I remarked extreme satisfaction in the King and Queen at seeing this grand marriage accomplished. The ceremony finished, as it was not long, only the King, the Queen, and, when necessary, the Prince and Princess kneeling; their Catholic Majesties rose and withdrew towards the left corner of their footcloth, talked together for a short time, after which the Queen remained where she was, and the King advanced to me, I being where I had been during all the ceremony.

The King did me the honour to say to me, 'Monsieur, in every respect I am so pleased with you, and particularly for the manner in which you have acquitted yourself of your embassy, that I wish to give you some marks of my esteem, of my satisfaction, of my friendship. I make you Grandee of Spain of the first class, you, and, at the same time, whichever of your sons you may wish[1] to have the same distinction; and your eldest son I will make chevalier of the Toison d'Or.'

I immediately embraced his knees, and I tried to testify to him my gratitude and my extreme desire to render myself worthy of the favour he deigned to spread upon me, by my attachment, my very humble services, and my most profound respect. Then I kissed his hand, turned and sent for my children, employing the moments which had elapsed before they came in uttering fresh thanks.

I had finished all my business. It was time to think about setting out. As soon, however, as I talked about going, there was nothing which the King and the Queen did not do to detain me. All the Court, too, did me the favour to express much friendship for me, and regret at my departure. I admit even that I could not easily make up my mind to quit a country where I had found nothing but fruits and flowers, and to which I was

---

[1] Saint-Simon's sons, the Vidame de Chartres and the Marquis de Ruffec, were bandy-legged specimens known at Court as 'The Dachshunds'.

attached, as I shall ever be, by esteem and gratitude. I made a number of farewell visits among the friends I had made; and on the 21st of March I had my parting state audiences of the King and Queen separately. I was surprised with the dignity, the precision, and the measure of the King's expressions, as I had been surprised at my first audience. I received many marks of personal goodness, and of regret at my departure, from his Catholic Majesty, and from the Queen even more; from the Prince of the Asturias a good many also. But in another direction I met with very different treatment, which I cannot refrain from describing, however ridiculous it may appear.

I went, of course, to say my adieux to the Princess of the Asturias, and I was accompanied by all my suite. I found the young lady standing under a daïs, the ladies on one side, the grandees on the other; and I made my three reverences, then uttered my compliments. I waited in silence her reply, but 'twas in vain. She answered not one word.

After some moments of silence, I thought I would furnish her with matter for an answer; so I asked her what orders she had for the King, for the Infanta, for *Madame*, and for M. and Madame la Duchesse d'Orléans. By way of reply, she looked at me and belched so loudly in my face, that the noise echoed throughout the chamber. My surprise was such that I was stupefied. A second belch followed as noisy as the first.

I lost countenance at this, and all power of hindering myself from laughing. Turning round, therefore, I saw everybody with their hands upon their mouths, and their shoulders in motion. At last a third belch, still louder than the two others, threw all present into confusion, and forced me to take flight, followed by all my suite, amidst shouts of laughter, all the louder because they had previously been kept in.

I left Madrid on the 24th of March, after having had the honour of paying my court to their Catholic Majesties all the afternoon at the Racket Court, they overwhelming me with civilities, and begging me to take a final adieu of them in their apartments. Whatever might be the joy and eagerness I felt at the prospect of seeing Madame de Saint-Simon and my Paris friends again, I could not quit Spain without feeling my heart moved, or without regretting persons from whom I had received so many marks of goodness, and for whom, all I had seen of the nation, had made me conceive esteem, respect, and gratitude.

On the 13th of April, I arrived, about five o'clock in the afternoon at Loches. On the morrow, the 14th, I arrived at Etampes, where I slept, and the 15th, at ten o'clock in the morning, I reached Chartres, where Madame de Saint-Simon was to meet me, dine, and sleep, so that we might have the pleasure of opening our hearts to each other, and of finding ourselves together again in solitude and in liberty, greater than could be hoped for in Paris during the first few days of my return.

Cardinal Dubois every day more and more firmly established in the favour of M. le Duc d'Orléans, pined for nothing less than to be declared prime minister. He was already virtually in that position, but was not publicly or officially recognised as being so. He wished, therefore, to be declared.

One great obstacle in his path was the Maréchal de Villeroy, with whom he was on very bad terms, and whom he was afraid of transforming into an open and declared enemy, owing to the influence the Maréchal exerted over others. Tormented with agitating thoughts, every day that delayed his nomination seemed to him a year. At last he resolved to make a last effort at reconciliation with the Maréchal, but mistrusting his own powers, decided upon asking Cardinal Bissy, to be the mediator between them.

Bissy with great willingness undertook the peaceful commission; spoke to Villeroy, who appeared quite ready to make friends with Dubois, and even consented to go and see him. As chance would have it, he went, accompanied by Bissy, on Tuesday morning. It was the day on which the foreign ministers had their audience. The audience being over, Dubois came from his cabinet, conducting the Russian minister, and immediately saw his sofa so well ornamented. He saw nothing but that in fact; on the instant he ran there, paid a thousand compliments to the Maréchal for anticipating him, when he was only waiting for permission to call upon him, and begged him and Bissy to step into the cabinet.

At first, nothing passed but reciprocal compliments and observations from Cardinal Bissy, appropriate to the subject. Then followed protestations from Dubois and replies from the Maréchal. Thus far, the sea was very smooth. But absorbed in his song, the Maréchal began to forget its tune; then to plume himself upon his frankness and upon his plain speaking; then by degrees, growing hot in his honours, he gave utterance to divers naked truths, closely akin to insults.

Dubois much astonished, pretended not to feel the force of these observations, but as they increased every moment, Bissy tried to call back the Maréchal, explain things to him, and give a more pleasant tone to the conversation. But the mental tide had begun to rise, and now it was entirely carrying away the brains of Villeroy. From bad to worse was easy. The Maréchal began now to utter unmistakable insults, and the most bitter reproaches. In vain Bissy tried to silence him; representing to him how far he was wandering from the subject they came to talk upon; how indecent it was to insult a man in his own house, especially after arriving on purpose to conclude a reconciliation with him. All Bissy could say simply had the effect of exasperating the Maréchal, and of making him vomit forth the most extravagant insults that insolence and disdain could suggest.

Dubois, stupefied and beside himself, was deprived of his tongue, could not utter a word; while Bissy, justly inflamed with anger, uselessly tried to interrupt his friend. In the midst of the sudden fire which had seized the Maréchal, he had placed himself in such a manner that he barred the passage to the door, and he continued his invectives without restraint.

'You are all powerful,' said he, 'everybody bends before you; nobody resists you; what are the greatest people in the land compared with you? Believe me, you have only one thing to do; employ all your power, put yourself at ease, and arrest me, if you dare. Who can hinder you? Arrest me, I say, you have only that course open.'

At last, carried away by anger and vexation, Bissy seized the Maréchal by the arm and the shoulder, and hurried him to the door, which he opened, and then pushed him out, and followed at his heels.

I had worked and chatted for a long time with M. le Duc d'Orléans. He had passed into his dressing room, and I was standing behind his bureau arranging his papers when I saw Cardinal Dubois enter like a whirlwind, his eyes starting out of his head. Seeing me alone, he screamed rather than asked, 'Where is M. le Duc d'Orléans?'

Dubois, who always stammered, could scarcely speak, so great was his rage and fear; but he succeeded at last in acquainting us with the details I have just given, although at greater length. He concluded by saying that after the insults he had received so treacherously, and in a manner so basely premeditated, the Regent must choose between him and the Maréchal de Villeroy, for that after what had passed he could not transact any business or remain at the Court in safety and honour, while the Maréchal de Villeroy remained there.

Upon this M. le Duc d'Orléans beckoned me over, and I said to him that hitherto I had always regarded the dismissal of the Maréchal de Villeroy as a very dangerous enterprise, for reasons I had several times alleged to his Royal Highness: but that now whatever peril there might be in undertaking it, the frightful scene that had just been enacted, persuaded me that it would be much more dangerous to leave him near the King than to get rid of him altogether.

The next day I went to M. le Duc d'Orléans whom I found with the Cardinal Dubois. M. le Duc entered a moment after, quite full of the adventure.

After we had chatted awhile, standing, Dubois went away. M. le Duc d'Orléans sat down at his bureau, and M. le Duc and I sat in front of him. There we deliberated upon what ought to be done. After a few words of explanation from the Regent, he called upon me to give my opinion. I did so as briefly as possible, repeating what I had said on the previous day.

As soon as I had finished, he asked M. le Duc what he thought. M. le Duc said his opinion was mine, and that if the Maréchal de Villeroy remained in his office, there was nothing for it but to shut up shop; that was his expression. M. le Duc again remarked that it must be done at once. Then we set about thinking how we could do it. I said there were two things to discuss, the pretext and the execution. That a pretext was necessary, such as would convince the impartial, and be unopposed even by the friends of the Maréchal de Villeroy.

I begged the Regent then to remember that he had told me several times he never had been able to speak to the King in private, or even in a whisper before others; that when he had tried, the Maréchal de Villeroy had at once come forward poking his nose between them, and declaring that while he was governor he would never suffer any one, not even his Royal Highness, to address his Majesty in a low tone, much less to speak to him in private. I said that this conduct towards the Regent, a grandson of France, and the nearest relative the King had, was insolence enough to disgust every one, and apparent as such at half a glance. I counselled M. le Duc D'Orléans to make use of this circumstance, and by its means to lay a trap for the Maréchal into which there was not the slightest doubt he would fall. The trap was to be thus arranged.

On Sunday, the 12th of August, 1722, M. le Duc d'Orléans went, towards the end of the afternoon, to work with the King, as he was accustomed to do several times each week; and as it was summer time now, he went after his airing, which he always took early. At the conclusion of this labour, at which the Maréchal de Villeroy was always present, and sometimes M. de Fréjus (when he made bold to stop), M. le Duc d'Orléans begged the King to step into a little back cabinet, where he would say a word to him alone. The Maréchal de Villeroy at once opposed.

The Maréchal, arising and stroking his wig, replied that he knew the respect he owed the Regent, and knew also quite as well the respect he owed to the King, and to his place, charged as he was with the person of His Majesty, and being responsible for it. But he said he would not suffer his Royal Highness to speak to the King in private (because he ought to know everything said to His Majesty), still less would be suffer him to lead the King into a cabinet, out of his sight.

Upon this, M. le Duc d'Orléans looked fixedly at the Maréchal and said, in the tone of a master, that he forgot himself; that he ought to remember to whom he was speaking, and take care what words he used; that the respect he (the Regent) owed to the presence of the King, hindered him from replying as he ought to reply, and from continuing this conversation. Therefore he made a profound reverence to the King, and went away.

Less than two hours after what had occurred, it was known that the Maréchal, bragging of what he had just done, had added that he should consider himself very unhappy if M. le Duc d'Orléans thought he had been wanting in respect to him, when his only idea was to fulfil his precious duty; and that he would go the next day to have an explanation with his Royal Highness, which he doubted not would be satisfactory to him.

All necessary measures had been taken as soon as the day was fixed on which the snare was to be laid for the Maréchal. Nothing remained but to give form to them directly it was known that on the morrow the Maréchal would come and throw himself into the lion's mouth.

All things being well arranged, the Maréchal de Villeroy arrived about mid-day, with his accustomed hubbub, but alone, his chairs and his porters remaining outside, beyond the Salle des Gardes. He enters like a comedian, stops, looks round, advances some steps. Under pretext of civility, he is environed, surrounded. He asks in an authoritative tone, what M. le Duc d'Orléans is doing: the reply is, he is in his private room within.

The Maréchal elevates his tone, says that nevertheless he must see the Regent; that he is going to enter; when lo! La Fare, captain of M. le Duc d'Orléans' guards presents himself before him, arrests him, and demands his sword. The Maréchal becomes furious, all present are in commotion. At this instant Le Blanc presents himself. His sedan chair, that had been hidden, is planted before the Maréchal. He cries aloud, he is shaking on his lower limbs; but he is thrust into the chair, which is closed upon him and carried away in the twinkling of an eye through one of the side windows into the garden, La Fare and Artagnan each on one side of the chair, the light horse and musketeers behind. The march is hastened; the party descend the steps of the orangery by the side of the thicket; the grand gate is found open and a coach and six before it. The chair is put down; the Maréchal storms as he will; he is cast into the coach; Artagnan mounts by his side; an officer of the musketeers is in front; and one of the gentlemen in ordinary of the King by the side of the officer; twenty musketeers, with mounted officers, surround the vehicle, and—away they go.

It was no agreeable task which had to be performed soon after by the Regent; I mean when he carried the news of the arrest to the King. He entered into His Majesty's cabinet which he cleared of all the company it contained, except those people whose past gave them a right to enter, but of them there were not many present. At the first word, the King reddened; his eyes moistened; he hid his face against the back of an arm-chair, without saying a word; would neither go out nor play. He ate but a few mouthfuls at supper, wept, and did not sleep all night. The morning and the dinner of the next day, the 14th, passed off but little better.

Immediately after the departure of the Maréchal de Villeroy, M. de Fréjus, the King's instructor, had been missed. He had disappeared. He had not slept at Versailles. No one knew what had become of him! The grief of the King had so much increased upon receiving this fresh blow—both his familiar friends taken from him at once—that no one knew what to do with him. He was in the most violent despair, wept bitterly, and could not be pacified. The Cardinal concluded by saying that no stone must be left unturned in order to find M. de Fréjus. That unless he had gone to Villeroy, it was probable he had hid himself in La Trappe, and that we must send and see. After some further consideration, Dubois pressed me to go and write to La Trappe. The letter finished, and I about to descend, Pezé, who had left me, returned, crying, 'He is found! he is found! your letter is useless; return to M. le Duc d'Orléans.'

Villeroy had persuaded the King that it was he, alone, who by vigilance and precaution had preserved his life from poison that others wished to administer to him. This was the source of those tears shed by the King when Villeroy was carried off, and of his despair when Fréjus disappeared. He did not doubt that both had been removed in order that this crime might be more easily committed. The prompt return of Fréjus dissipated the half of his fear, the continuance of his good health delivered him by degrees from the other.

Villeroy being banished, the last remaining obstacle in Dubois' path was removed. There was nothing, now, to hinder him from being proclaimed prime minister. I had opposed it as stoutly as I could; but my words were lost upon M. le Duc d'Orléans. Accordingly, about two o'clock in the afternoon of the 23rd of August, 1722, Dubois was declared prime minister by the Regent, and by the Regent at once conducted to the King as such. After this event I began insensibly to withdraw from public affairs.

1723

I was hopelessly wearied with M. le Duc d'Orléans; I no longer approached this poor prince (with so many great and useless talents buried in him)—except with repugnance.

I no longer deigned to speak to him. He perceived this: I felt he was pained at it; he strove to reconcile me to him, without daring, however, to speak of affairs, except briefly, and with constraint, and yet he could not hinder himself from speaking of them. I scarcely took the trouble to reply to him, and I cut his conversation as short as possible. I abridged and curtailed my audiences with him; I listened to his reproaches with coldness. In fact, what had I to discuss with a Regent who was no longer one, not even over himself, still less over a realm plunged in disorder?

Cardinal Dubois, when he met me, almost courted me. He knew not how to catch me. The bonds which united me to M. le Duc d'Orléans had always been so strong that the prime minister, who knew their strength, did not dare to flatter himself he could break them. His resource was to try to disgust me by inducing his master to treat me with a reserve which was completely new to him, and which cost him more than it cost me; for, in fact, he had often found my confidence very useful to him, and had grown accustomed to it. As for me, I dispensed with his friendship more than willingly, vexed at being no longer able to gather any fruit from it for the advantage of the State or himself, wholly abandoned as he was to his Paris pleasures and to his minister. The conviction of my complete inutility more and more kept me in the background, without the slightest suspicion that different conduct could be dangerous to me, or that, weak and abandoned to Dubois, as was the Regent, the former could ever exile me, like the Duc de Noailles, and Canillac, or disgust me into exiling myself. I followed, then, my accustomed life. That is to say, never saw M. le Duc d'Orléans except tête-à-tête, and then very seldom at intervals that each time grew longer, coldly, briefly, never talking to him of business, or, if he did to me, turning the conversation, and replying in a manner to make it drop. Acting thus, it is easy to see that I was mixed up in nothing, and what I shall have to relate now will have less of the singularity and instructiveness of good and faithful memoirs, than of the dryness and sterility of the gazettes.

First of all I will finish my account of Cardinal Dubois. On the 11th of June, 1723, the King went to reside at Meudon, ostensibly in order that the château of Versailles might be cleaned; in reality, to accommodate Cardinal Dubois. The King held at Meudon a review of his household, which in his pride the Cardinal must needs attend. It cost him dear. He mounted on horseback the better to enjoy his triumph; he suffered cruelly, and became so violently ill that he was obliged to have assistance.

On Saturday, the 7th of August, he was so ill that the doctors declared he must submit to an operation, which was very urgent, and without which he could hope to live but a few days; because the abscess he had having burst the day he mounted on horseback, gangrene had commenced, with an overflow of pus, and he must be transported, they added, to Versailles, in order to undergo this operation. The trouble this terrible announcement caused him, so overthrew him that he could not be moved the next day, Sunday, the 8th; but on Monday he was transported in a litter, at five o'clock in the morning.

After having allowed him to repose himself a little, the doctors and surgeons proposed that he should receive the sacrament, and submit to the operation immediately after. This was not heard very peacefully; he had scarcely ever been free from fury since the day of the review; he had grown worse on Saturday, when the operation was first announced to him. Nevertheless, some little time after, he sent for a priest from Versailles, with whom he remained alone about a quarter of an hour. Such a great and good man, so well prepared for death, did not need more.

The faculty, who saw the imminent danger of the slightest delay, sent to Meudon for M. le Duc d'Orléans, who instantly came in the first conveyance he could lay his hands on. He exhorted the Cardinal to suffer the operation; then asked the faculty if it could be performed in safety. They replied that they could say nothing for certain, but that assuredly the Cardinal had not two hours to live if he did not instantly agree to it. M. le Duc d'Orléans returned to the sick man, and begged him so earnestly to do so, that he consented.

The operation was accordingly performed about five o'clock, and in five minutes, by La Peyronie, chief surgeon of the King, and successor to Maréchal, who was present with Chirac and others of the most celebrated surgeons and doctors. The Cardinal cried and stormed. M. le Duc d'Orléans returned into the chamber directly after the operation was performed, and the faculty did not dissimulate from him, that judging by the nature of the wound, and what had issued from it, the Cardinal had not long to live. He died, in fact, twenty-four hours afterwards, on the 10th of August, at five o'clock in the morning, grinding his teeth against his surgeons and against Chirac, whom he had never ceased to abuse.

We have many examples of prodigious fortune acquired by insignificant people, but there is no example of a person so destitute of all talent (excepting that of low intrigue), as was Cardinal Dubois, being thus fortunate. His intellect was of the most ordinary kind; his knowledge the most common-place; his capacity nil; his exterior that of a ferret, of a pedant; his conversation disagreeable, broken, always uncertain; his falsehood written upon his forehead; his habits too measureless to be hidden; his fits of impetuosity resembling fits of madness; his head incapable of containing more than one thing at a time, and he incapable of following anything but his personal interest; nothing was sacred with him; he had no sort of worthy intimacy with any one; had a declared contempt for faith, promises, honour, probity, truth; took pleasure at laughing at all these things; was equally voluptuous and ambitious, wishing to be all in all in everything; counting himself alone as everything, and whatever was not connected with him as nothing; and regarding it as the height of madness to think or act otherwise. With all this he was soft, cringing, supple, a flatterer, and false admirer, taking all shapes with the greatest facility, and playing the most opposite parts in order to arrive at the different ends he proposed to himself; and nevertheless was but little capable of seducing. His judgment acted by fits and starts, was involuntarily crooked, with little sense or clearness; he was disagreeable in spite of himself. Nevertheless, he could be funnily vivacious when he wished, but nothing more, could tell a good story, spoiled, however, to some extent by his stuttering, which his falsehood had turned into a habit from the hesitation he always had in replying and in speaking. With such defects it is surprising that the only man he was able to seduce was M. le Duc d'Orléans, who had so much intelligence, such a well-balanced mind, and so much clear and rapid perception of character. Dubois gained upon him as a child while his preceptor; he seized upon him as a young man by favouring his liking for liberty, sham fashionable manners and debauchery, and his disdain of all rule. He ruined his heart, his mind, and his habits by instilling into him the principles of libertinism, which this poor prince could no more deliver himself from, than from those ideas of reason, truth, and conscience, which he always took care to stifle.

Dubois may have been all that Saint-Simon calls him; but modern historians rank him as a statesman of considerable ability.

As soon as Dubois was dead, M. le Duc d'Orléans returned to Meudon, to inform the King of the event. The King immediately begged him to charge himself with the management of public affairs, declared him prime minister, and received, the next day, his oath, the patent of which was immediately sent to the Parliament, and verified. This prompt declaration was caused by the fear Fréjus had to see a private person prime minister. The King liked M. le Duc d'Orléans, as we have already seen on account of the respect he received from him, and by his manner of working with him. The Regent always left him master of all favours, and of the choice of persons he proposed to him; and, besides, never bothered him, or allowed business to interfere with his amusements. In spite of all the care and all the suppleness Dubois had employed in order to gain the spirit of the King, he never could succeed, and people remarked, without having wonderful eyes, a very decided repugnance of the King for him.

The Court returned from Meudon to Paris on the 13th of August. Soon after I met M. le Duc d'Orléans there.

As soon as he saw me enter his cabinet he ran to me, and eagerly asked me if I meant to abandon him. I replied that while his Cardinal lived I felt I should be useless to him, but that now this obstacle was removed, I should always be very humbly at his service. He promised to live with me on the same terms as before, and, without a word upon the Cardinal, began to talk about home and foreign affairs. If I flattered myself that I was to be again of use to him for any length of time, events soon came to change the prospect. But I will not anticipate my story.

The new château of Meudon, completely furnished, had been restored to me since the return of the Court to Versailles, just as I had had it before the Court came to Meudon. The Duc and Duchesse d'Humières were with us there, and good company. One morning towards the end of October, 1723, the Duc d'Humières wished me to conduct him to Versailles, to thank M. le Duc d'Orléans.

We found the Regent dressing in the vault he used as his dressing room. He was upon his chair among his valets, and one or two of his principal officers. His look terrified me. I saw a man with hanging head, a purple-red complexion, and a heavy stupid air. He did not even see me approach. His people told him. He slowly turned his head towards me, and asked me with a thick tongue what brought me. I told him. I had intended to pass him to come into the room where he dressed himself, so as not to keep the Duc d'Humières waiting; but I was so astonished that I stood stock still.

I took Simiane, first gentleman of his chamber, into a window, and testified to him my surprise and my fear at the state in which I saw M. le Duc d'Orléans.

Simiane replied that for a long time he had been so in the morning; that to-day there was nothing extraordinary about him, and that I was surprised simply because I did not see him at those hours; that nothing would be seen when he had shaken himself a little in dressing.

The condition of M. le Duc d'Orléans made me make many reflections. Within the last year he himself had more than once told me that Chirac doctored him unceasingly, without effect; because he was so full that he sat down to table every evening without hunger, without any desire to eat, though he took nothing in the morning, and simply a cup of chocolate between one and two o'clock in the day (before everybody), it being then the time to see him in public. I had not kept dumb with him thereupon, but all my representations were perfectly useless. I knew, moreover, that Chirac had continually told him that the habitual continuance of his suppers would lead him to apoplexy, or dropsy on the chest, because his respiration was interrupted at times; upon which he had cried out against this latter malady, which was a slow, suffocating, annoying preparation for death, saying that he preferred apoplexy, which surprised and which killed at once, without allowing time to think of it.

Another man, instead of crying out against this kind of death with which he was menaced, and of preferring another, allowing him no time for reflection, would have thought about leading a sober, healthy, and decent life, which, with the temperament he had, would have procured him a very long time, exceeding agreeable in the situation—very probably durable—in which he found himself; but such was the double blindness of this un-happy prince.

I was on terms of much intimacy with M. de Fréjus, and since, in default of M. le Duc d'Orléans, there must be another master besides the King, until he could take command, I preferred this prelate to any other. I went to him, therefore, and told him what I had seen this morning of the state of M. le Duc d'Orléans. I predicted that his death must soon come, and that it would arrive suddenly, without warning. I counselled Fréjus, there-fore, to have all his arrangements ready with the King, in order to fill up the Regent's place of prime minister when it should become vacant. M. de Fréjus appeared very grateful for the advice, but was measured and modest as though he thought the post much above him!

On the 22nd of December, 1723, I went from Meudon to Versailles to see M. le Duc d'Orléans; I was three-quarters of an hour with him in his cabinet, where I had found him alone. We walked to and fro there, talking of affairs of which he was going to give an account to the King that day.

I found no difference in him, his state was, as usual, languid and heavy, as it had been for some time, but his judgment was clear as ever.

About an hour after, at most, I heard cries and a sudden uproar. I ran out and I found Madame de Saint-Simon quite terrified, bringing to me a groom of the Marquis de Ruffec, who wrote to me from Versailles, that M. le Duc d'Orléans was in an apoplectic fit. I was deeply moved, but not surprised; I had expected it, as I have shown, for a long time. I impatiently waited for my carriage, which was a long while coming, on account of the distance of the new château from the stables. I flung myself inside, and was driven as fast as possible.

At the park gate I met another courier from M. de Ruffec, who stopped me, and said it was all over. I remained there more than half an hour absorbed in grief and reflection. At the end I resolved to go to Versailles, and shut myself up in my rooms; I learnt there the particulars of the event.

M. le Duc d'Orléans had everything prepared to go and work with the King. While waiting the hour, he chatted with Madame Falari, one of his mistresses. They were close to each other, both seated in arm-chairs, when suddenly he fell against her, and never from that moment had the slightest glimmer of consciousness.

La Falari, frightened as much as may be imagined, cried with all her might for help, and redoubled her cries. Seeing that nobody replied, she supported as best she could this poor prince upon the contiguous arms of the two chairs, ran into the grand cabinet, into the chamber, into the ante-chambers, without finding a soul; finally, into the court and the lower gallery. It was the hour at which M. le Duc d'Orléans worked with the King, an hour when his people were sure no one would come and see him, and that he had no need of them, because he ascended to the King's room by the little staircase from his vault, that is to say his dressing room. At last La Falari found somebody, and sent the first who came to hand for help. Chance, or rather providence, had arranged this sad event at a time when everybody was ordinarily away upon business or visits, so that a full half-hour elapsed before doctor or surgeon appeared, and, about as long before any domestics of M. le Duc d'Orléans could be found.

As soon as the faculty had examined the Regent, they judged his case hopeless. He was hastily extended upon the floor, and bled, but he gave not the slightest sign of life, do what they might to him. In less than two hours all was over, and little by little the solitude became as great as the crowd had been. As soon as assistance came, La Falari flew away and gained Paris as quickly as possible.

At the first intelligence of apoplexy, Fréjus proposed M. le Duc to the King, having probably made his arrangements in advance. M. le Duc arrived soon after, and entered the cabinet where he saw the King, looking very sad, his eyes red and tearful.

Scarcely had he entered than Fréjus said aloud to the King, that in the loss he had sustained by the death of M. le Duc d'Orléans (whom he very briefly eulogised), his Majesty could not do better than beg M. le Duc, there present, to charge himself with everything, and accept the post of prime minister M. le Duc d'Orléans had filled. The King, without saying a word, looked at Fréjus, and consented by a sign of the head, and M. le Duc uttered his thanks.

The death of M. le Duc d'Orléans made a great sensation abroad and at home; but foreign countries rendered him incomparably more justice, and regretted him much more, than the French. Although foreigners knew his feebleness, and although the English had strangely abused it, their experience had not the less persuaded them of the range of his mind, of the greatness of his genius and of his views, of his singular penetration, of the sagacity and address of his policy, of the fertility of his expedients and of his resources, of the dexterity of his conduct under all changes of circumstances and events, of his clearness in considering objects and combining things; of his superiority over his ministers, and over those that various powers sent to him; of the exquisite discernment he displayed in investigating affairs; of his learned ability in immediately replying to everything when he wished. The majority of our Court did not regret him, however. The life he had led displeased the Church people; but more still, the treatment they had received from his hands.

The day after death, the corpse of M. le Duc d'Orléans was taken from Versailles to Saint Cloud, and the next day the ceremonies commenced. His heart was carried from Saint Cloud to the Val de Grace by the Archbishop of Rouen, chief almoner of the defunct prince. The burial took place at Saint Denis, the funeral procession passing through Paris, with the greatest pomp. The obsequies were delayed until the 12th of February. M. le Duc de Chartres became Duc d'Orléans.

After this event, I carried out a determination I had long resolved on. I appeared before the new masters of the realm as seldom as possible—only, in fact, upon such occasions where it would have been inconsistent with my position to stop away. My situation at the Court had totally changed. The loss of the dear prince, the Duc de Bourgogne, was the first blow I had received. The loss of the Regent was the second. But what a wide gulf separated these two men!

Index